My Life as a Night Elf Priest

TECHNOLOGIES OF THE IMAGINATION NEW MEDIA IN EVERYDAY LIFE

Ellen Seiter and Mimi Ito, Series Editors

This book series showcases the best ethnographic research today on engagement with digital and convergent media. Taking up in-depth portraits of different aspects of living and growing up in a media-saturated era, the series takes an innovative approach to the genre of the ethnographic monograph. Through detailed case studies, the books explore practices at the forefront of media change through vivid description analyzed in relation to social, cultural, and historical context. New media practice is embedded in the routines, rituals, and institutions—both public and domestic—of everyday life. The books portray both average and exceptional practices but all grounded in a descriptive frame that renders even exotic practices understandable. Rather than taking media content or technology as determining, the books focus on the productive dimensions of everyday media practice, particularly of children and youth. The emphasis is on how specific communities make meanings in their engagement with convergent media in the context of everyday life, focusing on how media is a site of agency rather than passivity. This ethnographic approach means that the subject matter is accessible and engaging for a curious layperson, as well as providing rich empirical material for an interdisciplinary scholarly community examining new media.

Ellen Seiter is Professor of Critical Studies and Stephen K. Nenno Chair in Television Studies, School of Cinematic Arts, University of Southern California. Her many publications include *The Internet Playground: Children's Access, Entertainment, and Mis-Education; Television and New Media Audiences;* and *Sold Separately: Children and Parents in Consumer Culture.*

Mimi Ito is Research Scientist, Department of Informatics, University of California, Irvine, and Visiting Associate Professor at the Graduate School of Media and Governance of Keio University, Kanagawa, Japan. She has published widely on new media and youth and led a recently completed three-year project, Kids' Informal Learning with Digital Media, an ethnographic study of digital youth funded by the MacArthur Foundation.

TITLES IN THE SERIES

Skate Life: Re-Imagining White Masculinity by Emily Chivers Yochim

My Life as a Night Elf Priest: An Anthropological Account of World of Warcraft by Bonnie A. Nardi

---

DIGITALCULTUREBOOKS is an imprint of the University of Michigan Press and the Scholarly Publishing Office of the University of Michigan Library dedicated to publishing innovative and accessible work exploring new media and their impact on society, culture, and scholarly communication.

MY LIFE AS A NIGHT ELF PRIEST

An Anthropological Account of *World of Warcraft*

Bonnie A. Nardi

THE UNIVERSITY OF MICHIGAN PRESS AND
THE UNIVERSITY OF MICHIGAN LIBRARY
Ann Arbor

Copyright © by the University of Michigan 2010
All rights reserved
Published in the United States of America by
The University of Michigan Press and
The University of Michigan Library
Manufactured in the United States of America
♾ Printed on acid-free paper

2013   2012   2011   2010   4   3   2   1

A CIP catalog record for this book is available from the British Library.

Library of Congress Cataloging-in-Publication Data
Nardi, Bonnie A.
  My life as a night elf priest : an anthropological account of world of warcraft /
Bonnie A. Nardi.
       p.   cm. — (Technologies of the imagination and digital culture)
    Includes bibliographical references and index.
       ISBN 978-0-472-07098-5 (cloth : alk. paper) — ISBN 978-0-472-05098-7
(pbk. : alk. paper)
       1. World of Warcraft.   2. Computer games — Social aspects.
    3. Korea (South) — Social aspects.   4. Virtual reality — Social aspects.
    5. Visual anthropology.   I. Title.
    GV1469.25.W64N37   2010
    793.93—dc22   2010007914

ISBN 978-0-472-02671-5 (e-book)

Acknowledgments

Although writing is a solitary pursuit, the influences of others are constantly present. I was fortunate in the guidance, advice, and encouragement generously extended by colleagues, friends, and family.

At the University of Michigan Press, I am grateful to Tom Dwyer, who helped shaped the manuscript from our earliest conversations. Series editor Mimi Ito suggested useful means of restructuring the flow of the book and provided sound advice about what to leave out as well as in. Heather Newman and Christopher Lehr produced images used in the book.

Anonymous reviewers made invaluable suggestions on reworking critical arguments and improving the prose. Many, many thanks—you know who you are.

I very much appreciate the feedback on various chapters provided by Trina Choontanom, Russell Crispin, Christopher Darrouzet-Nardi, Jeanette Darrouzet-Nardi, Scott Ditch, Alison Fish, He Jing, Yong Ming Kow, Wenjing Liang, Thomas Malaby, Linda Polin, and Celia Pearce.

Participants at the Productive Play Workshop hosted by Jason Ellis, Celia Pearce, and me at the University of California, Irvine, in May 2008, engaged in lively debate and discussion from which I profited.

I thank the Intel Corporation, which, at the behest of Eleanor Wynn, provided funding for the research I conducted in China. The National Science Foundation funded a separate study in China conducted by my student Yong Ming Kow (grant no. 446680-21260), as well as sponsoring the Productive Play Workshop.

I have many guildmates to thank—for good times as well as insights about game play. The guilds in which I conducted research must remain anonymous, but Terror Nova, a guild of colleagues with whom I play, was a source of scholarly input as well as friendly mayhem. My family guild, the Hoodoos, blasted through Azeroth with the tight coordination of people who know each other very well.

I would like to thank the players who agreed to be interviewed. They offered thoughtful commentary on their play experiences and called my attention to important matters that I did not pick up on from observations of game play. Many undergraduate students at the University of California, Irvine, where I teach, talked to me informally about their play, and I learned from, and very much enjoyed, those conversations.

Throughout my career, nearly all of my research has been about the use of technology at work. Moving to play, with its elements of whimsy, fantasy, freedom, and fun, was a pleasing turn to a novel arena of activity. But it entailed facing an unfamiliar literature going back 80 years. Surprisingly, very little of what I read was trite or uninteresting. I acknowledge with appreciation the analysis and theorizing of scholars from older traditions whose work remains fresh and pertinent, as well as those on the contemporary scene who are picking up and extending foundational work and moving ahead to lay out new paths of investigation.

At the present moment, we may well be in a golden age of games scholarship. Some amazing social scientists, computer scientists, educators, philosophers, media scholars, legal scholars, and journalists, many of whom you will meet in the pages of this book, have turned their attention to elucidating the import and meanings of play and games. I appreciate the quality of the work they have produced and their remarkable efforts to shape concerns about play and games into a rich multidisciplinary stream of scholarship.

Finally, I am grateful to the complex assemblage that is the *World of Warcraft*—players, designers, corporate purveyors, software artifacts— which has proved an endlessly fascinating object of discovery and inquiry.

Contents

PART ONE. Introduction to *World of Warcraft*

Prologue / 3

CHAPTER ONE. What Is *World of Warcraft* and Who Plays It? / 8

CHAPTER TWO. An Ethnographic Investigation of *World of Warcraft* / 27

PART TWO. Active Aesthetic Experience

CHAPTER THREE. Play as Aesthetic Experience / 39

CHAPTER FOUR. A New Medium / 52

CHAPTER FIVE. Work, Play, and the Magic Circle / 94

PART THREE. Cultural Logics of *World of Warcraft*

CHAPTER SIX. Addiction / 123

CHAPTER SEVEN. Theorycraft and Mods / 137

CHAPTER EIGHT. Gender / 152

CHAPTER NINE. Culture: *WoW* in China . . . and North America / 176

Coda / 197

Notes / 205
References / 213
Index / 227

PART ONE

Introduction to *World of Warcraft*

Prologue

0/12 19:36:38.533 [Raid] Loro: Now Slams and I have been talk-ing about a lot of events regarding our guild and how it can be improved.

0/12 19:37:14.349 [Raid] Robertoh: rofl why is everyone on tables

0/12 19:38:13.848 [Raid] Slams: I have always found that

0/12 19:38:23.224 Robertoh yells: I will be the right hand of loro. :)

0/12 19:38:47.301 [Raid] Slams: a guild that melds together as friends is one that essentially succeeds.

0/12 19:38:55.099 Noth kneels before Slams.

0/12 19:38:58.342 [Raid] Loro: Exactly slams.

0/12 19:39:15.218 [Raid] Leanallah: i agree

0/12 19:39:18.516 [Raid] Slams: you could essentially play this game alone

0/12 19:39:18.341 Robertoh bursts into dance.

0/12 19:39:34.315 [Raid] Aziki: cant to endgame alone tho :/

0/12 19:39:35.935 [Raid] Eleanor: uhh, Robertoh, did you forget your valium?

0/12 19:39:40.552 Sabina applauds at Robertoh. Bravo!

0/12 19:39:42.314 [Raid] Loro: Robertoh please settle down.

0/12 19:39:57.593 [Raid] Robertoh: :)

0/12 19:40:05.021 [Raid] Slams: While leveling up to get to higher level content is crucial—a strong sense of community is crucial as well.

0/12 19:40:11.816 [Raid] Loro: I find that by partying and questing together, we make the game a little more fun.

0/12 19:41:34.032 [Raid] Loro: social events tend to be successful in
    attracting other members.
0/12 19:45:49.638 [Raid] Slams: See, if our goal as a guild is to have a
    constant flow of 5 man raids . . . we've reached that goal.
0/12 19:46:08.531 [Raid] Slams: If we want to be able to do 40 man
    raids consistently . . . we haven't reached that.
0/12 19:46:52.846 Robertoh begins to eat in front of Sasha.
0/12 19:46:53.222 Noth flirts with Aziki.
0/12 19:46:59.508 [Raid] Eleanor: i think doing raids could be enjoy-
    able
0/12 19:46:59.213 Noth blows Aziki a kiss.

In the spring of 2005, I taught an undergraduate course on social aspects
of digital technologies. The students worked in teams on research projects.
One team reported on massively multiplayer online role-playing games.
I knew nothing of these games. But the students' presentation impressed
me—artistic screenshots, the students' excitement as players, the discussion
the topic sparked in class. Note to self: find out what this is about.

I listened when students talked about video games in casual conversation. Colorful but unfamiliar names jangled in my brain: *EverQuest, Ultima
Online, Final Fantasy, Guild Wars.* The game that kept coming up was
World of Warcraft. Based on this highly unscientific sampling, I decided to
try out *WoW,* as it is known, to further my broad research goal of studying
social life on the Internet. In December of 2005, I signed up for an account
with Blizzard Entertainment, the maker of the game, and began to play.
I planned to play for a few months until I knew enough to conduct some
interviews. I didn't expect to like the game—I had played board games as
a child and found them uninteresting. I tried to prevent my own children
from playing video games, which I considered a waste of time.

When I sat down with *World of Warcraft,* I had no idea what to do.
Luckily my son Christopher was home from college for Christmas break.
He helped me create an animated character with which to adventure in
the three-dimensional virtual world. Despite my antigame campaign,
Christopher had played text-based online role-playing games, and, although
he was not familiar with *World of Warcraft,* he seemed to understand basic
game semantics. We set forth on a quest. "Click on the monster and right
click!" he suggested. I obeyed. My frantic clicking produced the salutary

effect of killing the monster (which would soon have killed my character). Such activity seemed inordinately silly, but I was secretly smitten with the beautiful *WoW* graphics and charmed to be a character called a Night Elf.

The moment I began to find *World of Warcraft* truly interesting was when two small icons appeared on the top right portion of my screen. I had not placed them there, nor was I killing monsters; in fact I was relaxing in the woodsy hometown of the Night Elves, Shadowglen. My son explained that another player had caused the icons to appear—they were "buffs," or temporary magic spells to enhance my powers. In that moment I became aware of *other players*. I was not alone in the Night Elves' Garden of Eden but surrounded by real human players who would interact with me. I was touched that another player had given me something for free, without my asking or even having a way to thank him.

My son's brief tutelage ended as he returned to college. Unlike many players, I was not playing with friends or family members who could guide me through the new virtual world. I was a "newbie" (noob, n00b, nub, more derisively) of the first order. I soon learned that I could have thanked the player who buffed me in a couple ways—by typing a message into the chat window or by clicking on his character and typing a command, /ty, which would inform him of my gratitude. I was very happy to know this when I ran out of game money and had to ask a strange player what to do. He promptly gave me some coppers so I could repair my damaged equipment and go forth once more to slay the Webwood spiders lurking in the forest outside the village.

I have given many hours to the study of *World of Warcraft* since the Shadowglen days. I believe *World of Warcraft* is an exemplar of a new means of forming and sustaining human relationships and collaborations through digital technology. While video games might seem a frivolous footnote to modern technology (and video games researchers still get pitying stares from colleagues), the games have penetrated unlikely arenas of human activity, stirring interest in education, business, the military, and even religious organizations. Educators argue that video games have pedagogical value (Gee 2003; Squire 2005; Steinkuehler 2006; Barab et al. 2007; Fields and Kafai 2007; Ang and Zaphiris 2008; Hayes and Games 2008; Polin 2008; Sharritt 2009). Experiments with gamelike environments for work are under way at the world's largest multinational corporations, including Intel, Boeing, Hewlett-Packard, IBM, and Sun Microsystems (Cefkin et al.

2009; Nardi et al. 2009; Yee 2009). Many organizations have applications in *Second Life,* a 3D virtual world in which participants themselves build applications. An article in the *Harvard Business Review* reported research suggesting that people with experience in *World of Warcraft* make better corporate managers (Reeves et al. 2008). The U.S. Army produced and distributed, free on the Internet, a successful multiplayer video game, *America's Army,* designed as a recruiting and public relations tool (Delwiche 2007). DARPA, the research wing of the U.S. Army, funds research in the use of multiplayer games for combat and noncombat applications. Christian evangelists recruit new members through video games such as *America's Army* (Li 2004) and other games. In short, video games have entered the culture.

Some readers will have encountered *WoW* through media accounts that report the unusual, the sensational, the surprising—addicted players, Chinese gold farmers, online marriages, griefers, hackers, gender swappers. While these memes are not without interest, they do not embody the texture of the everyday experiences and emotions of the millions of players who constitute *World of Warcraft.* I will use the vehicle of the ethnographic monograph to provide a perspective on player experience that taps the ordinary, the mundane, the normal, the commonplace in and around *World of Warcraft.*

WoW players will recognize that references to the game belong to a moment in time. *World of Warcraft* is always changing, with software updates that extend the game with new content. The research for the book began in December 2005 and ended on October 11, 2008, when I attended the final day of BlizzCon 2008 (Blizzard's annual conference). I continued to study *WoW,* but BlizzCon marked the completion of the first phase of the research, and it is that which is reported in this book (with a few exceptions, which are noted).

Aims of the Book

For all that has been written about play, it remains a contentious subject. The first aim of the book is to develop an argument about *World of Warcraft* that examines play as active aesthetic experience, drawing on activity theory (Leontiev 1974) and the work of philosopher John Dewey. I am interested in the peculiarities of human play. Play links us to the upper reaches of the animal kingdom while at the same time generating distinctive cultural constructs. Sports, gambling, and a multitude of games, from mah-jongg to *Monopoly* to *World of Warcraft*, are some of *Homo sapiens'* most curious productions.

Understanding play in its contemporary digital manifestations is a second aim of the book. I argue that video games such as *WoW* are a *new visual-performative medium* enabled, and strongly shaped, by the capacities of digital technology, in particular the execution of digital rules powerful enough to call forth complex worlds of activity. This new medium orients human activity in a stimulating visual environment that makes possible a release of creativity and a sense of empowerment in conditions of autonomy, sociality, and positive reward. The importance and impact of design on human activities undertaken in the visual-performative medium is a key theme.

A third aim of the book is ethnographic reportage—interpreting experiences of playing *World of Warcraft* for those who will never play but wish to understand something of the role of video games in our culture. This aim shapes Part three in particular, which examines topics such as addiction and gender about which I am often asked when describing my work.

The research was carried out in three locales: the virtual world of the game itself; Southern California, where my students and I conducted interviews; and China, where my research assistants and I spent a month observing players in Internet cafes and talking to them about *World of Warcraft*.

CHAPTER ONE

What Is *World of Warcraft* and Who Plays It?

Once I got over my initial disorientation in the game, I developed a strong sensation that I had woken up inside an animated fairy tale. I was not just watching and listening though; I played a starring role. *WoW* is a virtual experience like reading a book or watching a movie, but also an active experience like playing a sport. The digital universe couples the richness of the experience of viewing the action in a film or play with the participatory experience of athletics. Many video games are structured around this powerful combination, so perhaps it is not surprising that they have surpassed film in revenue (Bainbridge 2007). Video games have global appeal; some of the most popular titles are from Asia. *World of Warcraft,* produced in California, has more Chinese players than any other national group. *WoW* is played in North America, Europe, Latin America, Asia, Russia, Australia, New Zealand, and elsewhere. It is available in English, two versions of Chinese, Korean, German, French, two versions of Spanish, and Russian.

As someone entirely new to video games when I began the research, I am aware of how foreign they seem to many, even how pointless, simplistic, fatuous. I will attempt to build a picture of the captivation and fascination it is possible to experience in *World of Warcraft,* mindful that the visual allure, and sense of discovery and serendipity that imbue *WoW* play, cannot be captured in descriptive prose. Like Borges's cartographers, one desires to create a map that coincides "point for point" with the richness of the real geography. But that is neither possible nor wise, so I will fall back on a selective portrayal that communicates some, at least, of what it was that got the undergraduates so excited.

A Day in the Life of a Night Elf Priest

To begin, I recount a day in the life of my character Innikka (a pseudonym). She belongs to a "guild" or club of players with whom she plays and socializes. The priest character type in *World of Warcraft* heals players being attacked by monsters or other players, restoring them so that they may defeat their opponents and avoid a trip to the graveyard, the penalty for death. Dead players must run back to the spot where they died to be resurrected.

It is 6:00 a.m. Before facing my emails, I login to *WoW.* I'm checking the stock of a computer character that sells herbs I need for potions produced in the alchemy profession. Dealer Sadaqat, who vends "Potent Potables," has rock-bottom prices. It's early, and no one else is around. Sadaqat has dreaming glory, felweed, and netherbloom, as well as some potions I can buy and resell for a profit at the Auction House. I spend about five seconds selecting and purchasing the herbs and logoff.

5:30 p.m. Time for a raid. It's early in the evening for me, but many people in the guild are on the East Coast, so we have to get moving before it's too late for them. The raid won't start until 6:00, but "invites" go out 30 minutes in advance. To make sure I get a spot in the raid, I login promptly.

Raiding is one of the most complex activities in *World of Warcraft,* involving 10 to 40 people who join together to defeat difficult monsters. Careful preparation and tight coordination are necessary. Raiders communicate through *WoW*'s text chat and nearly always use voice chat as well.

I still have fifteen minutes before the raid. I fly into the Terrokar Forest and locate some good fishing spots. In a few minutes I have lots of the Golden Darters needed for the Golden Fish Sticks buff. I cook them up and feel prepared for the raid.

It's time to head to Serpentshrine Cavern, the site of the raid, for our first attempt at "SSC." Most of us have read up on the SSC fights in out-of-game forums, blogs, and wikis created and maintained by players. Some of us have watched player-created YouTube videos to get a sense of what lies ahead.

We are nervous and excited. There's lots of silly banter in the guild chat channel. Players invoke small commands called emotes to dance, flirt, kiss, hug, and execute other amusing actions. I exchange "whispers," or private

A Player's Bags Carry Their Items: Items in bag slots are labeled with the number of each. A player's gold is displayed; Innikka had 560 gold, 61 silver, and 65 copper at the time the picture was taken.

chats, with several guildmates. We will encounter difficult raid "bosses," that is, high-level monsters with tricky, powerful abilities. The bosses will "drop" very good "loot"—or treasure—valuable pieces of equipment that empower characters to perform their roles more effectively.

SSC is situated behind an enormous waterfall that players can penetrate only when formally grouped in a raid. We run through the waterfall. Promptly someone is comically killed by the "elevator boss"—the player has dashed into an open elevator shaft and fallen to his death. I have read about the elevator in player descriptions of SSC and step carefully to wait for it to rise to our level.

Once on the elevator, we descend deep into the cavern. Finally we are facing the first "trash mobs," that is, guards who must be killed on the way to the bosses. (*Mob* is a generic name for monster, derived from *mobile*.) Players call them trash because, while powerful, they rarely yield good treasure. We buff the raid with several life-giving, damage-enhancing, mob-defeating spells and proceed.

We immediately "wipe" on the trash—that is, the whole raid is killed. Everyone runs back from the graveyard for another try. We pull ourselves together and successfully kill the guards.

Now we are at the first boss we will attempt, a creature called the Lurker Below. He lives in a pool and must be fished up. We stand on platforms surrounding his pool. We catch the Lurker on a fishing line and begin battle. The raid erupts into a chaos of loud, frenetic activity. *WoW*'s sound effects layer the roars of the monsters, a mélange of auditory signals associated with player actions, the noises of special events such as explosions, and a musical sound track.

Things are going pretty well until the Lurker issues a "spout," during which we are supposed to dive off the platforms into the water. Some dive too late and are killed. We try to keep going with a diminished raid but lack the resources to bring down Lurker. We wipe and run back yet again.

After wiping, it takes time to reassemble, rebuff, and discuss what went wrong. In voice chat, the raid leaders tell us what to do and provide assessments of our mistakes. We ask questions and crack jokes. My guild, "Scarlet Raven," is a "casual raiding guild," so, while people are intent on performing well, there are no recriminations.

After one more wipe, we are getting the hang of the Lurker. We know when to jump into the water and how to coordinate so the minions he summons will not kill us.

This time the Lurker goes down. The raid is deliriously happy. Through teamwork and personal skill, we have survived the Lurker's deadly spouts, geysers, and water bolts—or at least most of us have. The fallen are raised by the healers. A group screenshot is taken of us surrounding the dead Lurker and will be posted later to the Scarlet Raven website.

We roll virtual dice on the Lurker's loot to see who will win it. Miraculously, I win the Earring of Soulful Meditation, a very fine trinket. We congratulate those who won loot and exult in our first kill in Serpentshrine Cavern.

Now it's time to try Hydross the Unstable, so named because he has lost his mind under the duress of a lengthy imprisonment in SSC. The crazed Hydross has several powerful allies at his behest, which must be quickly dispatched. We get ready for a very different kind of fight. The same cycle of wipes and retries ensues. Finally we defeat Hydross.

It has been an amazing evening. It's 10:00 p.m. for me but 1:00 a.m. for

East Coast guildmates. We must end the raid even though there are more bosses to kill in Serpentshrine Cavern. Guildmates say good night.

After all the excitement, I fly back to my quiet post in Stormspire to resume the vigil of the Potent Potables vendor.

A Short *WoW* Primer

Based on a long line of fantasy themes derived from a variety of sources, including *Lord of the Rings* and its predecessors, *World of Warcraft* is staged in a medieval setting. Players create animated fantasy characters that adventure in a landscape of castles, dungeons, ogres, dragons, and beasts (Fawcett 2006; Tschang 2007). Players battle monsters, amass treasure, conduct business at an auction house, practice crafts such as alchemy and blacksmithing, and seek to improve their characters through the acquisition of ever better weapons and armor. Players start at level 1 and can advance to level 80, in a process known as "leveling," by slaying monsters and completing quests (minigames) that award "experience points." The character is seen in the third person, usually from behind.[1]

WoW is a game of movement. The game geography is huge. Characters travel on foot or by beast, boat, or air through fields, farms, forests, jungles, deserts, mountains, seas, and other distinctive scenery for which Blizzard artists have won many awards. Players quest to find and slay hundreds of different types of creatures from the game's "bestiary"—creatures dwelling throughout the varied landscapes of the world.

The construction of the world has strong appeal to the modern consciousness—everything is human scale. No building is more than a few stories high. (Some areas are reached by elevator but are only one or two levels once one arrives.) The objects players wear, wield, win, buy, and sell, including weapons, vials of magical potions, fishing poles, armor, crafting implements such as mining picks, and resources like herbs, cloth, and precious stones, are easily handled by the (virtual) human hand.

WoW provides respite from the incessant advertising which is the backdrop of so much contemporary activity. Most of the Internet can no longer be experienced without a barrage of ads; *WoW* has none. It is restful, even old-fashioned. The only claim on the player's consciousness is the game itself, allowing the kind of immersion one imagines Victorians attained

Innikka

with their hefty novels into which they could sink for hours of commerce-free entertainment. This focused experience provides a refuge—an "escape," as players say—from modernity. It is one of the ways in which the game creates its own reality apart from contemporary life, moving the player away from the ordinary into the alternative reality of a fantasy space.

WoW is a *virtual world*—a set of linked activities chosen by the player and carried out within a three-dimensional virtual space.[2] The goal of most *WoW* activities is to develop a character, enabling it to perform more and more difficult challenges. The orientation toward character development oddly echoes another Victorian meme; Victorians also worked at "character development," which for them meant striving to improve moral sensibilities. The notion that one's "character" can be shaped and refined through deliberate activity is a powerful motivational field in which cultures, or subcultures, may organize themselves. Many video games take up this theme; Hunter and Lastowka (2004) observed that in games such as *EverQuest*,

Dark Age of Camelot, and *Ultima Online* "the clear goal is to become a more powerful [player]."

WoW researchers are often asked, "But isn't *WoW* just killing monsters"? Media discourse around video games often centers on questions of violence, so it is a natural question. While my work is not about violence, I want to clarify for those not familiar with *World of Warcraft* that it is not a violent game in the tradition of first-person shooters or certain strategy games in which realistic violence is central to the games' visceral appeal.[3] Killing monsters is an important activity in *WoW,* but it is in some sense an abstraction, a way to keep score. Play theorists observe that play often involves a contest. The Anglo-Saxon *plega* meant game, sport, fight, or battle (Turner 1982). A game requires something to battle against. *WoW* monsters are cartoonish, often silly, and in no way terrifying or realistic. They waddle, many are corpulent and ungainly, they emit gurgling noises when they die—and of course they will soon be back for the next encounter. *WoW* has none of the graphic visceral realism found in other video games such as blood spatters or frightening weaponry.[4]

Taylor's comment (2003a) about violence in *EverQuest* could also describe *World of Warcraft:*

> While combat in the game is on the one hand quite extreme (you kill monsters and potentially other players) and on the other also muted (there is graphically no blood or gore), my sense is that the enjoyment of violence takes place at an abstract level. It is closely tied to the skills involved to take down a mob, the precise timings and movements required, the skill of playing your class well in a battle situation, the adrenaline rush involved with a fight and the general ability to even engage in this type of activity . . . In this way the actual fight is as much an opportunity to demonstrate the valued qualities of game mastery as anything.

Players can create multiple characters. Ducheneaut et al. (2009) found an average of eight characters per *WoW* account. Usually one is the "main" character and the rest "alts" or alternative characters. Eight characters may sound like a lot, but many players focus on their main and play other characters only briefly to try them out or occasionally for a change.

Players may join guilds—named groups with officers and a chat channel—so they will have others with whom to play. In the opening vignette in the Prologue, Innikka's guild is having a meeting. Guilds range in size from a small handful to several hundred players (Ducheneaut et al. 2006). A character can belong to only one guild. Many players are guildless at the lower levels (and some beyond). Guilds become more important as players gain interest in certain of the more challenging activities in the game or in leveling quickly by grouping with others. Officers control guild membership. They can induct new members as well as remove players. In the vignette, Loro and Slams are guild officers trying to move the guild toward more organized activities to engage new game experiences.

Much sociable chat takes place in the guild channel. Most is game related although players may remark on their local weather, mention that they have a test to study for, or supply other small details revealing something of their personal lives. *World of Warcraft* is not a chat room, however, and personal information in the guild channel is limited. Some guilds have websites with forums and player profiles, some with photos and personal information, so players may get to know quite a bit about each other. Many players know each other in real life; however, they speak infrequently about their real lives in public chat channels. Players get to know more about one another through whispers. A feeling of intimacy may develop, but it remains private; the guild as a social unit is devoted to the game itself along with a lot of jokey banter.

Players may maintain a "friends list" that includes players inside and outside the guild. When a friend logs on or off, the system notifies the player with a small sound and a text message.

Parties and raids are temporary groups formed to accomplish a goal such as a quest or raid. They are composed of players with different, interdependent skills. Players choose a "class"—priest, paladin, mage, warlock, rogue, hunter, shaman, druid, warrior, or death knight—each of which has its own distinctive skills. Skills are divided into *damage* classes, whose powerful weapons and spells kill the monsters; heavily armored *tank* classes which use their abilities to gain the attention of the monsters to keep them from attacking others; and *healing* classes which restore players as they are attacked. Healers must ensure the survival of tanks, without whom the group will almost certainly perish (see Taylor 2006).

WoW vernacular names the various groupings with a masculine adjective: 5-man parties and 10-, 20-, 25-, and 40-man raids. Raids are conducted in "dungeons"—elaborate fantasy structures such as a school for necromancy, a decrepit mansion, the underground control room of a vast reservoir.

Parties and raids have their own chat channels. *WoW* has several chat channels, including general chat which broadcasts to a fairly large geographic area in the game, "yelling" which reaches a smaller local area, and "say" for a small local area.

Characters are divided into races. Medievally accented, *WoW* races are rooted in earlier games such as the paper and pencil *Dungeons and Dragons* and Blizzard's *Warcraft* series. Race is largely cosmetic (although each race has a few abilities players may deem useful). Players are divided into two "factions," each with its own races. The Alliance races—Night Elf, Gnome, Human, Dwarf, and Draenei—are generally considered more genial. The Horde faction is a bit scruffier; the Orc, Tauren, Troll, Undead, and Blood Elf races are (except for Blood Elves), rougher, bigger, or more depraved (e.g., Undead cannibalize). Selecting a race is an important decision; players will be looking at their characters a lot. Players consider some races ugly and some beautiful. Ducheneaut et al. (2009) reported that players were very aware of the looks of their characters, noting that "hair matters" and that players carefully chose among interesting features such as horns or facial tattoos (see also Noël et al. 2009). Gender is also an important cosmetic attribute with implications discussed in chapter 8.

The core battle experience in *World of Warcraft* is killing computer-generated monsters. But another kind of contest is popular among a segment of the population—player vs player. In PvP, players can attack and kill the characters of other players.

This style of play is abhorred by some and adored by others. Blizzard thus created two types of servers: "normal" or PvE (player vs environment) servers, where PvP is not permitted except in limited areas, and PvP servers where players can be attacked by other players in most (but not all) of the game geography. Players choose their server type when creating a character. In PvP, players enjoy "pwning" opponents, that is, defeating them, in heated contests. The term *pwn* (pronounced "pone") comes from *own*, slang for *defeat*, and is said to have originated when a player mistakenly typed a "p" instead of an "o," the two being adjacent on the QWERTY keyboard. (Pwning is possible in many contexts, not just PvP.)

PvP increases contingency, ratchetting the game experience up a level—players must be constantly aware of surrounding players and ready to do battle (or flee) at any moment. Nonplayer characters (NPCs) are predictable and can usually be avoided if the player is not ready to fight. But human players bring cunning, sneakiness, and what I can only call orneriness to the game. Players trying to complete quests may be attacked and killed, slowing their progress. "Ganking" is the practice of attacking players at a lower level than oneself (and hence easy to kill) or attacking at sensitive times such as when a player is trying to complete a difficult quest or is almost dead from a fight. An extreme form of ganking is "corpse camping," wherein a player kills another player and remains by the corpse, "camping" it, killing the player after he resurrects and is in a weakened condition (sometimes repeatedly). These actions are perfectly legal in the game; the prescribed remedy is to get a posse of guildmates and friends to kill the ganker.

A third type of server is devoted to role-playing in which characters speak in a kind of humorous, ersatz Ye Olde English patois (see Kavetsky 2008). I have conducted no research on these servers, and they are much less popular than PvE or PvP servers. However, they have their devotees and are said to attract mature, serious players.

MMORPGs and Virtual Worlds

Another descriptor for *World of Warcraft* is MMORPG or massively multiplayer online role-playing game. Chess is an early example of a game whose pieces are humanlike characters instead of ciphers (as in checkers). A bit of backstory accompanies the chess pieces, but chess is a strategy game, not one in which players develop a unique character with a particular role, as in role-playing games. In role-playing games (whether pencil and paper, board games, or online), players choose a single character type. In *WoW* they choose one of ten types called "classes" and develop the character as they wish.

MMORPGs are role-playing games with hundreds, thousands, or millions of players. However, the acronym is awkward and not entirely accurate. *World of Warcraft* is a social world as much as a game. It is similar in some ways to environments such as *Second Life* in which participants create characters and activities in a three-dimensional virtual world (see Klastrup 2008).

I will refer to environments such as *World of Warcraft* and *Second Life* as virtual worlds. In these worlds, participants (1) create an animated character, (2) move the character in a three-dimensional space, (3) have means for communicating with others, and (4) access a rich array of digital objects. As elsewhere, the culture of a virtual world is enacted through human conversation and designed objects that mediate activity (Leontiev 1974; Vygotsky 1986). Virtual worlds perhaps feel more authentically like cultures than chat rooms because of the elaboration of space and objects.

Who Plays *World of Warcraft?*

While in a long line to purchase memorabilia at BlizzCon, an older man and a younger woman stood in front of me. The man (probably recognizing a familiar life form) turned around and said in a friendly way, "What characters do you play?" We got to talking, and he turned out to the be the woman's father. They both played, as did the man's son. The man said he played "so I have something to talk to my kids about." The woman had met her husband in *WoW*. They played together casually at first, then started talking in voice chat, then arranged a face-to-face meeting, although they lived across the country from one other. Things went well, and they got married, had a baby, and seemed to be living happily ever after. Baby was in the hotel with hubby and grandma, who also played, so that mom and granddad could have some free time at the conference.

By the time I got to BlizzCon I was not surprised to hear this story. But when I began my research, I assumed that the stereotype of the video gamer as self-absorbed young male with few social skills and little interest in anything beyond gaming was probably more or less true. ("A fat guy living in his mother's basement" is one satirical stereotype.) I was pleased to run into a much more interesting mix of people. My demographic data slowly accumulated as I got to know players in my guilds and as I chatted informally with players in "pickup groups" or "pugs" (ad hoc groups much like pickup basketball games formed for questing or raiding).

The *WoW* player population had considerable variance in age, gender, and social class. One of my online friends was a carpenter who worked in a factory making windows. Another was an intensive care nurse. An older guildmate had multiple disabling chronic illnesses. He took many medications, some of which kept him awake. *World of Warcraft* was a major part of his social life, and he played at odd hours, day and night. A former guild master in Scarlet Raven was a graduate student in chemistry.

A student we interviewed in San Diego described the demographic diversity of the 40-man raids he attended.

> You've got forty men—well, men in general, but they have women, and children there too, and it's pretty fun. You have a group of people trying to work for the same purpose.

No solid demographic information is publicly available for *World of Warcraft*. The problems of sampling 11 million players playing in seven languages and many more national cultures are daunting. Yee's self-reported data, collected on websites outside the game with a sample of 2,000 players, indicated about 21 percent female players (Yee 2005). My guess is that this figure is probably roughly correct for North American servers but almost certainly wrong for China, where my counts in Internet cafes showed about 10 percent female players. There are no public data of any kind for European, Korean, Latin American, and other players of which I am aware. My goal is not to pin down precise numbers (which is impossible) but to suggest that *World of Warcraft* is more open to females and older players than games such as first-person shooters (see Fullerton et al. 2007) and that *WoW* is a virtual world in which different social classes rub elbows.

How does one determine age, gender, and social class in a virtual fantasy world? Players themselves make this information available. The Scarlet Raven website had a photo gallery, so gender and approximate age were obvious for players who posted pictures. When players spoke on voice chat, gender was revealed. Age was trickier as voice quality was not always clear and age can only be approximately guessed through voice. Social class was often revealed as people used class-specific grammar (for example, uttering phrases such as "I seen the mob"). Photographs on the Scarlet Raven website showed homes and furnishings typical of particular social classes. Occupation is a good indicator of social class, and players often mentioned their occupations in chat or on the guild website. Smoking and social class are correlated (Jha et al. 2006). Players often paused for smoke breaks.

My sense is that the statistically modal player in *World of Warcraft* is a male in his twenties (see Yee 2005). But statistics do not reveal the nuances of the social atmosphere created by the presence of male and female, older and younger players. Scarlet Raven had a couple of young teens whose parents played in the guild. Occasionally the teens would make inappropriate remarks. One would often leave in the middle of a group activity when he had something else to do. While these events were annoying, it was part of the culture of the guild to tolerate the young people. Some of the older members such as an architect and a real estate agent were stabilizing influences, sometimes making calming remarks to defuse a tactless chat comment or ward off misinterpretation. The guild leaders were in their twenties and thirties, and one in his forties. They did not hesitate to remove players who behaved inappropriately. One evening a young male player typed the URL of a porn site into the chat line. The next night I saw him removed from the guild as someone had reported the incident to an officer. Scarlet Raven was far from a squeaky clean guild, but promulgating porn was outside its boundaries.

The presence of female players mitigated rough masculine discourse, toning down, although certainly not eliminating, profanity, homophobic discourse, and sexist comments. Language was negotiated. One evening a female player objected to a male player's liberal use of the F word in voice chat because her young children were nearby. The male player countered that he always talked that way and could not change. His girlfriend, who was also playing, said, "Come on, Tellison. You don't talk like that around my mother." Tellison managed to express himself more conservatively that evening. However, the dominance of male players statistically, and in terms of masculine rhetorical style, was assumed and protected (a topic explored further in chapter 8). When I first spoke on voice chat after joining a new guild, the raid leader said, "Oh, this is a girl." I said jokingly, "Yes, this is a girl, you have to be nice." He shot back, "No, we don't!"

Many players commented on the mix of players as a positive aspect of the game. A student at the University of California, San Diego, said:

> And, you know, as far as game play goes, like, there are people with different backgrounds that come together. Yeah, that really amazes me. I don't know what else to say. I mean, if I go on anymore it might sound corny, you know. So, yeah, but it's just that feeling.

Despite the reality of the diverse population playing *World of Warcraft*, the stereotype of the lonely gamer persists. I have been playing *World of*

Warcraft so long that I am startled when people ask about the lonely players who are cut off from "real" social life. (See Ducheneaut and Moore, 2004; Ducheneaut et al. 2006; Nardi and Harris 2006; Steinkuehler and Williams 2006; Williams et al. 2006; Bainbridge 2007; DiGiuseppe and Nardi 2007; Nardi et al. 2007; Lindtner et al. 2008 on social aspects of *WoW*.) In fact, I was inspired to write this book at a New Year's Eve party a few years ago when I found myself trying to explain multiplayer video games to my puzzled middle-aged neighbors in Half Moon Bay, California (where we spend vacations). Most have PhDs or law degrees and are generally well informed. But they had encountered only media stereotypes about games centered on themes such as addiction and lonely kids with no friends.

Many players played with friends and/or family members (see Taylor 2003b; Nardi and Harris 2006; Peterson 2007). The game was an extension of their existing social lives. This was true in both North America and China. Nightflower, a 53-year-old mother of seven, explained in an online interview:

> my oldest son just started playing last week and i am thrilled! he lives in NC [North Carolina] and we haven't been close for a while . . . but now we talk a lot more ig and irl [in-game and in real life].

One player, who played with two siblings and a nephew, said that they used a voice chat program to talk while they played. It was "like all being in the same room playing for a few hours a day." He had a brother who played with his wife and their 9- and 14-year-old daughters, re-creating the family through the characters. In one of my guilds, a mother of two who homeschooled her children used *WoW* as part of the curriculum to study typing and math. A married couple I interviewed played together and had chosen the character names Toast and Jam to identify themselves as linked. At BlizzCon I met a woman who proudly said she played "with three generations"—herself, her teenage daughter, and her mother. As will be discussed in chapter 9, in China people often played together in Internet cafes with friends from their immediate neighborhood.

Not only do people draw on existing social connections to explore virtual worlds, the virtual world itself is a stimulus to real world interaction. *WoW* was often a topic of offline conversation for people who played together and even for those who played but not together. One player said that he had gotten his brother to start playing, ". . . and, as a result we have new things to talk about, like in-game stuff." Another player, introduced to the game by his brother who was several years older, said, "Now we finally have something to talk about."

Study participants commented frequently in the interviews about the importance of socializing. A student at the University of California, San Diego, said:

> Well, I'd have to say, you know, getting with people, grouping, following the pack. You kind of get that—you get a nice feeling, like you're part of something. That's what it is.

Another player said:

> It's about interaction, it's about hooking up with people, it's about fighting with people. It's about—you know, that's where you build your game from. It's a people game.

And:

> This game is like, you know, real people, real talking human beings, you know. We can process, we can talk, we can think. So, you know, mostly it's about talking with people, hanging with people. You kind of get that—it's kind of like traveling the world without traveling the world, basically.

Those who come to the game on their own have ways of meeting new people in an open environment in which players expect to be approached by strangers (Nardi and Harris 2006; see also Brown and Bell 2004). The following chat log shows portions of an hour's play between my priest and a hunter, Delbarth, who formed a party. We approached a cave at the same time. I was on the quest Insane Druids, which required slaying Taneel Darkwood, Uthil Mooncall, and Mavoris Cloudsbreak. Delbarth and I switched from local area chat (the nearby vicinity) to party chat (just those in the formal party) at about 21:38.

1/8 20:59:41.690 To Delbarth: are you doing insane druids?
1/8 21:02:13.481 Delbarth says: do you want to party up?

1/8 21:02:20.599 Delbarth has invited you to join a group.

1/8 21:02:50.556 Delbarth says: what point in the quest are you at?

1/8 21:03:02.604 Innikka says: starting

1/8 21:03:12.441 Innikka says: how about you?

1/8 21:03:24.256 Delbarth says: I have killed two of them —need taneel still

1/8 21:03:30.935 Innikka says: ok

1/8 21:03:32.444 Delbarth says: lets give it a go :)

1/8 21:03:35.112 Innikka says: k

[many monsters are slain, including, finally, Taneel]

1/8 21:38:11.186 [Party] Innikka: ok got taneel!

1/8 21:38:11.809 [Party] Delbarth: oh yeah!

1/8 21:38:37.388 [Party] Delbarth: I am done with the quest, but you want to keep going?

1/8 21:38:44.612 [Party] Innikka: yes!

[several monsters later]

1/8 21:41:41.345 [Party] Delbarth: you ok with mana?

1/8 21:41:46.243 [Party] Innikka: yes

1/8 21:43:53.959 [Party] Delbarth: DING

1/8 21:44:00.636 [Party] Delbarth: 30th - wooh!

1/8 21:44:05.665 [Party] Innikka: hurray!

[yet more monsters]

1/8 21:54:00.856 [Party] Delbarth: shall we keep going?

1/8 21:54:06.858 [Party] Innikka: yes

[Innikka gets one more of the monsters she needs]

1/8 21:55:32.578 [Party] Delbarth: thanks for the healing :)

1/8 21:56:46.311 [Party] Delbarth: I need to stop for the night - my wife is getting ancy :)

1/8 21:57:03.302 [Party] Innikka: ok. thanks a lot for helping. and congrats on 30

1/8 21:57:20.881 [Party] Delbarth: thanks for the help, as well - can't do that dungeon solo, for sure!

The players I encountered had interests beyond *World of Warcraft*. I knew two players who bowled weekly. Members of Scarlet Raven participated in sports, including skiing, football, deep-sea diving, and river rafting. Others enjoyed offroading, martial arts, photography, international travel, and amateur theatricals. One player built a truck. Another was a professional wrestler who posted his (terrifying) YouTube wrestling videos on the website. Another played in a rock band. One player posted a picture of himself with the caption "Here I am in the middle of mixing mud for laying concrete block at a Habitat House in Georgia." Another served communion at his local county jail, which he jokingly referred to as the "hoosegow." He was involved in outreach activities for female prisoners. Parents in Scarlet Raven put up pictures of their children on the guild website. The general impression I had of many *WoW* players was that they were active people looking for intense, engaging, online experiences that complemented similarly engaging offline activities.

In addition to people with many varied interests, *World of Warcraft* also attracted parents whose lives were circumscribed by shift work and/ or young children. I met several young fathers at home tending sleeping children while their wives worked a shift. One of my guildmates sometimes left for several minutes to care for her young children who were watching television or playing together but needed a snack or other attention. As in many online communities, *WoW* had its share of people with disabilities for whom the game provided sociality, challenge, and variety difficult to attain in other venues.

One of the most striking things about *World of Warcraft* was the way it brought together social classes for authentic shared activity. I realized how limited my own social universe was when I began to perceive that I was spending many pleasant hours with people very different than I. One player was a military wife whose husband had been to Iraq three times on the front lines. Another lived on what he called a "hamburger farm," raising cattle in Missouri. Many players worked weekend or late-night shifts. One would logon telling us he smelled of grease from working in his brother's restaurant. A player who had been fired from Home Depot complained that his manager did not appreciate him even though he "did all the heavy lifting." This comment made me feel a little guilty since I use the expression "doing the heavy lifting" jokingly. For my guildmate, the words were not an arch jest but expressed a difficult physical reality. Through voice chat, I experienced varied North American regional accents (those so carefully cleansed from the mass media) from places like East Texas, Alabama, West Virginia, and Quebec.

A 21-year-old psychology major one of my research assistants interviewed commented on the diversity of players in his guild and how they had become skilled at designing and maintaining his guild's website.

> And most of them [don't do anything technical] for their living; most of them it's just random, you know, MAE [mainstream American English] teachers, and you've got all these crazy, you know, like, bus drivers. People from different backgrounds basically, just doing this amazing thing and they're not even computer technicians. They have no knowledge whatsoever, they just, you know, read the website and they come up with a really cool look or like a really flashy guild forum.

I found the following guild description on the Internet, posted on a guild website.

> Our guild is . . . growing daily as people see who and what we are: A group of players who casual Raid with a small core Elite Raid Group. We are all working class, have kids, family or other RL [real life] stuff to distract us from WoW. Afkkids is common for us and no one complains, even when we have to AFK 20 minutes as someone has to put their Kids to bed.

(AFK means away from keyboard. /afk returns a message to anyone who sends a message that the player is AFK.)

The glue that brought people together was the game itself. As a guild master in Scarlet Raven remarked on the guild website:

> Basically, Scarlet Raven is one big extended family. Some of us barely know each other. Some of us know each other in real life. Some of us know each other only in game. Some of us have spent years playing together. The one thing we all have in common is that we enjoy WoW and although we may sometimes stumble as a player, as a guild, even as a real life person, what makes Scarlet Raven a success is that we get back up, work out a solution, and we push onwards to the next obstacle. All while maintaining an enjoyable balance of gaming, community, and everything in between.

Some guilds were built around shared characteristics such as a religion or sexual orientation. There were Christian guilds, gay guilds, location-based guilds, family guilds, military guilds, guilds of coworkers, and guilds of professional colleagues. Such guilds tailored play to suit their values. Christian guilds, for example, usually requested that players avoid foul language (such avoidance not being the norm in *World of Warcraft*). While *WoW* has a profanity filter, even with the filter on players still see messages such as "that was f@#$%* stupid." In Christian guilds, no player ever need see such a message, at least not in guild or private chat. A list of Christian guilds at the CGAlliance website (CGAlliance n.d.) included evocative guild names such as God's Humble Servants, Mustard Seed Conspiracy, Carriers of the Cross, Servants of Faith, WWJD, The Forgiven, The Narrow Path, and Troop Agape.

A spoof at a widely linked website that pokes fun at fundamentalist Christians satirized Christian gamers and the lonely gamer stereotype:

> I think the reason so many people are open to hearing about Jesus in the World of Warcraft is because the majority of people who play the game are lonely kids who don't have any friends. I doubt any of them play sports so you can pretty much guess that there are lots of gay boys and fat little pale-faced Wiccan girls on the servers who hate themselves and escape into virtual characters so they don't have to deal with their pathetic lives. When they hear that someone loves them, even if it is just the Lord Jesus Christ, they always want to hear more! (LandoverBaptist n.d.)

The spoof playfully twists the characterization of gamers as isolated losers seeking solace in a video game. As more diverse populations take up video games, the notion of the lonely gamer, and games as the last refuge of the socially unfit, becomes parody, satire. My data, and that of others, suggest the fundamental wrongheadedness of the stereotype; instead of a withdrawal into fantasy worlds, we see the extrusion of the worlds into ordinary life as family and friends play together, as players gather in Internet cafes, and as they meet and socialize with others online.

CHAPTER TWO

An Ethnographic Investigation of *World of Warcraft*

When I began my study, I had no hypotheses or precise research questions. Unlike research in most academic disciplines, where investigation proceeds according to a scientific procedure involving hypothesis generation and testing, ethnography moves in a "go with the flow" pattern that attempts to follow the interesting and the unexpected as they are encountered in the field. I initiated the research with a desire to satisfy a deeply felt urge of the cultural anthropologist—to journey to a foreign land, to discover and experience the strangeness of a new culture, to find out what the natives are doing and what they think about what they are doing. The impetus to discovery (from the point of view of the discoverer, of course) has fueled anthropology at least since Henry Schoolcraft wrote accounts of Native American tribes 150 years ago. Schoolcraft was the first to systematically record the poetry, legends, and lore of indigenous cultures from Minnesota to the Eastern Seaboard. Longfellow based "The Song of Hiawatha" on Schoolcraft's publications. As Schoolcraft (1856/1990) wrote in a dedication to Longfellow:

> Greece and Rome, England and Italy, have so long furnished . . . the field of poetic culture that it is, at least, refreshing to find, both in theme and metre, something new.

Recently, opportunities for "something new" appear to have foreclosed in anthropology. Anthropologists have documented nearly every culture on earth, and the "primitives" to whom we have been devoted are disappearing into modernity. The blockage created by diminished opportunities to study cultures untouched by cosmopolitan markets and states has left contemporary anthropology somewhat unsettled. It is not surprising, then, that some turn to what appear to be new cultural forms emerging in virtual worlds. These social milieux offer up a chance to cast an anthropological gaze on fresh sets of natives and their exotic ways (e.g., Miller and Slater 2000; Wilson and Peterson 2002; Golub 2007, 2009; Williams 2007; Boellstorff 2008; Ito 2008; Malaby 2009; Pearce 2009).

Once the anthropologist has located some strangers in a strange land, how does she proceed? Simply by going down the rabbit hole; there are no formulaic plans to follow. As anthropologist Marilyn Strathern wrote:

> Ethnography is . . . the deliberate attempt to generate more data than the researcher is aware of at the time of collection . . . Rather than devising research protocols that will purify the data in advance of analysis, the anthropologist embarks on a participatory exercise which yields materials for which analytical protocols are often devised after the fact. (2004)

As an example of this style of data collection, I have amassed thousands of pages of chat logs recorded with a game function, /chatlog, which creates a file with a record of all chat in the chat window. I do not always know what I am going to do with the logs, but when a question begins to simmer I have rich data to consult.

The "participatory exercise" of which Strathern spoke is referred to in anthropology as "participant-observation." The ethnographer observes the culture in which he is situated but also *participates* to varying degrees. In studying *World of Warcraft*, my practice tilted toward the participant end of participant-observation. It would be impossible to penetrate the game without becoming engaged as a player.

Strathern's commentary builds on the history of anthropology, a discipline devoted to generating deep understandings of human activity and the cultures in which it is embedded. Such understandings require lengthy engagement with social groups and generally involve a good deal of qualitative data. Strathern pointed to the "generation of more data than the researcher is aware of at the time of collection." Anthropologists collect an abundance of materials: texts, audio and video recordings, observations, and any and all relevant artifacts. We attend to important events but also slavishly observe the everyday, the mundane, the boring (although it is not boring to us). People, objects, and events that a journalist would pass over as lacking newsworthiness we find deeply interesting. Since understandings of a culture develop as we collect data, we often cannot make sense of the data until we have "grown up" in the culture at least partially, gaining enough sense to analyze the materials we have accumulated. A journalist, by contrast, must immediately turn out a "story" with coherence and interest. Anthropologists take time to sink into a culture.

Most anthropological fieldwork requires a budget for foreign travel and the necessity to leave home. It often requires living under difficult circumstances. The cost of entering a virtual world is very low—in the case of *World of Warcraft* 50 dollars for the game CDs and 14 dollars a month for the subscription. No research grants or struggles with a foreign language were necessary to initiate the research. Nor was there a need to cope with disturbing food, large insects, filth, dangerous diseases, or homesickness. My entry point to the field site was a computer on my dining room table where I sat in a comfortable chair and played for many hours. And yet this fieldwork was nearly as immersive as the fieldwork I conducted for my postdoctoral research in Western Samoa or Papua New Guinea, where I accompanied my husband for his doctoral research. I typically played about 20 hours a week. I read fewer novels and slept a bit less. In addition to game play, I read my guild's website nearly every day and spent considerable time reading about *World of Warcraft* on the Internet.

Comforts of home notwithstanding, I grew curious about the largest group of *WoW* players—the Chinese. I traveled to Beijing for a month in August 2007 (no need to suffer: excellent food and a vibrant city) to investigate play in China. *World of Warcraft* was very prominent in the Chinese gaming scene.

Silvia Lindtner, a graduate student, assisted, conducting interviews in both Beijing and Shanghai with the help of a Chinese American assistant, Jui Dai. He Jing and Wenjing Liang, graduate students in sociology and anthropology at Peking University, collaborated with us, providing translation, analysis, and cultural interpretation. In the United States, I conducted interviews with the assistance of two undergraduate students, Nicholas DiGiuseppe and Tony Vu. Vu conducted interviews in the San Diego area and DiGiuseppe in Irvine. Justin Harris, a graduate student, conducted interviews and in-game observations. Stella Ly, a UCI employee, conducted observations in her guild. Yong Ming Kow, a graduate student, conducted interviews in China and North America on players who write software modifications. Trina Choontanom and Rubin Singh, undergraduate students at the University of California, Irvine, contributed to the research with studies of player customization. With these students, I have generated around 200 formal interviews resulting in thousands of pages of transcripts, as well as participant-observations from our various points of view.

I know far less of play in China than North America. General observations about *World of Warcraft* reflect North American practice unless noted. Most of what I have to say about China is in chapter 9. I sometimes use a quote from a Chinese interview if it expresses a sentiment common to China and North America.

My research methods were the standard methods of anthropology: interviews, observations, participant-observation, informal conversations, and document analysis. Most of the interviews were conducted face-to-face; I find I learn more when I sit down with someone for an unhurried conversation. The interviews were audiotaped and transcribed. Some interviews were conducted online. The interviews utilized a fixed set of questions, but, like most ethnographic interviews, they opportunistically followed the contours of the conversation. If the study participant said something interesting, the topic was pursued. I also read many *WoW*-related websites, blogs, forums, wikis, and news articles and watched *WoW*-related videos.

How does an anthropologist go about describing and analyzing a field site? There are two strategies. The first is through the application of theory. In this book I analyze *World of Warcraft* using activity theory and the closely related ideas of John Dewey. The second strategy is the accretion of a multitude of details that impart a sense of the everyday texture of experience in a culture. I present the details of the game in descriptions of the game itself, in specific episodes of activity, and through the words of players themselves.

An important part of my methodology in studying *World of Warcraft* was participant-observation. My primary guild, Scarlet Raven, was home to Innikka. Scarlet Raven comprised a diverse group of people including engineers, programmers, students, retail clerks, restaurant workers, a real estate agent, an architect, a truck driver, a machinist, traveling salespeople, a worker at a health spa, a commercial pilot, a bartender, a firefighter, an emergency medical technician, a stocker at a big box store, a city bus driver, a man who drove a billboard on a truck through a large city, and many others. There were about 200 people in the guild. Most were male, but about 20 percent were female (guild membership fluctuated). Female members included graduate students, a chef, a receptionist, a veterinarian, and a young girl who played with her brother and cousin.

A second guild, Terror Nova (its real name), on the Eitrigg server, was composed of people with a connection to games research. Participation in Terror Nova helped me keep up with research and was an occasion to play purely for fun. It was not a site of research. The third guild, which I will call The Derelict (a pseudonym), was a small guild of primarily working-class people, military personnel, and students. Scarlet Raven and Terror Nova were raiding guilds, where players took the game seriously and explored high-end content. They used tools that measure player performance and maintained a competitive atmosphere. The Derelict, by contrast, was a guild with limited raiding. I played there for several months to get a sense of dynamics in a small guild. In December 2008, my own family formed a small guild, the Hoodoos, on the Anatheron server for pwnage and family bonding.

Playing in several guilds was enormously time consuming (but fun!). Innikka was always busy, though my other characters led more circumscribed virtual lives. I did not participate in a "hardcore" raiding guild enforcing a strict schedule of required raiding, so even during the most intense periods of play, I maintained flexibility.

All names referring to guilds, guild members, and characters (except Terror Nova and the Hoodoos) are pseudonyms. All screenshots are from my research in North America and China, or from the Hoodoos, unless noted.

Scarlet Raven, on a North American server, was composed of members primarily from the United States and Canada but also Scotland and Australia. Despite time differences, the Scots and Australians managed to join in many guild activities and to serve in leadership roles. The Canadian presence was strong, as several guild leaders were from both the English- and French-speaking parts of Canada. The Australians and Scots joined Scarlet Raven through North American friends with whom they enjoyed playing.

My guildmates were incurious about my research. I told them about it, conducted short interviews online with some members, and posted mes-

The Hoodoos Visit Zul'Farrak

sages on the guild website. I did not meet any guild members offline. My research was not salient in my guild interactions. I hope making this point goes some way toward answering the question anthropologists are often asked: are you perturbing the culture you are studying by your very presence? As far as I can tell, I have caused virtually no perturbations in *World of Warcraft* apart from stimulating some players to reflect a bit more on their play experiences as a result of having been interviewed. I can identify no risks the research posed.

One of the first things an ethnographic investigation requires is finding a way to enter a new culture. In *WoW* that meant finding a guild since my interest was in social life. Landing a spot in a good guild takes some time if a player is not playing with friends or family. As a low-level, unguilded player, it is common to receive invitations to join guilds as they seek new members. Guilds want to expand to replace players who have moved to other guilds or left the game or to balance teams. I accepted my first invitation at around level 20. I spent a few weeks in the guild but did not feel much of a connection to its members. When a personable young player with whom I had been chatting issued me a guild invitation, I left my guild and joined his. Loro headed a wonderful guild that had several female players, including a social worker, a journalist from the Philippines, and an elementary school teacher, as well as vibrant personalities of both genders. We had a huge amount of fun PvPing, throwing guild parties, and convening guild meetings in which players humorously subverted Loro's efforts to conduct serious guild business.

As so often happens in *WoW* guilds, interpersonal conflict, i.e., drama, reared its ugly head. One day Loro disappeared without a word. The school-teacher took over but then broke up with her boyfriend who had gotten her into the game, and left *WoW*. The guild sadly disbanded.

After that guild came a third, in which again I did not make a good connection to the players. Loro, meanwhile, was still around and had been scouting guilds. He joined Scarlet Raven and got the officers to invite me. More drama surrounding Loro ensued, and he left Scarlet Raven (and then the server). But I found Scarlet Raven an excellent group of people with whom to play and stayed for two years.

Scarlet Raven was a little older and more mature than many guilds. "Mature" is a relative term; you had to be 18 to be in the guild. Even this restriction was only a rule of thumb, and the guild had some younger members who were the children or relatives of older members.

Many guild members were parents with small children. It was not unusual for game play to stop as a player settled an infant who had awakened or took time out to bandage a skinned knee. Part of the guild ethos was that members had real lives, so such actions were to be tolerated politely and patiently. In hardcore guilds, this would not be the case. Many Scarlet Raven members were professionals who traveled; they had little time for play when away and were not always available for group activities—again something that would not be possible in a hardcore guild (see Taylor 2003b; Malone 2007).

The following quote, from a discussion on the Scarlet Raven website, gives a sense of the kinds of materials anthropologists deploy to communicate understandings about a culture. (Spelling and grammar will be unchanged when I quote from websites and chats.)

Windsong: Before I got WoW, I had a lot of fun with my PS2, Xbox, Gamecube, and PC games. I loved checking out the latest games, and I played lots of RTS [real time strategy games] like Dawn of War and Battle for Middle Earth. Since WoW, I ain't bought a damn thing. Battle for Middle earth has both a sequel out now, and an expansion coing out xmas, and i won't buy either. I love Neverwinter Nights 1, had all expansions and tons of downloaded content. I won't buy the new one either. Other games are enticing, but in WoW what you do is persistent. It stays around. You can share your achievements with others. I mean, I heard that Oblivion was a simply awesome game . . . but I can't see the point anymore of playing a game where you increase level, get new cool looking armor and weapons that do neat stuff and you play your game on your own.

Here, I can not only show off my neat new gear that I can use now that I leveled yadda yadda, but I can use it to help your character through a tough [fight], and have a shared experience. The multiplayer experience really is the reason I can't stop playing this game.

Windsong was a reflective, articulate player. He posted regularly on the guild website. He did not "speak for" other players but expressed what I have heard dozens of players express in varying ways. Moreover, this text was addressed to guild members, not to me as an anthropologist.

Methodologically, there was not a great deal of difference between my work on *World of Warcraft* and my previous work. The ethnography involved considerable face-to-face contact in interviews with players and observations of players in homes, dorms, and Internet cafes, so it was not purely virtual. My goals were to understand the natives and try to make sense of their activities, as in any ethnography.

One difference in studying *WoW* was that the research inclined toward the *participant* end of participant-observation. I learned to play the game well enough to participate in a raiding guild. I looked just like any other player. For many practical purposes, I *was* just another player. I could not have studied raiding guilds without playing as well as at least an average player and fully participating in raids. By contrast, when I was walking around villages in Papua New Guinea or Western Samoa, I was obviously an outsider whose identity required explanation. When I investigated technological practices in a neurosurgery operating room, I donned scrubs, sat in the operating room, and looked like a doctor but, thankfully, was not given the opportunity to remove any brain tumors! Online, my *WoW* character appeared as any character, and I was a full participant in game activities. Pearce (2009) suggested the term *participant-engagement* to describe this style of work in which the researcher is deeply immersed in native practices.

Blending in, however, is not necessarily characteristic of research in virtual worlds; it does not distinctly identify "digital ethnography." In research I conducted in *Second Life* with IBM, my participation as a researcher was made clear to others to the point of having a halo over my character's head to identify my special status. Boellstorff (2008) and Pearce (2009) were identified as researchers in the virtual worlds they studied. It may be more natural to set up shop as an anthropologist in non-game worlds; in a game world, the overwhelming need to *play* dominates interaction much of the time. While it is easy to blend in online, the researcher's position with respect to those being studied depends on the nature of the virtual world and the activities under investigation.

A limitation of my research is lack of knowledge of the culture of Blizzard Entertainment. *World of Warcraft* is a product of that culture, and nearly everything that happens in *WoW* is linked in some way to Blizzard. As of this writing, Blizzard had not opened its doors to ethnographic examination as Linden Lab did (see Malaby 2009). I utilized whatever traces of Blizzard culture I could muster: aspects of the design of the game itself revealed corporate preoccupations, employee posts on official Blizzard forums demonstrated the shaping of corporate-player relations, and BlizzCon was an opportunity to hear what Blizzard movers and shakers had to say in media interviews and panel discussions.

PART TWO

Active Aesthetic Experience

CHAPTER THREE

Play as Aesthetic Experience

An obvious question about *World of Warcraft* is: Why do people like it so much? What is the nature of this human activity that captivates so many people? Why is *WoW* "addictive," compelling, absorbing, pleasurable?

It is tempting, and for good reason, to see *WoW*'s hold on players as the outcome of an elaborately designed Skinner box (Ducheneaut et al. 2006; Yee 2006). The constant, predictable forward progress of moving through the levels is a strong motivator. As one study participant, Mark, a teacher in his thirties, said:

> I think what drives the majority of the people is sort of goal orientation. You have goals. And so, there's this very easy goal of leveling, right? It's this numerically-defined kind of thing. You have this target. You get these rewards of experience. There's also goals of, say, improving your character's abilities through equipment. Things like that. So, you—really, you're trying to improve yourself.

In addition to the regularized progress of leveling, there was the intermittent reinforcement of unpredictable rewards. We know that intermittent reinforcement is the most compelling schedule for both rats and people (Perkins and Cacioppo 1950). Although I have not seen a clinical analysis of *World of Warcraft*, a Canadian player who was a psychology student with a specialty in addiction wrote to me in an email (used with permission):

> WoW rewards players systematically with level increases that happen fre-

quently at first and then less frequently as time goes by (and you and I both know the little thrill we get every time we "ding" [attain a new level]. This is also reinforced socially by the congratulations we receive from other players). So WoW uses the principle of shaping to reinforce play behaviour. There are also the randomly generated rewards of having good gear drop unexpectedly from mobs or [treasure] chests. This intermittent reinforcement may be the most powerful variable that maintains play. Gambling works on a similar principle. We've known since Skinner's work in the 30s that intermittently reinforced behaviours are the most difficult to extinguish, and WoW capitalises on that.

Players watched the "experience bar" which visualizes experience points. It always, satisfyingly, moved upward. In real life, progress is up and down when there is progress at all. In *WoW*, play was rewarded with advancement. Many players started new characters because they liked the leveling process so much. In the interviews, players reported that they enjoyed leveling and considered it a major attraction of the game.

But as the psychology student pointed out, it is perhaps the intermittent reinforcements that really kept players hooked. When one sits down to play *WoW*, there are a thousand little opportunities for intermittent reinforcement. A miner might acquire a rare jewel stone along with his everyday ore. A mob might drop a rare item of great value. As a member of Scarlet Raven commented in guild chat, such game events "can brighten your day."

One of the main forms of intermittent reinforcement in *WoW* was the acquisition of a piece of rare, high-end equipment. First there was a difficult mob to defeat. Then the equipment had to drop according to probabilities laid out in loot tables. Chances of the equipment dropping were often less than 10 percent (and in some cases much less). Then the player rolled the virtual dice against other players who might also want the equipment. When a player won, it was big! Players floated on the excitement for hours or even days. Skinner does indeed tell us something useful about *World of Warcraft*.

But there was more than Skinnerian dynamics at play in *World of Warcraft*. The gaming experience was woven of sociality, the visual beauty of the game world, and a sense of performative mastery. This chapter begins the task of exploring these themes, drawing on activity theory (Leontiev 1974; Kaptelinin and Nardi 2006) and the work of the American pragmatist philosopher John Dewey. Ideas from these sources will be used throughout the book to examine issues of design and to critique theories of play.

In his book *Art as Experience* (first published in 1934), Dewey developed a theory of *aesthetic experience* that I have found useful for thinking about player experience in *World of Warcraft*. Dewey argued that aesthetic experience is part of ordinary life and should not be confined to viewing the works of a few elite artists presented in museums. Aesthetic experience for Dewey is *participatory*—not merely passive "appreciation" as we think of it in relation to high-culture art. Dewey complained that the English language has no word to capture a notion of *active aesthetic experience*. He reconceptualized the term aesthetic experience to express an active, participatory relation to artful material and collective activity.

Dewey's work starts from the same fundamental principles as activity theory (Leontiev 1974; Kaptelinin and Nardi 2006), my own theoretical orientation. I will weave the two approaches together in what follows. Dewey appears to have independently arrived at certain formulations similar to those of activity theory. Many activity theorists read and appreciate Dewey, recognizing the resonance between the two approaches, as well as Dewey's distinctive, complementary contributions.

Dewey's account is in some ways less elaborated than activity theory's, but addresses aesthetic experience in unique, useful ways. On the other hand, certain of activity theory's concepts implicit in Dewey's work are made more accessible by their precise definition in activity theory. I will utilize, in particular, the activity theory hierarchy which distinguishes three levels of activity of a human subject (Leontiev 1974; Kaptelinin and Nardi 2006).

Activity, at the highest level, is motivated by an *object*. A motivating object gives shape and materiality to a subject's needs or desires (Leontiev 1974). Needs and desires are transformed to specific motivating objects which are a concrete instantiation of the need or desire. Motivating objects may be conscious or unconscious. They may indicate deep emotional engagement, what Kaptelinin and Nardi (2006) refer to as *passion*.

Actions are undertaken to fulfill the object. They are directed by conscious goals. Operations are unconscious, habitual movements underlying actions.

Let us develop an example to ground these concepts. A person feels a

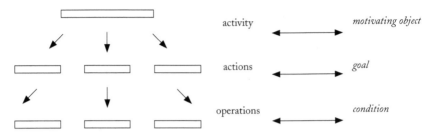

The hierarchical structure of activity. Activities are composed of actions, which are composed of operations. Activity is dynamic; it may move up or down the hierarchy.

strong desire to express herself, to organize and transmit her thoughts and experiences to others. She undertakes a novel. The novel is an object—a specific means by which to satisfy a desire for self-expression. The novelist engages the project with deep interest and attachment; it is a passion for her.

To realize the object of writing the novel, the novelist sets about completing certain conscious actions—devising a storyline, imagining characters, securing a publisher, revising the manuscript.

To capture her words, the novelist types—a practiced, habitual skill, or operation in activity theory terms, that requires no conscious attention.

The novelist develops carpal tunnel syndrome requiring that she input words into the computer differently. Since activity is dynamic, with potential movement between levels in the hierarchy, the novelist will, for a time, consciously attend to the necessary actions for inputting words such as using an ergonomic keyboard or voice system. Eventually she will become familiar with the keyboard or voice system, at which point her actions directed at input again become operations.

Any level of activity may transform to an adjacent level. If, after many years of writing novels, the novelist no longer feels passionate about expressing herself and is merely writing for money, writing becomes an action directed at the object of financial security (about which the novelist feels very passionate).

Going forward, I will use the terms *action, object,* and *activity* in the technical sense established by activity theory.

Dewey's Dimensions of Aesthetic Experience

We turn now to Dewey, who concerned himself with a particular kind of human activity: aesthetic experience. In Dewey's usage, experience is a very broad term. For our purposes, we can regard it as a kind of activity. Dewey paid attention to the *quality* of experience; he believed that explaining and understanding aesthetic experience would be a means of *promoting* it, something he very much wanted to do in line with the philosophical preoccupations that shaped his life (see Hook 1995; Jackson 1998).

Experience is subjective; that is, it requires an active self or subject. Dewey and activity theory regard human beings as biological organisms with biological needs satisfied through interaction with the environment. Humans developed culture as a special means of managing such interaction. Culture manages biological needs but at the same time generates its own social and cultural needs and desires. Within this conceptual framework, the self is an active agent responsive to culture but not determined by it. Dewey said:

> The self acts as well as undergoes, and its undergoings are not impressions stamped upon an inert wax but depend upon the way the organism reacts and responds. There is no experience in which the human contribution is not a factor in determining what actually happens. (2005)

Experience is subjective and thus variable across people. No experience is *inherently* aesthetic—the "human contribution" is always in play. As Dewey noted, the human organism is not an "inert wax"; the organism responds according to its own history. (See also Kaptelinin and Nardi 2006; Bardzell and Bardzell 2008; Spinuzzi 2008.)

Aesthetic experience is, then, a *subjective disposition toward activity*. Aesthetic experience incorporates the contribution of the subject as essential—aesthetic activity can never be realized purely through the structural or formal qualities of an artifact (such as a game). To understand aesthetic experience we cannot stop at analyzing an artifact as a text, or narrative or set of functions or composition of elements, but must also undertake to examine the actual activity in which the artifact is present.

Having established that aesthetic experience is a subjective disposition toward activity, Dewey went on to describe aesthetic experience more precisely. He characterized aesthetic experience as composed of means-ends relations, phases, and collective expression.

Means-Ends Relations

Dewey asserted that aesthetic experience is "whole," carrying with it "its own individualizing quality and self-sufficiency." Aesthetic experience moves toward its own fulfillment or end:

> Any practical activity will, provided it is integrated and moves by its own urge to fulfillment, have aesthetic quality. (2005)

Aesthetic activity is "a consummation and not a cessation" (Dewey 2005). Aesthetic activity flows toward a satisfying completion, or end, not simply the relief of being over with. The means to the end must satisfy in themselves.

> There are ends which are merely welcome cessations and there are ends that are fulfillments of what went before. The toil of a laborer is too often only an antecedent to the wage he receives . . . The means cease to act when the "end" is reached; one would be glad . . . to get the result without having to employ the means.

Under this broad definition, a very wide range of human activities are potentially aesthetic. Dewey offered, for example, "The intelligent mechanic engaged in his job, interested in doing well and finding satisfaction in his handiwork, caring for his materials and tools with genuine affection." In describing the aesthetic he enumerated:

> A piece of work is finished in a way that is satisfactory; a problem receives its solution; a game is played through; a situation, whether that of eating a meal, playing a game of chess, carrying on a conversation, writing a book, or taking part in a political campaign, is so rounded out that its close is a consummation and not a cessation.

In *World of Warcraft*, much of the pleasure of questing or running dungeons lay in devising the particular means by which to accomplish a quest or defeat a mob. The means themselves were of interest to the player, not merely the experience points. At the same time, the completion of a quest or the conquest of mob were moments of pleasure. Aesthetic experience entails a temporal flow of actions that are valued in themselves, ending in a satisfying "consummation."

Phases

Dewey, however, wanted us to understand aesthetic experience as something more complex. He pointed to the "successive phases that are emphases of [the] varied colors" of aesthetic experience. In other words, aesthetic experience requires an internal structure of differentiated phases. A simple repetitive behavior such as pulling the handle on a slot machine would not, for Dewey, count as aesthetic experience. Leveling a character in *World of Warcraft* (so long as the player enjoys the necessary actions) can be considered aesthetic because the completion of a series of quests, each unique, eventually leads to a new level. The successive phases of aesthetic activity in *World of Warcraft* recurse; the goal of reaching a new level is internally differentiated into a series of quests. Each quest itself is structured as a goal and a "description" which entails fulfilling the goal, with the description, or backstory, adding further "color."

A challenge for game designers is to create an environment in which a lot of paying customers will experience aesthetic activity—that is, they will enjoy the actions necessary to play the game.

But again no experience is inherently aesthetic. Take character leveling. While most study participants reported that they enjoyed leveling characters, others did not. What was a pleasing aesthetic experience for some was irksome to others. Some players simply wished to reach the level cap in order to access high-level game content (which for them was aesthetic). They may have been in a hurry or they may have leveled other characters and found repeating the same quests uninteresting. Our free market economy readily obliged these players; they could purchase an account on eBay and other places on the Internet (see Lin and Sun 2007). Players sometimes sold their characters when they left the game, as a side business, or when they got tired of a particular character. One of the young players in my guild sold his well-equipped warrior for 900 dollars when he lost his job

A *WoW* Quest Log
Showing Quest with
Goal and Description

at the Home Depot (gaining enough to live on for a month). There were businesses that offered "power-leveling" services and game gold (although they were against Blizzard terms of service and players could lose their accounts for using them).

Players were of two minds about buying and selling accounts. The vast majority of players I knew found the idea of buying a character nonsensical; the whole point for them was to actually *play*. They observed that you cannot learn to skillfully play a character unless you play it. They made derisive comments about "eBay characters" when, for example, they encountered a poor player in pickup groups. On the other hand, there were many online discussions about busy people who did not have time to level a character but wished to participate in *World of Warcraft*. Aesthetic experience, as Dewey formulated, is variable because it is subjective. We can understand these variable responses to the experience of character leveling only by attending to the subjective dispositions of players with their own personal histories, beliefs, and inclinations. As *World of Warcraft* itself ages, and players accumulate personal histories with the game, the game changes in response through the mechanisms of expansions and updates. Understanding the histories of the human subjects playing the game materially influences game design.

Dewey spoke of the "flow" of aesthetic activity from "something to something," that is, from a set of satisfying actions needed to complete an activity to the completion itself. The psychologist Mihaly Csikszentmihalyi developed a notion of flow somewhat related to Dewey's. Csikszentmihalyi observed that creative or accomplished people experience a state of deep focus that occurs when they undertake an activity that is challenging but still possible. The activity has clear goals and provides immediate feedback. Csikszentmihalyi's formulation pointed, like Dewey's, to the temporal flow of satisfying actions leading to completion (not cessation).

However, Csikszentmihalyi (and other theorists such as Stevens [1978]) emphasized means over ends. Csikszentmihalyi (1997) suggested that attaining an end can even be "anti-climactic." Dewey's conceptualization, by contrast, specified the *unity* of means and ends, their dependence on each other for meaning, purpose, and satisfaction. Part of the appeal of aesthetic activity, as formulated by Dewey, is a satisfying completion in which we eventually experience a distinctive, concrete moment of pleasure.

Collective Expression

Where Csikszentmihalyi focused on extraordinary, high-performing people, Dewey held to the promise of incorporating aesthetic experience into everyday collective activity. Dewey hoped to promote aesthetic experience in all walks of life:

> Works of art that are not remote from common life, that are widely enjoyed in a community, are signs of a unified collective life. But they are also marvelous aids in the creation of such a life. The remaking of the material of experience in the act of expression is not an isolated event confined to the artist and to a person here and there who happens to enjoy the work. In the degree in which art exercises its office, it is also remaking the experience of the community in the direction of greater order and unity.

For many who played *World of Warcraft*, the game was a stimulus to the "remaking of community" (see Steinkuehler and Williams 2006; Williams 2006; Williams et al. 2006). As Arian, a Scarlet Raven player, posted to the guild website:

> Welcome to a group of people who've built a guild "empire" around this game. Including: Forums, Vent, and Late-night hilarity.

Arian invoked ways in which players came to feel connected in and around *World of Warcraft:* forums on the guild website, the use of voice chat ("Vent"), and a spirit of fun, often heightened by the loss of inhibition induced in the late hours.

Collective expression in *World of Warcraft* constitutes a huge topic; I touch briefly on it here to introduce a tenet of Dewey's formulation of aesthetic activity. Notions of collective expression will be woven into subsequent discussions in the remaining chapters, all of which analyze, in varying ways, how aesthetic activity played out in multiple, varied game activities.

To summarize, Dewey's understandings of active, participatory, aesthetic experience incorporated community as well as decomposing the internal structure of aesthetic activity into temporal and structural dimensions. Dewey formulated aesthetic experience as participatory engagement in activity that is organized in distinctive stages and in which a satisfying completion is the end point of actions which are themselves pleasurable. To invoke concepts such as "pleasure" or "satisfaction" is to invoke an active subject for whom pleasure and satisfaction are products of a particular personal history rather than inherent characteristics of a set of actions. Aesthetic experience for Dewey required collective expression; it connects us to others in relations of community and "common life."

We might ask why Dewey selected these particular elements to identify aesthetic activity. Dewey was a philosopher interested in questions of virtue and excellence. He found much of modernity disappointing, criticizing its "monotony," "stasis," and mindless convention. (We will hear echoes of Dewey in the comments of *World of Warcraft* players in chapter 5 as they discuss the disappointments of their school and work lives.)

Dewey sought movement and development, noting their roots in our animal past. He observed:

> The live being recurrently loses and re-establishes equilibrium with its sur-
> roundings. The moment of passage from disturbance into harmony is that
> of intensest life.

He sensed that our animal energies are most satisfyingly discharged when
channeled in a pattern of "rhythmic and developing" activity:

> An engraver, painter, or writer is in process at every stage of completing his
> work. He must at each point retain and sum up what has gone before as a
> whole and with reference to a whole to come . . . The series of doings in the
> rhythm of experience give variety and movement; they save the work from
> monotony and useless repetitions.

Dewey thus argues (as activity theory does) that the human condition is
continuous with our existence as animals in productive interaction with the
environment:

> At every moment, the living creature is exposed to dangers from its sur-
> roundings, and at every moment, it must draw upon something in its sur-
> roundings to satisfy its needs. The career and destiny of a living being are
> bound up with its interchanges with its environment . . . in the most inti-
> mate way.

Dewey observed that these biological realities "reach to the roots of the
aesthetic in experience." He urged us to consider ourselves living creatures
primed by millions of years of evolution to engage deeply with our surroundings, to meet its challenges responsively, and to move, grow, develop.
For Dewey the "enemies of the aesthetic" were the inflexibilities of modernity that defeat such engagement: "convention in practice . . . rigidity . . .
[and] coerced submission." He was saddened that the modern economy
reduces much human activity to "the toil of a laborer" wherein living shriv-
els to the acquisition of a wage.

Given all this, it is not surprising that Dewey identified the aesthetic as
complexly phased action in which both the journey and the destination are
rewards and within which we can be "fully present." Stasis, monotony, submission, aimlessness were, for Dewey, antithetical to the potentialities of

the living being in intimate engagement with its environment—all senses on the *qui vive,* as he put it.

Dewey incorporated a notion of the collective into his ideas of aesthetic experience because his philosophy centered on society. His human subject is always present in a social matrix. Dewey perceived that collective life suffered distortions under the pressures of modernity—one social class was empowered to diminish the horizons of experience of other classes through the imposition of repetitive jobs undertaken only for a wage.

Dewey was no Marxist, but he had sharp words for plunderers and colonizers, observing that the aesthetic came to mean quiet, passive contemplation of "fine art" as a means of reinforcing the power of the ruling classes:

> Most European museums are . . . memorials of the rise of nationalism and imperialism. Every capital must have its own museum . . . devoted to . . . exhibiting the greatness of its artistic past, and . . . to exhibiting the loot gathered by its monarchs in conquest of other nations. [This] testifies to the connection between the modern segregation of art, and nationalism and militarism.

Perhaps most important, Dewey wanted to "recover . . . the continuity of aesthetic experience within normal processes of living." He was genuinely disturbed by what he called the "compartmental conception of fine art" in which art is literally picked up and moved to controlled cultural citadels, separating what is deemed excellent from everyday life:

> [In times past,] [d]omestic utensils, furnishings of tent and house, rugs, mats, jars, pots, bows, spears, were wrought with such delighted care that today we hunt them out and give them places of honor in our art museums. Yet in their own time and place . . . they [were a] manifestation of group and clan membership, worship of gods, feasting and fasting, fighting, hunting, and all the rhythmic crises that punctuate the stream of living . . . The arts of the drama, music, painting, and architecture thus exemplified had no peculiar connection with theaters, galleries, museums. They were part of the significant life of an organized community.

Modernity sequesters the aesthetic in regulated institutions outside normal processes of living. Dewey suggests how deeply *peculiar* this is. He argued that active aesthetic activity must be reconceptualized and reintegrated into everyday life to infuse normal processes of living with the "delighted care" and "genuine affection" that move collective life toward excellence of experience.

CHAPTER FOUR

A New Medium

In an Internet cafe in Beijing, Huatong, a young female player, showed us her *World of Warcraft* character. She played a druid—a class that "shape-shifts," or takes on different forms, including several beautifully rendered animals. She found these shifting forms stimulating, and presented to us, one by one, the druid's shapes and abilities. Without being asked, she mentioned that she thought about the game when she was not playing because it was so "interesting."

In this chapter, I argue that video games like *World of Warcraft* constitute a new digital medium. The fusion of immersive visual experience with intense, skilled performative activity, represents a significant evolution in the history of digital culture. Video games afford rich stimulation to visual sensibilities while at the same time developing complex spaces of performance with opportunities for mastery and active participation.

Each of these elements—visual experience and performance—is compelling on its own. Together they are intoxicating. In Huatong's descriptions, both the visual and performative qualities of the druid's varying forms were deeply interesting to her, and she elaborated on their manifestations in each form.

Visual and performative experience in *World of Warcraft* were entwined, feeding back into one another. Accessing new visual experience and advancing in the game were mutually efficacious; attaining a level of performative mastery was necessary for "seeing new content," as players said, while at the same time experiencing new content opened possibilities for performative challenge.

The term *performative* refers here to activity that demands conscious

Druid Forms

attentiveness and skill. It is time delimited, entailing a specific instance of performance, and engages an audience, either others or oneself. I do not use "performance" as a metaphor for the reproduction of culture through certain actions (see, e.g., Butler 1990) in which people are unaware that they are "performing" but rather as it is used in sports or theater, where participants engage in specific, recognizable instances of performative activity.

Contemporary culture offers many activities that afford either a strong visual experience *or* a venue of performance. Film and theatergoing, for example, involve immersive visual experience, but the audience has no part in the performance. Bowling is an enjoyable performative activity, but bowling alleys are visually austere and uniform, as are the sites of most sporting activities.

Interesting visual-performative activities occur in the real world, and they seem to spark the same enthusiasm as video games. Dance clubs that feature square dancing, salsa, or ballroom dancing combine visual and performative experience. Participants wear colorful, stylized costumes and perform complex dances. Members of church choirs, alongside parishioners, sing in churches decorated with seasonal flowers and religiously themed accoutrements. Paintball pits teams against one another in competitive play in woodsy environments. Hunting and fishing take place outdoors, often in locales of beautiful open country or on picturesque waterways. Participants in U.S. Civil War reenactments recreate the extravagant clothing of the era and enact elaborately staged mock battles and other historically inspired activities. Fantasy masquerade balls invite guests to appear in costume to dance and revel, as do events such as Burning Man and Mardi Gras.

World of Warcraft is very much like these activities. But it is a packaged, self-contained, computer-based medium created and reproduced on a massive scale enabled by digital technology powering immersive graphics and complex game mechanics. *WoW* is more accessible than most real world visual-performative activities because the entry point was a cheap commodity—a networked personal computer. The genius of *WoW,* and other video games, lies in allowing millions of people to attain skilled performance in artistically designed spaces entered through an ordinary computer.

One of my guildmates succinctly captured the notion of *WoW* as a visual-performative medium when he said, "*WoW* is baseball in elf costumes." The term "elf costumes" evoked the visuals so vital to players. Baseball was a metaphor for the competitive contests central to play in *World of Warcraft:* quests, raids, duels, battlegrounds, and arenas.

When I first started giving talks about *WoW,* I emphasized community and collaboration. An audience member who played the game said, "Well, that's interesting, but you've left out the most important thing—mastery of the game." The comment indicated the need to attend to the development of skilled performance as critical to player experience. The emphasis in the interviews on leveling, constant player chat about attaining better equipment, and the seriousness of the collective organization undertaken to support raiding argued for mastery as crucial to game experience.

A notion of mastery complexifies an account of *WoW* as primarily a series of Skinnerian rewards. Yes, players wanted the loot and the experience points. But mere acquisition was not the sole source of satisfaction; the loot and points accumulated, over time, toward the player's object of becoming a better player—of "improving yourself," as Mark said. Focus on the object of activity proscribes reductive accounts such as Skinner's as the end point of analysis. Attention to higher levels of activity moves analysis beyond the moment of reward to the larger historical trajectory of the activity, recalibrating the time horizon in which human activity is intelligible and for which analytical logics must be devised.

In the following sections I discuss the contours of performance in video games, the means by which visual/performative activity is encapsulated in digital rules, and the place of video games in mass culture.

Performance

Let us discuss *WoW* raiding as an example of the centrality of performance.[1] (We might also investigate ordinary quests, 5-man instances, battlegrounds, and arena play, all of which entail performative challenge.)[2] In a raid, as in a sporting contest, the outcome can turn on the smallest mistake or advantage. A spell cast a moment late can kill a player or wipe a raid. A player hanging on by a few points of health can still battle to victory. Raid action is in constant dynamic change. Players spoke of the importance of "situational awareness" (a military term), denoting the ability to mentally process rapid multidimensional environmental changes. The same ability is mandatory in team sports, where the positions of the ball (puck/Frisbee/ . . .) and the positions of other players, as well as their specific movements, must be tracked and responded to rapidly.

Golub (2007) provided a detailed account of the 25-man Magtheridon raid that nicely captured its performative demands:

> Because the party will wipe if they attempt to fight both Magtheridon and the magicians, the magicians must be killed in under two minutes . . . Magtheridon will release a dangerous "blast nova" that will also kill the entire party. In order to prevent the blast, players must *simultaneously* click on the [magicians'] cubes to delay the blast for one minute. However, because a . . . player can only click a cube every two minutes . . . two teams of five players each must take turns . . . Finally when Magtheridon is at [a certain stage] he . . . will begin collapsing the walls of the room. Players must avoid the pieces of falling rock which will kill most of them instantly.

In this encounter, players are required to achieve precise timing in clicking the cubes. They must be vigilant of the magicians' imminent demise and the point at which Magtheridon will issue the blast nova. Toward the end of the encounter, players perform the duties of their class while simultaneously moving their characters around Magtheridon's Lair to avoid the collapsing walls. As Golub remarked, "The fights . . . can be quite intense."

In my own raiding experiences I was acutely aware of the need to perform. During one encounter Scarlet Raven was just learning, the raid leader admonished the raid, "Innikka had demons three times and she survived and she's a healer!" The comment was a rebuke to more powerful players. Though many had died, I had squeaked by even though healers have reduced power against mobs (demons here) which must be fought, in this encounter, by individual raid members.

Such scrutiny of player performance was deployed to direct and improve performance. Bardzell and Bardzell (2008) observed that a character in a virtual world is known to others through the performance of its actions. A character is "a subjectivity constituted by actions in-world." (Their use of the word *subjectivity* is the same as the use of the word *subject* in activity theory.) A character is not merely an image or static representation but a performance. In Magtheridon's Lair, either you can click the cube at the right moment or you cannot. There is no way to disguise an inability to perform this action precisely and accurately. Bardzell and Bardzell said, "A subjectivity . . . cannot lie; it is as it does."

The centrality of performative mastery in video games was noted by Kennedy (2005) who reported that the female *Quake* players she studied used terms such as *athleticism, balance, coordination,* and *taking risks* to describe why they liked *Quake,* a first-person shooter game:

> Although it is the avatar that performs these feats of athleticism or coordination within the game space, it is the players' skill in controlling the interface that shapes this performance. The sense of agency the players experience is doubled; the player experiences a freedom of movement and sense of authority and mastery within the game, alongside a sense of empowerment through their skill in mastering the technology.

Kennedy pointed to the same issues of performance, mastery, agency, and empowerment I discovered among *WoW* players (see also Turkle 1984). Drawing a further connection between games and performance in sports, Kennedy (2005) reported a comment from a woman who ran a gaming site:

> "Women are starting to realize that they have the same abilities in sports— and things like sport—as men," said Leann Pomaville, a 38 year old former school teacher who runs the girl gaming sites Da Valkyries and *Quake* Women's Forum. "Quake is a game where your own personal skill makes all the difference, like in a sport."

In the same vein, Taylor (2003) observed of *EverQuest* players that "the actual fight is as much an opportunity to demonstrate the valued qualities of game mastery as anything." *WoW* players were deeply attracted to "the competitive atmosphere," as one player put it, noting that she was fascinated with "learning what strengths and weaknesses your character has against another's" (Choontanom 2008). Wine (2008) emphasized the "drive to be a good player" in her analysis of discourse on a *WoW* priest forum.

As in contemporary sports, performance in *WoW* was expressed in a series of publicly reported metrics (see Taylor 2008). Performance was measured and displayed in tables and logs. The "combat log" was a history of game actions, reporting in minute detail what transpired during a particular encounter, including metrics such as who delivered a "killing blow" and how much damage or healing resulted from a player action. Players seeking to improve their performance, and raid leaders critiquing an encounter, studied these logs carefully.[3]

Players embraced performance measures. Going far beyond the tools provided by Blizzard, player-created software modifications computed and reported performance metrics. ("Mods" were available for free download on the Internet and placed in a folder provided by Blizzard.) One of the most popular categories of mods was "damage meters" (see Taylor 2008). Damage meters gathered game data, computed metrics, and output the results in a window. The results could be reported in chat. Meters measured not only damage, but healing and many other quantities related to game performance. The illustration shows a window from Recount, a player-created software modification.

Raiding guilds studied these oracles religiously. Players kept an eye on their own performance, striving to be near the top of the meters. After each raid, Scarlet Raven posted detailed statistical results generated by a program called WoW Web Stats (WWS). These metrics, archived on the guild website, became a permanent part of guild history.

Players' obsession with gear derived from their interest in performance. *WoW* required skill, but if two players of equal skill competed the better geared player won. The impact of gear on performance was made plain in reports provided by meters; players could see the effects of the gear they were accumulating. Players often posted questions in guild chat of the form "Is X or Y better?" where X and Y were similar pieces of gear. Guildmates would discuss why a particular piece of gear might be better for the particular player asking the question.

Another series of player metrics ranked performance in terms of guild "progression" through more and more difficult raiding dungeons. Websites such as wowjutsu.com ranked guilds according to progression measured as dungeons completed and bosses downed. Players dedicated to raiding eagerly read these websites. Sean, an undergraduate player I interviewed and got to know as a student in several of my classes, was excited about the "leap in rankings" his guild experienced after completing the Serpentshrine Cavern and Tempest Keep dungeons. Progressing through dungeons "felt fantastic," he said. *WoW* was "not a Harry Potter fantasy game," as he put it, but a site of serious competitive play and performative challenge.

Damage Done	⟲ ✿ 🗎 🗎 ◀ ▶ ✕
1. Darkmike	2273745 (5536.0, 19.7%)
2. Bloodienight	2227441 (5292.8, 19.3%)
3. Uriell	1985720 (4438.9, 17.2%)
4. Soktana	1671981 (4432.7, 14.5%)
5. Tam	1286872 (3066.8, 11.1%)
6. Aoshii	1059414 (2588.4, 9.2%)
7. Partykiller	1022486 (2670.4, 8.8%)
8. Calvieri	27953 (71.0, 0.2%)
9. Bxinscoe	2007 (5.7, 0.0%)
10. Fannie	1112 (3.2, 0.0%)

A 10-Man Raid on the Kilrogg server

A member of an internationally known guild, Nihilum, wrote on their website:

> Well, storming through BT [an advanced dungeon] and basically putting the smack down like we did killing Illidan [a difficult boss] way before many others would see him dead was probably a better experience than AQ40 [another difficult dungeon] was. God we owned BT! When Illidan died it was an amazing feeling.

Like Sean, who said it felt fantastic when his guild progressed, the Nihilum guild member expressed a release of positive emotion—"God we owned BT! When Illidan died it was an amazing feeling." "First kills" in *World of Warcraft* were famously moments of performative ecstasy. Players savored them for days, they posted accounts and pictures on guild websites (see also Golub 2009).

At the other end of the spectrum of performative experience, when a boss or dungeon was under control, players having mastered it, the encounter was said to be "on farm status." (Farming will be taken up in the next chapter; it referred to game activities lacking challenge.) Players linguistically marked the quality of dungeon experience according to the level of challenge, accenting the importance of performance. When encounters could be handled with aplomb, players engaged them not for performative experience but for loot—with loot, of course, always feeding forward to the next opportunity for performance and improving a player's numbers on the charts and meters.

A further indication of the salience of performance in *WoW* was player humor. Players made fun of each other's abilities, joked about how opponents cheated when a duel was lost, or facetiously suggested raiding low-level dungeons. For Alliance players, a running gag was mock discussion of organizing a raid to kill "Hogger," a level-11 "elite" mob (i.e., difficult-at-level mob). When a player in my guild would ask on a non-raid night "we doing anything?" someone might reply, "get ready for Hogger." The player-created thottbot.com website contained comical accounts of fictional attempts to defeat Hogger. Players drove the satire home by invoking *WoW*'s performative constructs and lingo. Below is the first Hogger post and a few others. The first brief post inspired a cascade of ever more preposterous Hogger stories, some quite lengthy and one with original artwork:

Hogger
by Zvert

Tried 2 solo him with my 70 hunter, got him 2 65% and i wiped. He hits like a truck.

Re: Hogger
by Jasmela
My guilds current progression [ratio of bosses downed in a dungeon]:

12/12 - Karazahn
6/6 - Zul'Aman
2/2 - Gruul's Lair
1/1 - Magtheridon's Lair
6/6 - SSC
4/4 - TK
5/5 - Hyjal
9/9 - BT
6/6 - Sunwell
0/1 - Hogger

Re: Hogger
by belegamarth

Even with your guide, we had 2 40-man raids (lvl 80s with tier 12 gear) there and only brought him down to 64%. When he got to 70% he summoned the boars and most of our healers went down. Then he uber pwned us with his paw. One of these days we are going to get that Huge Gnoll Paw . . . As for the water, that sweet succulent spring water, I'll keep grinding till I get it.

(http://thottbot.com/c448)

The jokes played off *WoW* metrics—"[we] brought him down to 64%" and "when he got to 70% [of his health]"—as well as character and gear levels and progression ratios such as 0/1 Hogger.

The Software Artifact

This section turns to the implications of the visual-performative medium as a *digital* entity encoded in rules. Among games, video games uniquely digitize rules of play, encoding and containing them in a software artifact. As Fron et al. (2007b) observed, "Video games . . . dictate and enforce rules automatically through software." Taylor (2004) noted, ". . . we cannot overlook the role software and design play in shaping online life."

In *WoW,* play was nearly perfectly reduced to performance and mastery of digital rules. Mechanical encapsulation (Kallinikos 2006) established and enforced rules automatically through the agency of the "black box" of software closed to user inspection and alteration. The kind of interpretive flexibility that, for example, a referee or umpire brings to a sport was absent. Mechanical enforcement of rules removed a source of social authority with whom to negotiate and rethink rules of play as they were followed (or not followed) during actual performances of play.

Digital encapsulation curtails (but does not eliminate; see Consalvo 2007) the possibility to engage rules at their margins to gain advantage. In sporting contests, by contrast, players are constantly aware of rules they might usefully bend and manipulations players on the opposing team might be planning to leverage. The software artifact's mechanics permit constant, reliable vigilance and enforcement that give little quarter to ambiguity or interpretation; they eliminate the vagaries of the different personalities and proclivities of human agents such as referees and the impact they might have on the interpretation of the rules.[4] As inscriptions within a machine, digital rules are not established and reestablished in interactions between human agents meeting in a shared space of performance; rules are removed from such influences.

WoW players could not critique or question human judgments about particular instances of play during play, but they could air their concerns and grievances about rules of play on official forums maintained by Blizzard. A different mechanism, then, for moving the game in new directions was in place.[5] Rather than actual performances instigating change, player discourse about performance was encouraged and analyzed. As each new patch was issued, it was obvious that players' opinions had been considered and their concerns rewoven into the software artifact. The black box was thus breached, although indirectly, through conversations about the game that occurred outside the game.[6]

The dialectic between players and the corporate provider was an important means by which *World of Warcraft* was altered and refined. However, this set of interactions, and their useful consequences, should not cause us to be inattentive to the force of the software as a designed entity. Activity theory and actor-network theory posit that technology embodies a powerful agency not strictly under human control (Callon 1991; Latour 1994; Kaptelinin and Nardi 2006; see also Mumford 1934; Ellul 1964; Kallinikos 2004, 2006, 2009). Technology forcefully shapes human activity and invariably entails unintended consequences (Winner 1977). In formulating *WoW* as a performative medium, I want to draw attention to the importance of the design of the game itself, its potent agency as a particular kind of medium that engaged players in certain kinds of regulated performances.

A revealing instance of the powerful shaping of the game's design occurred in the wake of the first software expansion of *World of Warcraft*. The expansion, for which players purchased and installed new software, extended the game with significant content. "The Burning Crusade" added new geographies, quests, and dungeons. It was released in North America and Europe in January 2007 and in China in September 2007. Players spoke of "TBC," as it was known, and "pre-TBC," indicating its importance as a critical juncture in the history of the game.

The expansion brought the addition of ten levels of play. Players could level their characters from level 60 to 70. The 20- and 40-man dungeons became obsolete. They still existed, but new, superior 10- and 25-man dungeons were introduced. The loot in these dungeons was so amazingly better than the old loot that players abandoned the pre-TBC dungeons (although after awhile some players started conducting nostalgia runs).

TBC dungeons were exciting venues for fresh performative challenges in new visual surroundings. They contained clever storylines, imaginative graphics, and crafty bosses.

All this new content sounds like a great thing. And, in many ways, it was. It enabled players to improve their characters through enhanced loot and to enjoy novel visual-performative events—exactly what I am arguing *WoW* provides as its core experience. However, amid the happiness was a decidedly negative outcome. For many guilds, TBC entailed a transmogrification of guild social dynamics. Guilds such as Scarlet Raven, in which players had been playing peaceably together for months or years, suddenly fractured into two groups: players who advanced quickly through the new levels and acquired desirable new loot, and players who progressed more slowly and could not keep up with the swift progress of their peers.

The single biggest source of the fracture was a new 10-man dungeon named Karazhan. Acquiring equipment from Karazhan was necessary in order to advance to 25-man content. For guilds going from, say, raiding Molten Core, an old 40-man, to a sudden focus on 10-man was jarring. Only 10 people got a chance to raid. And they all had to perform to a high standard. In good old MC, a few players not really doing their jobs would not wipe a raid. In Karazhan, every player had to know what they were doing and be reasonably geared. The composition of the raid involved a precise balance of classes. On raid nights often there was a single group going to "Kara," leaving behind many players who had previously been raiding.

An apparently simple solution would have been to start another Kara raid with an additional 10 people. But often the right combination of player classes was not available. Players grew discouraged at not getting a raid invite and would sign up for raids less frequently, exacerbating the problem.

Within Scarlet Raven, considerable disturbance ensued. Incipient guild cliques became more visible. Players advancing quickly wanted to play with others doing the same. They expressed irritation at slower or less skilled or geared players. The advanced players did not consider it their obligation to help the slower players, who were described in Scarlet Raven website posts as "less dedicated." The design change from 20- and 40-man raids with some latitude for error, and openings for nearly all who wanted to raid, to a 10-man raid requiring better performance and precise class composition, generated a situation in which the rich got richer and the poor got poorer. Skilled, geared players preferred raiding with skilled, geared players. They did so, getting better and better equipment. Others, squeezed out of the raids, progressed even more slowly.

Not surprisingly, when the "dedicated" were geared and ready for 25-man, they found that having left others behind, they were impeded in their efforts to form a large raid. One solution was to recruit from other guilds. Scarlet Raven recruited successfully, although this action created fresh tensions among existing members. The 25-man raids came onboard much more slowly than everyone thought they would.

A little over a year after the launch of TBC, frustration among the ambitious raiders reached a tipping point. Raid progress had been too slow. Some of the most serious, best-geared players defected to hardcore guilds where they would be assured a rigorous schedule of disciplined raiding. Scarlet Raven tried raiding with those available, but gear limitations made it impossible to defeat new bosses. Within three months of the departure of key raiders, the guild closed down 25-man raiding. Scarlet Raven's rapid descent from the server's most successful casual raiding guild (according to wowjutsu.com rankings) to a guild with limited 10-man raiding was wrenching.

Many of the Scarlet Raven players who left had been with the guild a long time and were popular, visible members. They had hung in, waiting for others to catch up. But by refusing to institute a systematic program of helping the less geared, their departure was inevitable—if we understand *WoW* as a visual-performative medium. The social glue was insufficient to sustain the community building necessary to properly equip enough players to perform in the difficult dungeons. Nor was the simple fact of community adequate to retain geared players. It is a cliché of multiplayer games that players "come for the game and stay for the people." But relations between game and people must be understood in more complex terms. *WoW* was engineered to require sociability for the most challenging content, but it only weakly developed community as shared commitments and durable social bonds.

It was players' desire to grab the TBC opportunities to enhance performance and experience new visual content that led more advanced players to push forward with their own progress, altering social dynamics. Hypothetically, it would have been possible for Scarlet Raven to devise a social solution for a challenge imposed by a technological design decision. The guild could have slowly accommodated the less geared or skilled members. But such a solution would have abrogated the logic of the game, which was to perform to one's fullest ability. *WoW* was a voluntary space of performative play, not a place in which players wanted to spend hours helping the less fortunate. Efforts to mitigate the disruptions entailed by TBC were difficult to institute because they violated the spirit of free play and the very reason to play the game, which was to perform and see new content—to engage the visual-performative medium. Once the new content was locked up in the 10-man dungeon with its limitations and constraints, and once this dungeon became a bottleneck to other content, guild dynamics altered dramatically.

This powerful design dynamic created what activity theory calls a *contradiction*. A contradiction is a *systemic* inconsistency or discrepancy (Engeström 1987; Groleau et al. 2009). Raiding guilds were formed for the purpose of raiding. At the same time, guilds were supposed to be friendly, supportive groups that a player could count on. These two purposes stood in relations of tension with the changes brought by The Burning Crusade; it was difficult for guilds to accommodate both.

The contradiction between raid progression and group support led some well-geared players to depart. On the other end of the gear spectrum, players who identified themselves as "nonelite" also became frustrated and /gquit. For example, one player wrote on the guild website in her good-bye message:

> I came into the guild about 7 months ago and was quite aware of the elites versus the non, and I persevered to make my character good enough. I built some great friends and wish them all nothing but good fortune however in all my time here my class captain did not address me even once and even ignored me one day I sent him 3 whispers asking for a good time to help

me. I read all the forums and did research on my own however sometimes
you just need some advice from those who have gone through it. I made
myself available for raiding at least 4 times per week and often was called
in to fill a vacant spot. I believe I was respectful and tried to help all my
guildies when asked.

She ended somewhat bitterly:

> I am sorry this was not the type of mature player you needed and again
> wish you the best.

Thus, one change in dungeon design—a change that had some positive
effects—also had a significant negative impact on many guilds.

Sean described how he left his guild because he desired "an environment that I want to play in" which he defined as

> players that are same skill level as me or better, people who share the same
> goals of progression, a guild with my friends that I select and who respect
> me.

He said that in TBC, "I could not do my job"; in other words, he could
not perform adequately because less skilled players were unable to raid
effectively. He invoked the social: "a guild with my friends that I select
and who respect me." However, the nuances of "social" in this discourse
were linked to the performative; Sean wanted to be surrounded by other
performers of similar skill level who shared mutual respect for the "jobs"
they did.

A Scarlet Raven player wrote sadly on the guild website:

> i remember the old guild, the ones who would always be up for Scholomance
> or ubrs even strat [dungeons] to help people get there gear. this guild was
> built on helping . . . but tbc has changed all that.

I have spoken with European players who told the same story of post-
TBC disruption. (At the time I was in China they were still waiting for
TBC.) Scarlet Raven was irreversibly altered after The Burning Crusade.

The relaxed atmosphere in which guildmates engaged each other in playful player-designed activities and a lot of wacky humor was gone. Pre-TBC, for example, Scarlet Raven had "gnome races" in which guild members created level-1 gnome characters and undertook various challenges (of a very silly, very delightful nature). The guild used to conduct competitive timed runs of one of the old dungeons, Upper Black Rock Spire. (I have fond memories of being on the first winning team in which we did UBRS in 53 minutes.) Such activities, and the guildwide camaraderie that generated them, fell away from the guild.

I left Scarlet Raven in June 2008 for a new raiding guild. My research in Scarlet Raven was extensive enough for the analysis I wanted to do, and I wished to continue to learn from raiding both as a researcher and a player. I kept in touch with friends from Scarlet Raven, and found the new guild through a former Scarlet Raven player. I often checked to see who from Scarlet Raven was online (using a simple *WoW* command). Usually only a few people were logged in; the guild was on life support awaiting the next expansion. Eventually the guild was dissolved, and players split into two small guilds.

Why did Blizzard institute such an abrupt change? Karazhan was created with the best of intentions—to open raiding to small guilds that could not muster enough players for larger raids. This was, in some respects, a good thing. The Derelict would never have been able to experience 25-man content unless it partnered with another guild, a difficult exercise in coordination undertaken by few guilds. However, the Derelict enjoyed Karazhan. The problem was in positioning a difficult 10-man dungeon as an obstacle for 25-man and in instituting such a change in a context in which many guilds had been raiding with large groups which could no longer easily be accommodated.

The design of a software artifact, then, may powerfully shape human activity. The pervasiveness of the disruption of guild dynamics following the TBC changes, across guilds, countries, and cultures, suggests the enormous directive influence inherent in rules encoded in digital technology. In the next section, I consider the disquiet often aroused by the power of digital rules and ways in which they have been analyzed in the literature. I argue for seeing rules as a potential resource rather than a hindrance to positive human activity.

Rules Rule

The story of TBC indicates that we pay special attention to the influences of artifacts on human activity. While it is clear that player experience refigured *World of Warcraft* in significant, meaningful ways (chapter 7 will address this topic), on balance I argue that the software artifact was uniquely powerful in creating the world experienced by players.

In examining such software artifacts, we turn to their *encoded rules* which embody directive force, giving designers the tools with which to transmit designed experience. While all artifacts mediate our relation to reality in important ways (Vygotsky 1986), the expressive flexibility of software rules entails not merely mediation—as a hammer mediates our relation to a nail—but the remarkable ability to conjure worlds of participatory aesthetic activity which can continually develop and change, generating historical depth and context. Karazhan was an important moment in *World of Warcraft* that occurred at a point in time. Through new content embodied in rules, *World of Warcraft* has moved on and will continue to do so as long as it is a viable commercial product. *WoW* is thus in some ways like life itself. But it is very much unlike the ineffable processes of ordinary life in that software artifacts can be deliberately constructed and implemented according to strict, articulated design goals authorized by designers. Rules are the vessel in which designers' intentions and creativity are expressed in a machine-readable format and delivered to a large public.

In the context of this discussion, "rules" are taken as structures in a software program. In digital games, software rules also embody game rules. We might use the term *algorithm* to refer to the software structure, but for our purposes the emphasis on control connoted by rules is needed (rather than sequencing of instructions).

In his analysis of enterprise resource planning systems,[7] Kallinikos (2004) noted:

> The study of technology and its social impact cannot be exhausted at the very interface upon which humans encounter technology. Essential strips of reality are not observable or even describable at the level of contextual encounters.

Kallinikos urged that we examine the qualities of software itself, in particular its capacity to direct activity through encoded rules. In studying only "contextual encounters," we miss the stuff of the artifacts themselves—the powers flowing from their form and function. In essence, Kallinikos says there is something to learn about hammering not from "contextual encounters" involving watching people hammer but from addressing the hammer itself. How much does it weigh? What is its shape? Of which materials is it constructed and why? How does the hammer fit into a human hand? (An analysis certainly more easily done when the hammering is not taking place.)

This line of inquiry would appear to contradict the emphasis in Dewey and activity theory on studying the actual activity of human subjects. However, what Kallinikos noted was that we seem to find it difficult to attend to *both* the artifacts themselves—with their capacities for mediating activity—and the lived experience of engaging them. Kallinikos observed that in studies of software artifacts examination of the artifact itself is often sidestepped in favor of asserting the importance of user resourcefulness in dealing with the artifact. Studies center on managing software in practice. Analysis often addresses the ways in which people work around the perceived ill effects of the execution of software rules in human activity or how rules are manipulated. Orlikowski (1992), for example, conceived a notion of interpretive flexibility through which workers managed problems created by computer-aided software engineering tools in their organization. Other research celebrates resistance to the power of rules—for example, that of hackers (see, e.g., Consalvo 2007; Jordan 2007)—or ways in which human actors such as game masters (employees who provide in-game customer support) and guild leaders smooth the bumps that invariably issue from the inflexibilities of rule-driven systems (Ryan 208).

Kallinikos argued that such analyses of "contextual encounters" construct a user control that is largely illusory, downplaying or even denying the astonishing capacity of software to call worlds of human activity into being and to sustain, within narrow limits, specific actions in those worlds. While user actions such as devising workarounds or hacking are important, Kallinikos (2004) suggested that the user contribution in a rule-generated world (such as a video game or enterprise resource planning system) "must be attributed its right proportion." The world created by the rules is huge; user response is relatively small, reactionary in nature, and sited within the framing established by the rules. It is the very rules that give meaning to the activities of hackers trying to break them, to employees finding local solutions to the inflexibilities of large software systems, and to game masters and guild leaders patching over the rough spots. Rules direct and motivate the activity of these actors, not the other way around. As Kallinikos (2009) observed:

> Emerging use of artifacts and workarounds are efforts to reinvent or resist the expectations tied to a technology, and in this regard are inescapably framed by the functions and forms embodied in the artifacts.

To a considerable degree, we are products of our technologies. Kallinikos provides a strong version of this claim:

> The agent that acts upon, interprets, or reshapes technology has, to a significant degree, been made an agent by, among other things, technology itself.

At a workshop on "productive play" sponsored by the National Science Foundation and hosted by Jason Ellis, Celia Pearce, and me in May 2008, virtual worlds pioneers Chip Morningstar and Randy Farmer touched on the debate, remarking on what they called the "tyranny of emergence." They observed that we all hope that online communities will emerge in bottom-up fashion from participatory activity, and we approve as participants take whatever technical affordances they are offered and appropriate them to their own ends. But at the same time these veterans cautioned that we cannot forget the "hand of God" that is the software artifact and the power of designers to shape activity (see Nardi et al. 2009). As Kallinikos said, it is the "right proportions" of the relative contributions of users and software we seek to apprehend.

Pickering's (1995) notion of the "mangle" is a distinctive formulation of the relative contributions of user practice and technology. Unlike Farmer, Morningstar, and Kallinikos, who urged attention to the primacy of software rules and their directive force, Pickering proposed that a mangle—a mélange of user practices, socioeconomic conditions, and technologies—produces experience. This vivid metaphor suggests the entanglement of diverse elements; taking the metaphor at full face value, the conceptual mangle "mutilates" the varied elements it passes over, pressing them into one another.

Engaging Pickering's notion, Steinkuehler (2006) discussed ways in which player practice modulated undesirable effects of the rules in the video game *Lineage*. She described how high-level players traveled to areas with new, low-level players and repeatedly killed them. As upsetting as this was for the low-level players, such activity was permitted by the rules. In response, *Lineage* clans (i.e., guilds) organized themselves to periodically sweep through low-level areas to establish order by killing offending players.

Clan action was a resourceful response to a perceived problem of the rules. Following Pickering, Steinkuehler argued that a mangle of player practice and game rules "interactively stabilized" the game world, relieving new players of the predations of advanced players. She observed:

This "interactively stabilized" system (Pickering, 1995) emerged from the mangle of both designed-in technologically instantiated rules and human intentions.

However, it would have been trivial—a matter of a few lines of code—for the game's designers to change a rule to make it impossible for a high-level player to kill a low-level player in designated areas (as in *World of Warcraft*). *Lineage's* rules were in place to promote a certain style of play. The story of the rescuing clans presumes that we cheer them on as they scour the countryside meting out justice to errant players. But we must also acknowledge the fun high-level players were having pwning nubs—actions *Lineage's* designers chose to preserve through the rules. A world in which ganking is possible was precisely the world intended by designers, and it was that world they encoded into the rules.

While "interactive stabilization" is one possible outcome of the function of any system, the mangle suggests that equilibrium is the expected outcome of dynamics within a set of interacting variables or factors. The events surrounding Karazhan did not result in stabilization but destabilization. Notions such as mangles appear to be a small subset of general systems theory, which elaborates varying system dynamics (beyond stabilization) (see Ashby 1956; von Bertalanffy 1968).

The mangle, it seems to me, underplays not only relational dynamics but also temporality. In the account of the *Lineage* clans, the temporal flow of events is clear. Clans acted in response to realities entrained by game rules. The necessary accommodations, reactionary in nature, followed events engendered by the rules. Rules established conditions that made killing low-level players possible, which in turn led to clan posses. I see less a mangled hash of interacting elements in which rules lose their directive force, surviving simply as one element in the mix, and more a temporal progression from rules to reaction.[8]

Paradoxically, the clans' (re)actions served to reinscribe the very rules whose outcomes distressed them. *Lineage*'s designers had no need to exercise their power to change rules because the clans instituted a workaround. Clan actions, rather than asserting dominion over the rules, redoubled the rules' power.

Metaphors such as mangles are useful in calling attention to a heterogeneous mix of practices, economic conditions, and technologies that shape experience. But in the context of digital artifacts, such metaphors may camouflage the outsize contribution of software shapings, imputing, indirectly, a sort of equality between elements. Notions such as stabilization mask asymmetrical accommodation to the power of digital rules. Steinkuehler (2006) described the lengths to which she went as clan leader to ensure that her guild participated in policing low-level areas, including an elaborate rewards system. Rather than a natural merge of practice and rules, practice was forced to stretch and extend itself to accommodate the rules—which remained untouched.

In assessing user response to rules in enterprise resource planning systems, Kallinikos (2004) observed:

> Interpretation and local reshaping of the package can take place *only within those narrow limits allowed for by the constitution of technology* . . . To navigate effectively in the engraved routes of large-scale information platforms entertains the hope (or illusion) of gradually acquiring control over them. (emphasis added)

Attention to the "constitution of technology" is necessary for understanding how we encounter digital technologies. Kallinikos's argument that we attend to the precise ways in which digital rules shape experience suggests that theories that itemize elements of experience without assessing their relative contributions and particular means of influence (such as the narrow range of possible customizations in enterprise resource planning systems), cannot account for the capacity of digital technology to direct activity (see also Taylor 2006a; Fron et al. 2007b). A kind of figure-ground reversal seems to occur in which actions such as the heroism of the *Lineage* clans, which was a relatively small adjustment to the world shaped by the rules, become emblematic, defocusing the larger shapings entailed by the execution of rules. Kallinikos's argument indicates a need to rise analytically to the level of the world of human activity created by the rules of software systems, examining, in the large, the quality of experience produced by the rules in dynamic interplay with human action.

Rules May Nurture

It is just that quality of rule-based worlds to which I turn now. Notions such as mangles and interpretive flexibility suggest that, with some effort, the ill effects of digital rules can be managed. A different response to the power of rules is to denounce them as "totalizing"—figuring rules as entities that brook no interpretative activity and restrict the moves a subject can make (see, e.g., Jordan 2007). Based (somewhat loosely) on the work of theorists such as Foucault and Lyotard (1984), the notion of totalizing rules in computer games draws attention to the foreclosure of "metagaming" in which players alter the rules to suit themselves, as we all (putatively) did with *Monopoly* and other board games (Jordan 2007).[9] From this perspective, the fact that we cannot alter rules within digital games is troubling. Jordan pointed to the problem, proposing hacking as a solution:

> Academic programs in game studies are in the unique position to offer institutional support for hobbyist emulation and ROM-hacking communities, and it is our obligation to utilize the resources of thousands of programmers and gamers in our common goal of reverse-engineering and documenting, recontextualizing, and reworking these products beyond mere objects for consumption.

It is through hacking, Jordan argued, that we may "transform, adapt, and distribute the systems of rules themselves."

Whether viewing rules as manageable because they can be flexibly gotten around, or declaiming rules locked down and in need of being broken into, both arguments cast digital rules in a bad light. Analyzing *World of Warcraft* invites us to examine rules from a different angle, considering them as *resources preserving good design.* In *WoW*, the artistry of the graphics, the excitement and imaginativeness of the quests and raids, the careful progression through increasingly challenging levels of play, the interdependencies of character classes were undeniably grounded in the creativity and ideations of *World of Warcraft*'s designers. Their labors were caught up in the inscriptions encoded in the software and made available to players in replicable form through execution of the rules.

Anyone who has played *World of Warcraft* knows how vibrant and present player interaction and negotiation are in the experience of play. I will give an example of such interaction and negotiation, indicative, I hope, of the texture of everyday play. At the same time, I argue that such texturing is largely (though not fully) engineered by the rules, as it was in *Lineage.*

As noted, when players are grouped and a mob drops a valuable item, players must decide who will receive it. The decision can be highly charged, as a desirable new item invariably and inevitably enhances the player's abilities (themselves a product of the rules of the game encoded in the software).

In group play, it was sometimes unclear which player was most deserving of an item. In a raid, perhaps a member of an appropriate class rolled for an item but another player of the same class was equipped with inferior gear. It would benefit the guild as a whole were she to get the item. The raid leader might step in and allocate the item to the player who lost the roll but appeared to need it more. Even when guilds used systems in which players bid for items based on points accumulated through raid participation, raid leaders might dictate or suggest that a player who had bid fewer points receive the gear. The point systems, intended to remove ambiguity, were, in practice, deployed flexibly in response to judgments about guild and player needs rendered in the thick of play. Guild leaders sometimes negotiated these matters among themselves in voice and chat channels reserved for officers. It was not simply game rules that decided the crucial matter of who attained prized gear; complex, occasionally contentious assessments, shaped the process. These assessments, and the negotiations that generated them, loomed large in player consciousness, producing an ambience of constant human interplay.[10]

Player practice shaped loot distribution in another way; under some circumstances, in particular in pickup groups, but also 5-man guild runs, players had to decide whether to cheat. One of the game's mechanisms for allocating loot was a roll of virtual dice by typing the /roll command into the chat window. The odd thing was, players could cheat by using an addon that mimicked the output of the roll:

Zeke rolls 75 (1 -- 100)

The player who won picked the item up from the mob.

Cheating could not be detected by other players unless someone recorded a series of rolls and came forward to say that so many rolls in the nineties were statistically impossible. Some players did not even roll; they simply walked over to the mob and picked up an item, a practice known as ninja-ing. Player practice materially figured into loot distribution; it was trivial for a player to defeat the virtual dice or ignore them altogether.

Players could also choose a system of loot distribution in which they selected "need" or "greed" for an item. If the item was appropriate to their class, need would be the correct choice. If more than one player chose need, the system rolled the dice and the player who won would find the item automatically placed in his or her bag. But sometimes players chose need even though another player clearly deserved the item more—another type of ninja-ing. When a ninja struck, a good deal of ill feeling ensued.

One of the most important aspects of play, then—loot distribution— was subject to player intervention; crucial decisions about whether to cheat, and assessments regarding who should receive loot, were shaped by player practice and interaction.[11]

Without denying the centrality of such practices and interactions, we must regard them as materially constituted through the engineering of the rules. *World of Warcraft* might easily have been designed differently so that a high roll would automatically place gear in bags, or so that classes could not roll on gear they could not use. The design of a game dictates where opportunities for human intervention shall be offered; a hand of God is embroidered into the software. It was not simply player inventiveness that gave rise to the negotiation and sociality that molded game experience; latitude for such player activity depended on specific rules of play. Just as fractious *Lineage* players were permitted to rampage, so were *WoW* players afforded means by which to cheat, as well as means by which to share wealth if they so chose.[12]

Hunter and Lastowka (2004) observed of an early virtual world, *LambdaMoo*, that its founder, Pavel Curtis,

> . . . and the other four [programmers] who worked with him could quite literally reshape *LambdaMoo*'s heaven and earth, which was nothing more than a database of textual representations and coded rules that governed the objects within that represented space.

Hunter and Lastowka recounted that when Curtis and the programming team came to a point at which they wanted to abdicate responsibility for running *LambdaMoo* (which became a burdensome responsibility), they realized they could not because the software, which they controlled, was so definitive of participant experience.

The design of a software artifact dominates experience while not completely determining it. This asymmetry of player and software shapings is desirable when good design is encapsulated in digital rules with their capacity to reliably reproduce experience. In the case of video games, invariant execution of rules constitutes a resource for preserving and propagating vision and artistic imagination. *World of Warcraft*, whose software encoded elegant artwork, clever game mechanics, and support for specific forms of social activity, gave rise to play experience that found appeal to millions of people from diverse national, cultural, and socioeconomic backgrounds. I suggest that we examine outcomes of rules as situated in particular artifacts rather than as a monolithic category, conceiving rules of *well-designed* software artifacts as neither inflexibly totalizing nor calling out for user remedy but as nurturing, protective, caring.

In *WoW*, the enforcement of game rules conserved a rich, complex play experience. The design was hardly perfect, and the experiences surrounding Karazhan indicate the troubles that may issue from design decisions, but, taken in the large, *World of Warcraft* was an out of the park, bases-loaded home run, becoming a de facto standard for multiplayer games according to most any metric we might consult, including sustained player base, formal awards, and (presumably) profitability.

Let us now consider a case in which participants in a virtual world are responsible for its creation and content is not pregiven, locked down in rules, by designers working for the corporate entity. A point of comparison with the highly designed universe of *World of Warcraft* comes ready to hand.

We will inspect a virtual world devoid of its own content, dedicated instead to participants' creations: *Second Life*.

In *Second Life*, participants construct content using tools provided by Linden Lab, *Second Life*'s purveyor (Malaby 2006, 2009; Boellstorff 2008). Malaby conducted extensive field research at Linden Lab, reporting that the design of *Second Life* was guided by a philosophy of emancipation endorsing whatever creativity might spring from the hands and minds of *Second Life* "residents," as they are called. From the beginning, Linden Lab's ideology centered on the importance of furnishing participants tools to build whatever they wanted (Malaby 2006, 2009).

Launched in 2003, *Second Life* has had considerable time (in an Internet sense at least) to establish its trajectory. The practical results of the radical freedom envisioned by *Second Life*'s designers, have been, I would say, mixed. While *Second Life* contains a rich assortment of diverse activities (Boellstorff 2008), on the whole, participants have gravitated toward creating content devoted primarily to two activities: shopping and sex.

In a world in which people can do whatever they want, the reproduction of consumption as a primary activity is, in my view, a somewhat disappointing turn (though consistent with the larger culture). The prevalence of sexually themed activity is a draw for some but uncongenial to others. Hansen and his colleagues (2009) analyzed the written responses of senior business executives who spent time in *Second Life* as part of an assignment for an MBA class:

> Anonymity is considered a likely contributing factor to the often alarming pornographic activity within *Second Life*. In the words of a program management executive, "In my 40 years of life I don't think I have ever run into so many sexually-motivated characters." Stories of sexually-oriented activity and rudeness abounded in the data. Executives reported a multitude of situations where they were harassed, stalked, and on one occasion, sexually violated. One executive indicated that he cannot see a way to control such activity, which greatly limited any significant conceivable role for the medium in organizations.

Another executive observed:

> In addition, even if you filter out mature content, the risqué clothing, skin,

and parts business is unbelievable, so you are never safe from a flash of some body part while walking through a Herman Miller studio or Coldwell Banker's HQ.

One executive highlighted the impact this could have on business:

> If we recommended our customers to use this site, and they subsequently were propositioned or mistreated in any way, I believe that our reputation would suffer irreparable damage.

In practice, the freedoms cherished by *Second Life*'s designers resulted in the dominance of certain activities, pushing away other activities into which potential participants, disaffected by the dominant activities, might have entered.[13] This is not to say that sex and shopping are bad, or should be dismissed, but that they constitute a narrow range of experience. Sexually themed activity has a powerful dynamic; its presence in *Second Life* draws sharp lines between those who will enter a world where it is pervasive and those who will not.

A partial solution to the problem of off-putting content is to pay for private spaces within *Second Life* that are inaccessible to the general public. Many businesses and organizations maintain them. They serve an important purpose and are integral to the success of *Second Life*. But at the same time we may view such spaces as a retreat to walled gardens, defeating the ideal of an agora of diverse activities in which we might browse and learn and be enchanted. If participants enter only into restricted areas in *Second Life* and must stay off the streets, so to speak, the impact of the creativity Linden Lab's founders envisioned is diminished in its capacity to generate abundant, varied experience.

Malaby (2006) noted another sequela of residents' activities. Visually, the virtual world evolved into something of a junk heap. Malaby reported that Linden Lab employees complained that *Second Life* was "ugly, trashy, and junk-filled." Malaby remarked that

> the *Second Life* built landscape is remarkably variant, with giant advertising signs next to enormous modernist skyscrapers next to medieval castles next to five story dinosaurs next to perfect recreations of art deco gas stations. With no gravitational limits on building, the skyline is cor-

respondingly unconstrained, and the word that springs to mind . . . is, indeed, "trash."

Without the gifts of artists to compose the landscape and rules of governance to channel participants' creations, the ensuing hodgepodge dismayed those who worked at Linden Lab, and even sympathetic observers such as Malaby commented on the infelicitousness of the visual prospect in *Second Life*.

That some *Second Life* residents rejected its "trashy" aspect was evident in the practice of residents moving to private spaces in which elements of order and unity were exactly those reintroduced. Malaby reported that one of the first things owners of private spaces did was establish rules. Private spaces asserted "sovereignty . . . to build . . . in a particular style . . . with restrictions . . . and covenant[s]" (2006).

It is perhaps ironic to locate finer sensibilities in a video game centered on killing cartoon monsters than in a virtual world devoted to the creativity of the citizenry. But there is no substitute for good design; a well-designed digital artifact such as *World of Warcraft*—with its rules and constraints and limits—can be constitutive of a "work of art . . . not remote from common life," as Dewey said. The design of *Second Life*—its bid for tools-without-rules—and the pursuant disorder and disunity, made its public spaces less works of art for common life and more environments that provoked the "lamentations" of its own designers that it was not more beautiful (Malaby 2006).

Second Life is, of course, a digital object with its own software rules; rules per se guarantee nothing. My argument is that digital rules provide a special kind of resource with which good design can be preserved and protected through encapsulation in the black box. In this sense, rules may nurture by providing a safe haven for cultural objects of integrity and excellence. I see the design encapsulated in the rules of *World of Warcraft* as a work of art—one that gives rise to participatory aesthetic experience, to the remaking of experience and community, as Dewey formulated.

Thus, I view with caution proposals to instigate more player control and "community participation." Taylor (2006b) suggested that participatory design techniques could be utilized in multiplayer video games for the purpose of "according [players] some power and responsibility to govern their own community and world." While there is appeal in this idea,

I believe it is quite difficult to determine where the design of a game such as *WoW* leaves off and "governance" begins. Obviously players shape game experience, as Taylor (2006b) and others have pointed out and as I have discussed. But I wonder if allowing players latitude in matters such as character design is a workable idea. Taylor (2006b) described a protest that took place within *World of Warcraft* instigated by players displeased with changes in their characters. She noted that multiplayer games have few spaces for such protests and that corporate entities such as Blizzard do not encourage them.

I am skeptical that those gathering to protest were representative of the millions of people playing *World of Warcraft* or that there is any way to develop representative political processes within a game such as *WoW*. I am skeptical that the protesters were better equipped than Blizzard designers to alter character design. I have discussed ways in which Blizzard consulted players. They had their own methods for doing so; it is hardly the case that players were silenced by the corporation.

Methods of participatory design are intended to balance power among stakeholders. Participatory design is deliberately democratic. I cannot speak too highly of democracy as a political system, but artistic production is, to me, another matter; it is inherently singular, anomalous, moving on the edges of culture. It has no interest in balancing competing claims through fairness or compromise, although it is, of course, not immune to influences outside itself.

When I attended the "UI and Mods" session at BlizzCon, I was cheered to hear one of the panelists declare that *World of Warcraft* was intended to be an immersive experience of a lively visual world in which the mobs are moving, the scenery interesting, buildings and landscape features designed to be woven into strategies for fights. In other words, the gestalt of the designed world was the basis of play experience. The designer said:

> Don't play the user interface, play the game . . . [We want you] to look at the world not the bars.

Another panelist said that *World of Warcraft* should be "organic and fun."

In contrast, many player-created software modifications redirected the game, moving it toward a focus on numbers. The interface to these numbers became a central focus of player attention. As with much quantification, numbers rarely tell the whole story, but they become the salient point of contact between actor and world.

I confess I loved Recount. But at the same time, it frustrated me that certain aspects of my healing activity were not represented in its calculations. Recount computed only direct heals, ignoring the mitigation of damage provided by the "shields" a priest can cast or the fact that priests have an ability to increase the armor of the player being healed, also preventing damage. Many guilds chastised players whose WWS numbers were not as high as a class or raid leader thought they should be (see Taylor 2008; Wine 2008). At one point, a (misguided) priest captain in Scarlet Raven declared that I was casting too many "Prayer of Mending" spells, which he had determined by studying WWS reports. This efficient spell did not reveal all the healing I was actually doing because, in the modification that measured heals, healing activity from Prayer of Mending was attributed to the players who received the healing (due to a technical complexity in the design of the modification). The class leader wanted me to move up in the rankings by reducing my use of the spell, even though the spell was beneficial for the raid.

I have seen more and more use of player-created software modifications in *World of Warcraft*. Mods often push the game away from the gestalt identified by Blizzard as core to *WoW* play experience toward a world of meters, alarms, shortcuts, and annoying announcements cluttering the chat window. I was forced to adopt the mods Clique and Grid in order to speed my healing to maintain my position on the meters. The use of Clique did nothing but allow me to mouseover to heal more quickly. *WoW* encounters were designed to allow players enough time to click on a target and then select a spell. (Blizzard did not design a game impossible to play.) My use of Clique was a defensive maneuver in response to the power of player-created meters. Likewise, I was pressured into using Grid, which I grudgingly admit had some very useful features not found in the standard *WoW* UI, but which also lacked some features (such as the ability to move individual raid group windows).

Golub (2009) argued that mods help players in difficult raid encounters. This is certainly true, but many of the mods players used simply were not needed once an encounter was learned. For example, Deadly Boss Mods (DBM) warned players of impending events, allowing them to prepare and take action. I used Deadly Boss Mods until it stopped working (I tried everything to restore it, and eventually did). But for a time I got used to not having it. Golub observed that players used mods like DBM for mobs such as Akil'zon the Eagle Lord who casts a devastating electrical storm that can only be avoided if players run to him. But if a player's situational awareness is switched on, there is a warning from the game and time to run.

Golub reported that players in his guild used an audio alert mod when battling the dragon Sartharion to anticipate when lava walls rise up and must be negotiated by running to a gap between them. I died several times in the lava walls but became an ace at them in pretty short order. Sartharion was one of my favorite encounters in part because it was so visually stimulating. Lacking mods, I was forced to maintain visual attentiveness.[14]

So, while mods were helpful without question and I see them as critical to player experience, as I will discuss in chapter 7, some mods served to hasten progress in the game rather than to make it "organic and fun." I would not trade the fun of having gained command of the lava walls for quicker progress in the game, and, indeed, some of my guildmates who used mods got the hang of the lava walls after I did. It is not always the case, then, that "the community" is invariably right; there are competing perspectives on what makes for good play. Although she is in favor of strong player participation, Taylor (2008) observed that

[T]hrough [modifications'] rationalization and quantification of action, they . . . strongly inform (and potentially limit) what is seen as "good play" or what is viewed as reasonable.

In analyzing discussion on a priest forum, Wine (2008) remarked:

The mistakes healers make are some of the most public, and posts in the forums try to head this off by letting priests know the "right way" will be expected of them in a raid.

The limitations entrained by modifications and narrow concepts of the "right way" do not open games to a wider variety of experiences and personal preferences but move to rationalized systems of control. With respect to player-centered governance, we may need to be careful what we wish for.[15]

I am doubtful of the feasibility of participatory design methods in large virtual worlds. At the time of this writing, *World of Warcraft* had 11 million players. These players lived in countries as different as Denmark and Dubai. They spoke different languages and came from diverse cultures. How are we to engage them in exercises of participatory design? While I am sympathetic to the aims of participatory design, its techniques were developed in the context of a specific local culture (Scandinavian trade unionism), and the techniques it devised are accountable to particularities of that culture (see Kensing and Blomberg 1998). There is little evidence that participatory design techniques scale to large multinational, multicultural venues.[16]

The question, then, is how best to sustain and develop communities that spring up in and around video games and virtual worlds. My discussion of design and governance is intended to problematize participant input, to call into question a propensity to see all participant input as an a priori good.

Indeed, the very notion of *community* must itself be reexamined. It is perhaps not so simple as community = players, when surely community is a complex assembly including, in the context of *World of Warcraft*, Blizzard and the corporate entities behind websites such as Wowhead.com, from which players derive critical information, as well as advertisers who support these sites.

Developing nuanced understandings of the varying roles of participants and corporations in online worlds is a daunting task. Devising ways to attain dialogue between interested parties remains a challenge, one we will struggle with for some time to come. Productive interchange must reckon with the diversity and complexity of authentic participant experience, the visions of artists who design games, and corporate realities.

I mention a final testament, in the context of *World of Warcraft*, to the power of a well-designed software artifact to preserve and propagate vision and inspired imagination. The potency of *WoW*'s artistry gave rise to the player practice of conducting "nostalgia runs" in old, pre-TBC dungeons. Having gained a foothold in TBC, some players journeyed back to old content they had not seen. Dungeons such as the Temple of Ahn'Qiraj and Blackwing Lair, extremely difficult at level, offered imaginative settings and contests players wished to experience. Players whose characters were not geared enough when TBC arrived, or who had not had time for advanced content, went back to see what they had missed. These players could not obtain a single piece of equipment better than that of the new TBC dungeons; acquiring gear was moot. Doubling back to the old dungeons was purely for the pleasure of novel visual-performative experience.

Since players were equipped with powerful new gear, the old dungeons provided visual experience for the most part, although players were sometimes surprised at their performative difficulty. They still had to figure out what the mobs were up to and how to defeat them.[17] Some players upped the ante by returning with small groups, refiguring performative challenge by attempting, say, the 40-man Blackwing Lair with a smaller group.

Players' sustained drive to "see the content," as they put it, whether in high-end dungeons or quotidian quests, owed much to the care and nurturance afforded by the black box, sheltering, as it did, code in which was registered the desires and visions of talented designers. Empowered through digital technology to call forth complex worlds of human activity, creators of the virtual world preserved their artistry, ensuring its continuance through inscription in digitally encoded rules.[18]

Performance and Participation

I have proposed that video games constitute a unique visual-performative medium, affording—on a massive scale, by way of cheap, commodity technology—visual-performative experience available in the real world in more limited ways. The accessibility of desirable participatory experience has enabled a significant evolution in digital culture with global impact.

Dewey's notion of participatory aesthetic activity, on which I have relied, is one of many concepts of participation in the literature on video games. Raessens (2005) observed:

> Many authors refer to concepts such as . . . "participation" to characterize the distinctiveness of computer games and the media culture that has developed around them . . . [But] these terms are used in various and sometimes contradictory ways, a situation that leads to confusion.

Huisman and Marckmann (2005), for example, suggested that participation must involve "an open dialogue between user and designer." Unless players are extending a game through their "own imagination," play activity is merely consumption. Huisman and Marckmann observed, "[I]t turns out that [participation] is interesting only when the number of users is limited . . . The smaller the number of users, the greater the influence each one can have." This formulation excludes *World of Warcraft* and other popular multiplayer games and seems limiting.

Without exhaustively analyzing notions of participation (see Raessens 2005), let us examine Raessens's thoughtful construction of participation in video gaming. I will suggest that it has some limitations, while recognizing that it identifies certain critical aspects of participation.

Raessens's notion of participation is theorized at the action level of the activity hierarchy. He formulated video game participation as comprised of three elements: interpretation, reconfiguration, and construction. Interpretation is figuring out how game rules work. Reconfiguration builds the player's game world by selecting objects and actions from a fixed set offered by the game. Construction adds new game elements such as player-created software modifications.

These elements of participation were present in *World of Warcraft*, and they faithfully capture a good deal of the texture of everyday *WoW* activity. Structural decomposition of participation into its actions, as Raessens has done, is useful and necessary. What is missing for me in Raessens's depiction is the passion that animated participatory activity in *World of Warcraft*—the object of activity that imbued actions with intensity and interest.

I began my investigation wondering about the undergraduates' excitement over multiplayer video games. The actions of interpretation, reconfiguration, and construction, while pleasurable in themselves, were deeply absorbing, not merely momentarily diverting, in building toward something bigger, specifically, the development of performative mastery. Dewey noted that the flow of aesthetic activity moves from "from something to something." Actions such as interpretation and reconfiguration satisfy in themselves, but at the same time they advance toward an object—a horizon of fulfillment in a larger trajectory (see Kuutti 1998).

In analyzing participation, it is useful to attend to both short and long time frames, as activity theory and Dewey's conceptualization of aesthetic experience indicate. Ethnographic methods play well with this strategy, mindful as they are to nuances of small moments that embody larger themes, while sticking, over time, with the subject (in both senses of the word) to trace paths visible only as they emerge in their particular temporality. For analyses grounded in notions of texts (such as Raessens's), temporal flows of human activity may be less salient as structural characteristics of artifacts predominate the analytical field of view.

Game design that provides pleasurable means building toward the possibility of a kind of greatness in a player's personal history produces a compelling form of participation. Sean's discussion of his choice of guildmates, frustrations with certain players, and elation at progression were indicative of a larger object of continually improving his performance in *World of Warcraft*. For him, knowing rules, configuring objects, and reconstruction were organized and motivated by the object of becoming a better player. By themselves these actions cannot explain Sean's attachment to *World of Warcraft* or the meanings of the game for him. The object of performative mastery imbued his actions with significance and interest.

The Spectacle of Images

I want to end this chapter by looping back to Huatong's fascination with the druid character type and her contemplation of its varied renderings. Performative activity in *World of Warcraft* took place in a rich visual matrix. Analogizing video games and sports takes us only so far, lacking, as it does, acknowledgment of the brilliant visual spectacles that constitute contemporary video games.[19] Metrics and competition suggesting sportslike activity tell half the story, but instead of the literal uniformity of sporting uniforms and the plainness and predictability of, say, basketball courts or soccer fields, video games conjure striking visual worlds remarkable in their vivid realizations of unique imagined universes.

In the interviews, players often discussed and evaluated *WoW*'s visuals. They talked about the game artwork, mentioning colors, character images, animations, buildings, and game geography as important aspects of play experience.

An American player was touched by the animation of a leaf falling from a tree.

Sheryl: I love the scenery. It's just beautiful, the animals, everything. You know the little leaves that they'll have falling. Or, like a feather on the ground. It's just like, out of all the things they had to do in this game, they remembered to do a little leaf.

Chinese players commented:

Chen: It seems the game is done with a lot of devotion and heart by its producers and every [visual] detail is elaborate.

Bao: I like the characters, the pictures, the production. And the characters have a vivid performance.

A player in Shanghai said:

Liu: My guild members and I fight the monsters and then we rest and look at the area together. We explore and wander through different areas . . . Looking at the scenery is recreational.

Players conversed about how gear looked:

Herold: Not all AQ40 [a dungeon] sets are ugly, personally I like the leather ones for rogues n drood [druids].

They expressed delight when a new piece of gear (or an enchant) was sparkly, showy, unusual (in a cool way), evocative of the class, or otherwise well designed.

Dimminix: Priest T6 [a category of gear] is HAWT[20]

Players registered disappointment in gear that copied old designs, was clumsy looking, or ugly. It was especially regretful when a piece of gear had "good stats," that is, powerful attributes, but poor design:

Rigg: man, I hate it when ugly sets have good stats.

The notion of seeing new content alluded to both visual and performative experience, but new content had tremendous visual impact when first encountered, bringing forth complex visual worlds no one had ever seen before. Juul (2005) observed:

> Most video games . . . project a fictional world: The player controls a character; the game takes place in a city, in a jungle, or anywhere else.

Juul theorized that fictional worlds are, in part, imagined by players who "fill in any gaps." While agreeing that video games bring forth imagined worlds, my data suggest that these worlds are less a fiction in which players fill in gaps and more a powerful visual experience like viewing a striking landscape—the world is fully realized, and one need only gaze at it.

This emphasis on the visual is not to say that textual representations were not important in *World of Warcraft*. They were very important—in chat, quest descriptions, character statistics, and other game elements. We might call video games such as *WoW* visual-performative-textual media, if it weren't so inelegant. But I don't think we need do that. "Baseball in elf costumes" crystallizes what brings video games into the realm of the deeply compelling for a vast audience; the marriage of performance and stimulating visual experience impels players to spend long, dedicated hours engaged in activity in game worlds.

We have a handy comparison with which to argue for the primacy of the visual. Text-based role-playing games (such as *Arctic* or *Avalon*), while similar in certain ways to their image-rich cousins, never attained the wide appeal of video games. Text-based games utilized similar storylines, offered opportunities for performative excellence, and engaged players with challenges. But despite a core audience of enthusiasts, text-based games have always been, and remain, a niche. The performative element, *sans* visuals, seems insufficient to enable these games to break into the big time, even though they go back to the 1970s (Jerz 2007). Players today could choose such games, which are cheaper to produce and require less bandwidth, but they overwhelmingly select games with graphics.

The notion that video games are themselves texts, i.e., a form of narrative (see Murray 1997), is another sense in which we may consider the question of textual representation. Games such as *A Tale in the Desert* engage true narrative; game play changes based on a clever mix of player activity and designer storytelling (see Fujimoto 2005). However, the blockbuster games, including multiplayer role-playing games and first-person shooters, are only weakly narrativized as far as play goes. One can play without knowing a shred of what players call "lore." Contemporary video games utilize narrative, but they are not essentially stories in the way that "narratologists" have argued (see Aarseth 1997).

World of Warcraft was indeed based on a rich textual backstory. In the forests of Tirisfal Glades, the Scarlet Monastery, once devoted to the Light, was conquered by fanatical zealots. The rocky environs of Shadowmoon Valley sheltered the powerful warlock Gul'dan, who transformed the Black Temple into headquarters of the Shadow Council, an organization bent on destruction. Silithus, an insect-infested desert, was home to the fallen Aquiri Empire, whose capital, Ahn'Qiraj, housed a temple sealed off by Night Elves in an effort to prevent complete infestation.

This is beautiful stuff, but I had to look it up on WoWWiki. The lore does not come through seamlessly in play experience as the surface of the visual world does. Some players loved *WoW* lore and would have known what I looked up. But they were a minority; guild chat almost never mentioned lore while players constantly talked about how their equipment looked and discussed their desires to see new content.

WoW's visual world borrowed elements of theater; characters accumulated wardrobes of colorful, fanciful costumes and props and participated in encounters in stagy settings. A cast of fantasy beasts, such as the druid forms Huatong loved, were on display, as well as demons, ogres, trolls, giants, dwarves, and dragons. The costumes, props, and characters afforded direct visual experience that did not require the mediation of narrative or the need to "fill gaps" in an incomplete fictionalized world. Visual elements were intact and complete in themselves. As Andy Warhol said of the importance of surfaces:

> If you want to know all about Andy Warhol, just look at the surface of my paintings and films and me, and there I am.

The impact of *WoW*'s visual surface was evident in consistent player comments about animations, landscape, gear, and so on—players were sensitive to, and liked the way things looked.

But the visual surface of the game had other important work to do. Players interacted with visual elements with more than gaze; much of what they saw was intended to be interpreted for purposes of play. The visual environment contained quest items, friendly and unfriendly NPCs and players, flowers to be picked, ores to be mined, bodies of water to dive into, forges at which to smith weapons and armor. In battle, "line of sight" was critical; players carefully arranged their characters around walls, buildings, and hills so that their spells could reach those they were healing or fighting or to prevent an onslaught of mobs which would be riled if approached "in the open" rather than from behind the safety of a door or wall. Players knew well what the fantasy world looked like from a performative standpoint: where a flag carrier might be hiding in the Warsong Gulch battleground, how to jump from a ledge to a balcony in Blackrock Spire to get to the entrance of one of its dungeons, ways to use the pillars in the Ring of Trials arena to competitive advantage.

Players not only interpreted visual elements; their actions altered the visual world—unlike other visual media such as television or film. One of the most satisfying aspects of play was the impact of action on the world—watching an enemy's (usually rather comically enacted) death, seeing a raid member appear beside one through the magic of a warlock's summoning ability, calling forth a "pet" such as a baby wolf or tiny, psychedelically colored bat.

WoW's design, then, was a kind of theatre in which audience and performers were one.[21] There was plenty to look at,[22] but at the same time, players themselves were onstage. In boss fights, players performed in spaces very much like stages; in some, bosses stood on literal platforms exactly like stages. In others, a confined space such as a cave or library delimited a stage in size and orientation. The Zul'Gurub dungeon, for example, was gaudily theatrical—amid Mesoamerican ruins decaying in a jungle, crocodiles, panthers, tigers, serpents, and giant spiders guarded bosses who, during battle, transformed to huge, powerful animals. The biggest boss was Hakkar the Soulflayer, visible on a high platform as players moved through the instance killing lesser bosses.

It was an exciting moment when players assembled on the virtual stage in anticipation of a challenging fight. The relation of player to play was given literal form in the Opera encounter in Karazhan. A stage manager, Barnes, invites the "audience" of players to watch a play. But when the curtain rises, the characters onstage transform from actors to mobs, attacking the players—who are required to perform to avoid death. The flip from viewer to actor dramatizes players as agents who do not merely watch but

Barnes invites the audience to. . . .

. . . a performance of Little Red Riding Hood.

themselves act. The encounter subverts pervasive cultural instructions to sit quietly, passively, one's activity constrained to viewing (recall Dewey's impatience with high-culture art). By abruptly inverting audience and actor, the directive authorizes, indeed demands, participatory activity.

WoW's visual surface, then, did double duty; players could gaze appreciatively at their surroundings, but, simultaneously, the world's visual features invited players to participatory activity.

Within commodity culture such as television, visual elements lack the capacity to instigate participation. Baudrillard (1983) asserted that mass media produce a "narcotized," "mesmerized" consciousness of passive immersion in a spectacle of simulated images. Turkle, a pioneering media theorist, noted that with television, "the body of the television spectator is not in the picture" (1984). While television may have its social side (see Jenkins 1992; Mankekar 1999), I believe Turkle's powerful observation, and the arguments of theorists such as Baudrillard, are generally descriptive of the medium.[23]

In the early 1980s, Turkle began to report the engaged, active experiences of computer users, including gamers, arguing that computers afford an experience in which the (virtual) body *is* in the picture. Even before Turkle's work, in the late 1970s an immersive text-based game, *Colossal Cave Adventure*, generated a cult following. *Colossal Cave Adventure* established a digital space that described a game geography in words, offering players interesting performative opportunities. The game began:

> Somewhere nearby is Colossal Cave, where others have found fortunes in treasure and gold, though it is rumored that some who enter are never seen again. Magic is said to work in the cave . . . You are standing at the end of a road before a small brick building. Around you is a forest. A small stream flows out of the building and down a gully. (Jerz 2007)

Players remembered:

> The game spread like wildfire across the Internet, inspiring such obsessive efforts to solve the game that it is rumored numerous college seniors did not graduate that year as a result.

> The entire computer industry was set back by a week. (Rickadams n.d.)

Though tongue-in-cheek exaggerations, these statements indicate the excitement and intensity players experienced in response to *Colossal Cave Adventure*'s performative challenges—the same excitement that suffuses today's video games, which reach a much wider audience through their image-rich design.

New text-based games, worlds, and communities continued to develop after *Colossal Cave Adventure* such as *LambdaMoo* (Cherny 1991; Mnookin 1996; Damer 1998, 2009), *Habitat* (Morningstar and Farmer 1991), and the Well (Rheingold 1993), as well as console and arcade games (Hunter and Lastowka 2004; Huhtamo 2005; Malliet and de Meyer 2005). Mass culture, with its accumulation of images, seems quite capable of generating participatory experience; video games afford arenas of activity in which visual experience is unified with active performance. Baudrillard's fear of the "simulacrum," i.e., simulation that devolves to ersatz experience, and his rejection of the virtual appear to have been based on too narrow a sampling of virtual media, one that neglected the rapid development of interactive networked media.

Participation in virtual worlds is not simulation but performance. There is no faking performance; it is brutally honest. The software enforcing the rules and the players watching to see whether you click the cube at the right moment compel honesty. Postmodern theory asserted the delusional quality of mass-produced images, but even as those images were proliferating, new means of authentic expressive performance, embedded in vivid visual spaces, were emerging as forms of mass culture.

CHAPTER FIVE

Work, Play, and the Magic Circle

Gaming is of course a kind of play. This chapter connects *World of Warcraft* to long-standing debates about the nature of play, in particular, examining issues of play and its putative opposite, *work,* that have preoccupied play theory for decades. Entangled in these debates is the idea of play as a magic circle—a protected space defended against the encroachments of everyday life such as work, school, and domestic duties.

Play theorists have struggled to define work and play. While seemingly straightforward notions, when scrutinized, they seem to dissolve into inconsistency and contradiction. I will inquire into play theorists' notions of work and play, as well as those of *World of Warcraft* players. The analysis is grounded in Dewey's broad concept of active aesthetic experience, of which game play is one example, and draws on the work of theorists whose focus is more narrowly on play and games. The discussion maintains a distinction between "game play"—i.e., the performance of a game—and "games" as cultural entities such as hide-and-seek or *World of Warcraft.* A good deal of games scholarship focuses on *games,* in particular, their structural characteristics, e.g., Juul 2005. For Juul, games are games whether played professionally or for leisure. That distinction is important for me (as I will discuss). The chapter develops a conception of game play as constituted in part by subjective dispositions toward activities involving the cultural entities we call games.

Work and Play

Dewey contrasted aesthetic activity with the "the toil of a laborer" in which the wage is the sole reward. Taking certain forms of play as a kind of aesthetic activity, the contrast implies the traditional work-play dichotomy. While it seems only common sense to suppose that work and play stand in relations of opposition, this opposition has been questioned by scholars observing that, on the one hand, video game players often engage in worklike activities, and, on the other hand, sometimes our jobs can be fun (Stevens 1978; Pearce 2006, 2009; Yee 2006; Poole 2008; Rettberg 2008).

WoW players seemed to agree with Dewey, as well as play theorists such as Turner (1982), Callois (1961), and Huizinga (1950), that play is not work. Early in my research I was struck by the explicit and emotional juxtaposition of work and play in chat conversations and posts on the Scarlet Raven website. The website had a forum thread in which prospective guild members introduced themselves and applied to join the guild. The following messages were exchanged between an applicant and two guild officers:

Hello, I filled out an application pretty recently [and I have a question] . . .

Okay, gotta get back to work

Thanks!

~Myrna

Reply:

Wait, Myrna. . . . what is this "work" you speak of?

I'll go google that word.

Arian

Second reply:

Im not really sure but . . . but . . . i tell ya, I have heard nothing but bad things about "Work"! If i was you I wouldnt even go there . . .

Takamu

Arian and Takamu bracketed work by putting it in quotes, setting it outside the realm of the game. The pretended unfamiliarity with "work" indicated its disjunction from play and suggested that it might have a pretty bad reputation. In a similar post, Zaq, a bartender, wrote:

> since the date [of the guild event] was moved from tuesday to monday, I won't be attending. I do that thing called "employment" on monday.

A player preparing for exams for graduate school explained why he had not been in-game much recently. Darkstorm wrote:

> just on the off chance that anyone from [my company] is reading this and knows who i am, i was just kidding before about leaving my job this spring. i love working in accounting. i . . . um . . . set up vendor codes. and i ask for w-9 forms. and i . . . um . . . receive them. and write reports about it. what could possibly be soul-crushingly boring about that?! nothing! hoooray for accounting! and hooray for beer! i was kidding about the beer just then.

An uncannily similar piece of dialogue occurred in the opening episode of the popular American television comedy *The Office*. Jim, a young employee, says:

> My job is to speak to clients, um, on the phone about, uh, quantities and uh, type of copier paper. You know, uh, whether we can supply it to them, whether they can, uh, pay for it and, um, I'm boring myself just talking about this.

The Office, based on a British show of the same name, plays on the boredom of work and the stratagems employed by a group of office workers to make it through the day. Many worker/viewers identify with the acerbic portrayal of the tedium of work and its characterization as "boring."

In describing Scarlet Raven, a guild leader wrote on the website:

> Our main priority is to have fun! World of Warcraft is a game, not a job.

A Chinese player said:

Let the game be a game and not work.

Players commonly gave precise times when they would have to return to work or school, marking the transition out of *World of Warcraft* and back to real life. Guild chat:

> Beehive: well people, i think it's bedtime . . . gotta be at work in 6 hours, so i MIGHT need sleep if they're going to get anything outta me. g'night all

Party chat:

> Malita: k i have about 10 mins then i have to go to sleep lol school tomorrow blah![1]

> Malita: i have to be up at 5 am, and out at 6 am . . . it's 10:38 now

It was 1:00 a.m., and a player who had to leave in the middle of a quest typed:

> Malinstrife: gtg [got to go] really sorry, i have to be at work at 9

Johan Huizinga, a Dutch play theorist, affirmed Dewey's distinction between work and play (1950). Huizinga observed that play is "never imposed by physical necessity or moral duty." In our culture, work, as well as school, are, by and large, involuntary and imposed by a range of physical and moral duties.[2]

But it is also true that shifting subjective boundaries between voluntary and involuntary, work and play, problematize a simple dichotomy. The fluidity of the boundaries is nicely illustrated in chapter 2 of Mark Twain's *Tom Sawyer,* "Tom Sawyer Whitewashing the Fence."

Aunt Polly has given Tom the onerous job of whitewashing a large fence. This task, imposed by moral duty as well as the potential depredations of Aunt Polly's slipper, has sunk Tom into a "deep melancholy" as he contemplates his foiled plans:

> [Tom] began to think of the fun he had planned for this day, and his sor-

rows multiplied. Soon the free boys would come tripping along on all sorts of delicious expeditions, and they would make a world of fun of him for having to work . . .

Freedom and necessity, work and play, seem to inhabit clear categories. But Tom knows that these categories are open to manipulation precisely because they are subjective. Tom's rival, Ben Rogers, approaches, mocking Tom.

> "Say—I'm going in a-swimming, I am. Don't you wish you could? But of course you'd druther work—wouldn't you? Course you would!"
> Tom contemplated the boy a bit, and said: "What do you call work?"
> "Why, ain't that work?"
> Tom resumed his whitewashing, and answered carelessly: "Well, maybe it is, and maybe it ain't. All I know, is, it suits Tom Sawyer."
> "Oh come, now, you don't mean to let on that you like it?"
> The brush continued to move.
> "Like it? Well, I don't see why I oughtn't to like it. Does a boy get a chance to whitewash a fence every day?"
> That put the thing in a new light. Ben stopped nibbling his apple. Tom swept his brush daintily back and forth—stepped back to note the effect—added a touch here and there—criticized the effect again—Ben watching every move and getting more and more interested, more and more absorbed. Presently he said:
> "Say, Tom, let me whitewash a little."

With a bit of intersubjective work, Tom enlists Ben, and then the other boys who come along, to whitewash the fence as he idles pleasantly in the shade. Here work and play are disjoint not by virtue of specific actions that are inherently "work" or inherently "play," but as separable subjective experiences. I see no reason to dispute Tom Sawyer, Huizinga, or Dewey on the subjective voluntariness of play (see also Garvey 1977). Dewey said, "Play remains an attitude of freedom from subordination to an end imposed by external necessity."

While *WoW* was a voluntary activity, players experienced certain aspects of play as worklike. The pressures of raiding and the need to continually "farm" materials for raid consumables began to feel like work for some. Farming referred to repetitive actions undertaken to acquire game materials such as killing the same type of monster over and over again. (The term *grinding* was also used.)

Both Chinese and North American players reported that sometimes *WoW* felt like work. Peng, a 24-year-old employee at a small venture capital firm in Beijing, and Chiu and Lefen, two students from Beijing, were guildmates. In an interview in an Internet cafe, they explained:

Peng: Our guild is like a work unit, you belong to a certain team.

Chiu: You have to participate [in raiding] everyday from 7 p.m. to 12 p.m. That feels like work.

Lefen: It is very exhausting to participate in regular guild activities, especially for classes whose task it is to watch the combat for a very long time. Thus, after finishing a guild activity, we are too exhausted for anything else.

Yee (2006) observed that players may "burn out" as gaming becomes too similar to work.

In a gaming context, the nuances of the word "work" were context dependent. When Chiu said raiding could "feel like work," he expressed a wearying shift from enjoyment to obligation. By contrast, raiders might also experience the preparation needed for raiding and its seriousness as "dedication" or "hard work." In this context, "work" was energizing and positively valued; it connoted focus, concentration, and empowerment.

"Work" was sometimes invoked in a celebratory mode to acknowledge teamwork and success in performative activity. The Scarlet Raven website posted raid progress:

From 2/6 in SSC to 5/6 in one week! Let's keep up the hard work!

The guild progressed in one week from defeating two of six bosses in the Serpentshrine Cavern dungeon to defeating five out of six. This rapid progress was hailed as a result of "hard work." Likewise, after killing Illidan, Nihilum posted on its website:

Half of us don't realize what was behind all of it. Hard, grunt work. The determination to learn this encounter to its fullest extent. The next day—after 3 hours of tries on Illidan, he finally fell, and his cruel grasp on the world of Outland had been released by Nihilum.

Raiders sometimes likened raiding to the seriousness of a job:

> When you are raiding, remember that upwards of 24 other people are counting on you to do your job and do it well

wrote one player on the Scarlet Raven website. (Recall also Sean's reference to "doing a job.") In describing how he felt about raiding and the preparation required, another player, Jerzey, posted:

> My raid time is precious (with family and work), so I invest much into the 1–2 raids I can attend and commit to each week. For this I actually work very hard in my other time, grinding heroics for gear, and getting mats [materials] to craft almost half of my raiding gear.

He ended the long post (of which these sentences were a part) with a comment that underscores the subjective separation of work and play:

> I hope that made sense. Wrote this from work . . .

When Scarlet Raven experienced the crisis in which players were leaving for hardcore raiding guilds, the guild master posted:

> So where does that leave everyone? People are free to remain here or to go their separate ways if they so choose. If guild is more important than raid to you, that is fine. If raid is more important than guild to you, that is also fine. It's your game, you choose how you want to play it.

It is rare to have such latitude at work or school. Mandated activities in these settings entail strict schedules and obligations inside of which people have limited room for negotiation or choice. The guild master's words were not mere rhetoric; players weighed their preferences and desires. Some stayed; some left to participate in guilds structured very differently than Scarlet Raven.

Dewey captured the paradox of the freedom of play and its coupling with seriousness:

Play remains an attitude of freedom from subordination to an end imposed by external necessity, as opposed, that is, to labor; but it is transformed into work in that activity is subordinated to production of an objective result. No one has ever watched a child intent in his play without being made aware of the complete merging of playfulness with seriousness.

In sum, play is, at the highest level, a freely chosen activity while at the same time opening the potential for worklike results. A notion of freedom must be understood in its social matrix, not as a philosophical absolute. Jerzey delimited three categories of activity he managed: family, work, and play. Family and work entailed serious obligations in which he was enmeshed, while the "precious" raid time was handled as an activity subordinate, and requiring accommodation to, demands of family and work.

Miller (1973) observed that play is characterized by "a degree of autonomy for the actor who manipulates the processes at his disposal." Vandenberg (1998) noted, "The excitement of play results from the sheer exercise of freedom over necessity." The voluntariness of play is evident in the relative ease with which people abandon play activities. Players leave *WoW* (and other games) all the time, making deliberate, conscious, thoughtful choices. A Scarlet Raven player posted the following:

Since a few weeks ago, WoW has been well . . . boring . . . The hardest part is to say farewell to the friends I've made, so I won't do that until I've made my decision. In addition, i'm thinking about giving away my account, so if anyone wants it, send me an email at . . . @gmail.com. Better not to waste 3 [characters] and I wouldn't feel comfortable auctioning the account on ebay.

The consequences of cutting loose from work and family are much more serious, tied to the "moral duty" of which Huizinga spoke, as well as a great many practical constraints. Freedom in the context of play is not to be taken in a heroic Ayn Randian sense, but certain aspects of contemporary life are chosen; our society is predicated on the buying and selling of "leisure" activities in which corporations compete for discretionary dollars and hours.

Within play, then, elements of "work" enter in two ways. First, play may manifest seriousness and dedication which players refer to as work. Second, play may demand obligatory actions such as farming that are necessary to accommodate the larger play activity—the activity that players find pleasurable. Dewey observed that few aesthetic experiences are "wholly gleeful"; they require some actions that afford less pleasure than others. It is useful here to analytically separate actions and activities in a hierarchical manner, as activity theory does; a pleasurable activity can proceed even as some of its required actions are, in themselves, less pleasurable.

Huizinga further specified that play occupies a "magic circle" separating it from other activity. He observed that play, as a domain separate from work (and anything else), inhabits its own space or "sphere." Play is, according to Huizinga (1950):

> a stepping out of "real" life into a temporary sphere of activity with a disposition of its own.

Play takes place within a magic circle into which players move in order to adopt a particular, recognizable set of rules and practices (Huizinga 1950). Boellstorff (2008) noted that crossing such boundaries "can strengthen the distinctiveness of the two domains that [the boundaries] demarcate."[3]

To summarize, play theorists assert that play is characterized by:

1. A subjective experience of freedom
2. An absence of social obligation and physical necessity
3. A subjective experience that is absorbing, compelling, or pleasurable
4. Occurrence in a separate realm sometimes referred to as the magic circle

I add that play requires active cognition and/or physical skill. Juul (2005) described games as requiring "effort." Malaby (2009) spoke of play as engaging "a readiness to improvise," indicating active, creative participation on the part of the player. Play happens when the imagination is stimulated, when there is an alertness to the surroundings and sometimes an engagement with physical activity. We may distinguish between, say, a child listening to a story being read and taking her dollies on an imaginary picnic. The activities are not unrelated, but one requires a more vigorous exercise of the imagination with the possibility of ending up in new places of the mind rather than more predictable outcomes of a story. Both are valuable experiences but distinctive in their potentials.

This notion of play is very broad, descriptive of many activities. *Game* play is a specific form of play, involving all the elements of play and three additional elements: contingency, rules, and "limited perfection."

Huizinga observed that game play "brings a temporary limited perfection" through activity that involves "uncertainty" and "chanciness." Players want to "achieve something difficult, to succeed, to end a tension" (Huizinga 1950). The notion of limited perfection recalls Dewey's emphasis on the satisfying completion of aesthetic activity, but specifies a relation to contingency ("chanciness"). Callois (1961) also emphasized the importance of "chance" in games. Garvey (1977) remarked:

> A game has a clear beginning and end, and its structure can be specified in terms of moves in a fixed sequence with a limited set of procedures for certain contingencies.

Malaby (2007) noted that games provide "contrived contingency." A game establishes a table of contingencies in which players take their chances, through skill and/or luck, to attain a desired outcome. Contingency is necessary for the activity to be playfully interesting and for the gratification of limited perfection that apparently satisfies psychological needs (Huizinga 1950). Play involves a "contest for something," resulting in activity that is "absorbing" (Huizinga 1950), "compelling" (Malaby 2007), "fun" (Juul 2005), or "pleasurable" (Miller 1973; Taylor 2003; Hayes 2005; Kennedy 2005).

Game play is characterized by:

1. A subjective experience of freedom
2. An absence of social obligation and physical necessity
3. A subjective experience that is absorbing, compelling, or pleasurable
4. Occurrence in a separate realm sometimes referred to as the magic circle
5. Activation through cognitive and/or physical skill
6. Contingency
7. Rules
8. Opportunities for limited perfection

This characterization draws on the work of several theorists. While I believe it is descriptive of *World of Warcraft*, as well as the game play familiar to most readers, whether baseball, bowling, poker, pinball, or Pong, we do not have sufficient cross-cultural data with which to assess whether such a characterization describes play in every culture or even whether every culture has a concept of play (see Malaby 2007). However, I think it tenable to argue that game play is an identifiable human activity whose structure includes both subjective dispositions, such as a sense of freedom, and specific cultural constructs such as rules. Game play is complex precisely because it comprises both subjective dispositions toward activity and concrete, culturally defined elements. Attention to the subjectivity of play is particularly important; the formal characteristics of games, such as contingency and rules, are not the same as the activity of game play. Participating in a lottery to be selected to receive a Green Card (which establishes certain rights for foreign visitors to the United States) involves rules and contingency but is hardly play; getting—or not getting—a Green Card may have extraordinarily serious consequences for individuals and families. One would choose to just get a Green Card if one could, not to enter a space of contingency through a lottery with an uncertain outcome.

How do game play and active aesthetic experience relate to one another? Neither fits neatly within the other; they crosscut. Dewey's notion of aesthetic experience, while broad, does not subsume all game play. It incorporates two elements missing from a baseline definition of game play; aesthetic experience involves a collectivity and it is phased. Game play should include a game such as Solitaire, for which a significant collective element is absent, and it should include playing slot machines, an activity with a simple repetitive structure. We must, then, stretch across two related theoretical approaches to understand the activity of playing *World of Warcraft*, seeing it broadly as aesthetic experience and more narrowly as a kind of game play.

With these conceptualizations in mind, let us return to the *WoW* players and their discussions of work and play. The explicit separation of work and play in player discourse is especially notable in light of the sizable numbers of students and working-class people playing *World of Warcraft*—those most likely to be confronted daily with boring, insufficiently rewarded activity. Player discourse expressed a desire to "step out" of "real life" as, in part, a response to the boredom of school and work embodied in their lack of both playful and aesthetic elements. At the end of August, as school approached, guild chat featured laments about the impending doom such as:

> Leorith: night ppl [people] c u [see you] after the first day of hell i mean skool

A Chinese player said:

> When I stopped playing *WoW* because of my exams, I felt like I did not want to stop. The way of playing is very creative.

Darkstorm called his job "soul-crushingly boring." Nylere, a druid in Scarlet Raven, wrote on the guild website:

> I am stuck back at work, and it's blessidly quiet enough for me to do some research on becoming a better [player] . . . I found the following page to be incredibly helpful and by far the most comprehensive so far http:// elitistjerks.com/f31/t17783-druid_raiding_tree/. It even goes into gems, flasks and enchants! (. . . I am bored, lol!).

Nylere, who was employed in a low-level job so undemanding that she had time to surf the Internet, became absorbed in the "incredibly helpful," "comprehensive" website about her character class, druid. She juxtaposed the action of studying the website to being "stuck back at work" and "bored, lol!" Her statements separated work and play, consistent with other players' characterizations. Even though she was "at work," she removed herself through immersion in the gaming website. Her actions demonstrated the dedication and seriousness of play as she did "some research on becoming a better player," delving into the particulars of her character's options for "gems, flasks and enchants!"

A guildmate indicated that he was not afraid of homework as long as it was interesting:

> Carloh: i do more homework for wow than I do for school lol

Another player, surreptitiously reading humorous posts on the Scarlet Raven website while at work, wrote:

And I am now laughing so hard I'm drawing stares from the other cattle in
the cube farms . . . I'd better stop.

The bleak image of "cattle in the cube farms" is a devastating comment
on modern workplaces, making a desire for vivid, challenging play spaces
unsurprising.

Darkstorm's account revealed his work as entirely routinized, without
contingency or challenge. While not all jobs are as boring, many do not provide regular, orderly satisfaction of needs to succeed at something difficult.
Activities at work and school not only fail to yield perfection, they are ces-
sations not consummations, as Dewey said—activities in which the actions
needed to attain ends are not in themselves absorbing or compelling.

The activity of "gold farming" nicely exemplifies the riddle of work and
play. Gold farmers play *World of Warcraft* (and other games; see Dibbell
2006; Steinkuehler 2006) as a job, generating game gold to sell for real
money (Dibbell 2007). But are they *playing?* I argue that gold farmers are
not engaged in the same activity as players who voluntarily play for what
they call fun. Game lingo reflects this disjuncture; the very term *gold farmer*
is intended to establish a firm boundary between ordinary players and gold
farmers.

Gold farmers may find gold farming preferable to other work that their
education would enable them to obtain (Dibbell 2007), but that does not
mean they are playing. As with the Green Card, it is useful to distinguish
the formal characteristics of cultural constructs (such as *World of Warcraft*)
from a more complex entity identifiable as play involving a subjective disposition yielding absorbing or compelling activity. Dibbell reported that the
Chinese gold farmers he interviewed were entirely focused on farming—
during 12-hour shifts they repetitively killed the same monsters. Farming
was not subordinate to other exciting game activities; it was all the gold
farmers did. Confinement to farming activity was, of course, not the pattern of normal *World of Warcraft* play among gamers.

Gold farmers worked "twelve hours a night, seven nights a week, with
only two or three nights off per month" (Dibbell 2007). It is difficult to
interpret such a pattern of activity as playful. Dibbell reported that gold
farmers sometimes played *World of Warcraft* as a leisure activity after work.
While the lack of leisure time in the gold farmers' schedule makes this a
surprising claim, assuming that at least some gold farmers played *WoW*

after work, Dibbell's story of a gold farmer known for after-hours play is telling—the player did not farm after his shift, but enjoyed difficult dungeons, testing, and showing off, his performative abilities.

Professional gaming appears to blur the lines between work and play. Work that is subjectively experienced as deeply pleasurable may merge, at least sometimes, with play. Paid work, however, tends to rapidly develop strong elements of obligation—obligations to make money, to be accountable to interests such as corporations, universities, advertisers, or family members, and obligations to be performed at certain times and in certain places, with constraints imposed by others. I continued to be impressed by *WoW* players' self-determination in deciding if, when, and how to play *World of Warcraft*—something rare and difficult with paid work.

Rea (2009) discussed gaming in Korea, including its amateur and professional aspects. He noted:

> The Korean language encodes a strict conceptual boundary between what counts as "work" and "play."

Gaming was unambiguously identified as play, but some young players aspired to gain paid work as professional gamers, who are celebrities in Korea. Rea designated the activity of these young gamers "aspirational gaming"—not yet paid but directed toward the object of professional status and high income. Rea (2009) observed:

> In order to hope to become a pro-gamer, one must begin honing one's skills early and invest a considerable amount of time practicing, often in PC Bangs [Internet cafes]. I call this phenomenon "aspirational gaming," meaning that it indeed does count as "work" in the Korean context because it is an activity performed by those that aspire to become professionals.

The actions of gaming were the same for aspirational gamers as for any young player, but their disposition toward gaming activity was markedly different, oriented toward the object of professional play. Rea observed that aspirational gamers had a clear object in mind; they were keenly aware of the rewards of a life as a professional gamer:

> Professional gamers, recruited from around the country usually through

success in local tournaments sponsored by PC Bangs, can make six-fig-
ure salaries and receive corporate sponsorship and room and board from
the leagues they join. The top pro-gamers occupy celebrity subject positions similar to music and movie stars and are even seen as sex symbols by
Korean youth.

For some Korean youth the object of going professional, expressed in a
vivid scenario of life as a pro, moved gaming from play toward a form of
education in preparation for a specific kind of work and career.

A Partial Separation of Play and Not-Play

The notion of a magic circle asserts that play is separate from the rest of
life. Malaby (2007) suggested that play is "*relatively* separable from everyday life" (emphasis added). Taking up this more qualified notion, I will
discuss ways in which *WoW* game play impinged on nonplay and vice versa.
Malaby reminds us that play has consequences outside itself and cannot, by
definition, be entirely separate. Castronova (2005), for example, examined
ways in which activity in virtual worlds extruded into the economy and
polity outside the worlds, such as people selling characters on the Internet
or litigating issues related to game activity. Play does not, and cannot, exist
in an imperturbable magic circle; it is always in dynamic relations of tension to other activities in which a player might engage. Play is calibrated
against competing activities, as we saw in Jerzey's accounting of his time.
Play is linked to the demands of the body, to others in the player's social
environment, and to notions such as work, which it partially defines. Let us
examine how these links were manifest in *World of Warcraft*.

WoW was so absorbing that it was sometimes difficult to find time to
eat, drink, and go to the bathroom while playing. When these activities
became urgent, players typed "bio" into the chat line, a signal that collaborative play must cease for at least a few minutes while the needs of the
body took precedence. The mind encased in the body came into play as
well. Game activities entered the conscious and unconscious mind outside
playtime; players said that they daydreamed about *WoW* when not playing
or dreamed about it at night.

Game play was entwined with the demands of others in the player's social milieu. Players spoke of "spousal aggro," or "family aggro," metaphorically invoking the term for the game mechanism by which monsters are engaged in hostile interaction. In the context of family and friends, *aggro* signified that play might be interrupted by the needs of others who were not-playing, and who might evince a certain level of hostility. In the wee hours one evening, a player in The Derelict who had laboriously assembled a pug had to leave shortly after we began to play.

Gork: sorry guys, gotta go. gf [girlfriend] pissed

In a more positive vein, Sutton-Smith observed that play may result in "adaptive potentiations" in which people take vocabulary, practices, and attitudes from play into other arenas of life (1975). We form the "A Team" at work to tackle a difficult problem or use sports metaphors to describe our actions or urge people to adopt a "winning attitude" (see Dutton 2008). Sutton-Smith argued that differentiated spaces of play encourage potentiations to emerge. People enjoy opportunities to "step out," to be creative, to think outside the box, to experiment, to fool around with doing things differently.

A website in which players discussed how *WoW* linked to the rest of life included the following post showing a way in which *WoW* game mechanics could inform personnel management practices:

When I was assigned to an HR [human resources] project in the company I work for, I noticed how WoW can be useful in real life. After much debate, we realized we could structure our career plans as talent trees on WoW—as people studied and made progress, they would improve certain "talents" that were linked—so after being considered fully prepared in a certain "talent", a person could pursue two or three different specialization paths related to that talent, with an increasing salary the "deeper" that person went in one of the trees. They could also go for a "hybrid build", incorporating talents from different trees. Career choices became pretty much like deciding if you're going to be an Elemental/Enhancement/Restoration or Hybrid Shaman!

Since *WoW* is a big hit among the people who work at this company, everyone quickly understood the concept and what they needed to learn in order to evolve and grow within the company, and where they could eventually get if they invested their time and effort in developing certain talents.

The only hard part was convincing the "conventional managers" that they would have to respec in order to understand these new ideas ;)

Posted at 9:35AM on Jun 14th 2007 by Kabbalah (Schramm 2007).

Talent trees allowed players to specialize a character by emphasizing and strengthening certain abilities (Choontanom 2008). Kabbalah formed a creative link between game mechanics and workplace needs in imagining how talent trees could be used to structure employee advancement. This is a striking example of taking a game construct—a talent tree—and transporting it to a new arena of activity. Such transposition embodied a cultural critique of an existing practice; Kabbalah not only examined current practice and saw that it could be improved, she called out "conventional" managers in need of "respeccing" if they were to see the larger issue her suggestion addressed. In this way, play may be subversive, moving to arenas in which its modes of activity suggest new ways of acting (see Turner 1982).

There is another sense in which we may argue that work and play are only partially separated. Conceptually, work and play are linked; as opposites we use them to define one another. Does this opposition come into play in active relations *between* work and play? How does one affect the other? These are complex questions, but I believe farming in *World of Warcraft* entails an interesting interplay between work and play. I focus here not on gold farming but the native player practice of farming.

As noted, farming boils down to a lengthy set of repetitive actions with little contingency. (Juul 2005 observed that such actions are often part of games.) Killing mobs to gain gold or specific items dropped by mobs (typically needed for crafting), or repetitively collecting resources such as herbs or minerals, are typical farming activities. A close synonym in game lingo is *grinding*—suggesting the onerous nature of the actions.

Farming could take hours and hours of playtime. I once spent nearly six hours (not at a stretch, thankfully) collecting materials for a set of gear used to fight only one boss, a powerful gal named Mother Shahraz. During this time, Innikka did not die once; she simply flew around Shadowmoon Valley on her mount, swooping down to extract motes of shadow (the required element for the gear) when they appeared on a little map in the corner of the screen.

Given that players agree to undertake such activities, some researchers have suggested that repetitive actions in video games (not just *WoW*) constitute preparation for the work world. Yee (2006) remarked:

> . . . video games are inherently work platforms that train us to become better workers. [T]he work being performed in video games is increasingly similar to actual work in business corporations.

Poole (2008) observed:

> [Games] hire us for imaginary, meaningless jobs that replicate the structures of real-world employment . . . If games are supposed to be fun . . . why do they go so far to replicate the structure of a repetitive dead-end job?

Rettberg (2008) asserted that in players' "subconscious capitalist minds" farming is an expression of the "Protestant work ethic" and, moreover, a "sustained delusion" that play equates to work.[4]

I was puzzled that so many *World of Warcraft* players spent so much time farming and did not complain very much (given that player forums were replete with grievances about minutiae such as the color of the glow of a weapon enchant or the degree to which pieces of armor coordinated visually).[5] The sheer boredom of farming and players' acceptance of it were surprising. Chinese players, too, commented on farming; they used the evocative term "brushing" to connote the execution of small, simple, repetitive game actions.

But from the players' point of view, farming in *World of Warcraft* was a logical activity undertaken for well-defined ends. Players wanted to acquire materials with which to craft equipment or enchantments or make gold with which to buy these items in order enhance performance. We might ask, though, why such an activity was part of the logic of the game at all. Why did Blizzard include so much farming as part of *World of Warcraft*? I cannot agree that video game companies have taken it upon themselves to train us for the workplace. Is farming in *WoW* like being a bank teller or checking groceries or performing secretarial work? If there is a move on the part of game corporations to prepare us for capitalist jobs, such a claim needs to determine for itself how it can be substantiated, how it can be more than a moment of radical mischief.

Rather than games as training grounds for the workplace, a more straightforward explanation is ready to hand, at least for farming in *World of Warcraft*. Farming was woven into the game as a design element to provide game content at a cost that increased corporate profit margins. Farming slowed players so they did not rip through months of careful content development in a few days or weeks. Blizzard's incorporation of farming reduced its need for development by inserting a necessary but time-consuming activity into the game that kept gamers busy. Blizzard did not want to create so much content that the game's scope became unmanageable (such as having 250 levels and items that offer +10,000 stamina). Farming said to players, "All right, you want to be marginally better (enough to pwn them!) than the other players on the server? You want something in return for the hours and hours you put in? Okay, you can get that extra little bit, but it's going to cost you. Go farm." This allowed ambitious players to work hard for an edge.[6]

That Blizzard wanted to slow players was pervasively evident throughout the game. Travel times across the game geography were egregiously long. Blizzard must have received player feedback on this issue because I heard players complain about it *often,* but Blizzard steadfastly required players to laboriously travel long distances. At one point I established a set of metrics for myself involving how much housework I could get done while traveling from one spot to another. For common journeys on mounts that delivered players to their destinations without the need for player control, I could, for many travel paths, unload a whole dishwasher full of dishes, gather up and put in a load of laundry, and take one out of the dryer. That seemed like too much work accomplished while "playing." There were many other mechanisms to stretch out game play such as "cooldowns" on crafting activities, which required players to wait a day before a new item could be crafted (or even longer to "discover" new crafting recipes). Blizzard altered the timing on certain actions in professions such as mining and alchemy (e.g., how long it took to mine a node), so I know they were paying attention to player feedback. But these were reductions in seconds, not minutes as with travel.

While Yee's statements about relations between game play and capitalist labor were broad claims about video game companies' inclinations toward repetitive activities, Poole (2008) was more direct in attributing conscious purpose to the inclusion of these activities, calling them "a malignly perfect style of capitalist brainwashing." Even allowing for rhetorical flourish, such provocative words indicate something very wrong with farming. Rettberg's notion of a "sustained delusion" suggests a major hoodwinking. While I share the interest these investigators have put forward in drawing attention to the surprising appearance of repetitive activity in video games, I have come to see farming in *World of Warcraft* as an activity with its own potentialities and affordances, meaningful inside the magic circle.

To think about farming, let us consider a conception of play as a complex activity expressive of a duality in its relation to ordinary life. Turner (1982) theorized play as underwriting cultural norms and, at the same time, providing an arena of potential cultural critique (see also Sutton-Smith 1975). Play may both conserve and reject cultural themes outside itself, and is powerful precisely because it affords grounding through a capacity to reproduce the familiar while simultaneously yielding the potential for transformative activity.

Farming in *World of Warcraft* transformed the pervasive, familiar cultural experience of boredom—which we all undergo, to varying degrees, in school and at work—into one with positive valences. It allowed players to confront anxieties about boredom and recast and reshape them in a context where they were played out and resolved differently than in ordinary life. In the everyday world, boredom is frequently an isolating, frustrating experience. The end result of perseverance in sticking to necessary but boring activities is too often an inadequate paycheck or report card or just another load of laundry. The culmination of farming in *World of Warcraft*, on the other hand, yielded a meaningful, exciting reward. A new piece of gear or an enchantment emerged as the product of the tedium, advancing a player in the game and enabling measurably better performance. (And it might be sparkly, too!) The reward directly addressed a player's object of performative excellence and continual striving to "improve yourself," as Mark put it.

The acquisition of the reward—certainly a moment of limited perfection—was also a moment of social consequence. Other players offered congratulations, remarking on the attainment of the new gear in a spirit of shared celebration. In a raiding context, farming mats (materials) was a social obligation. For some encounters, success depended on players acquiring specially crafted gear, as with Mother Shahraz. I once mailed assiduously farmed mats to a player who could craft them for me. He returned the crafted gear in mail with a message saying, "Way to be on top of the

Note Stamina in Base Stats in the box on the bottom left.
Stamina is an important stat for warriors.

The warrior adds +3 stamina by equipping the Knight's Gauntlets
of the Bear, replacing the Sentry's Glove of the Monkey.

raid's needs Innikka!" I was pleased about this, though farming the mats had been irksomely repetitive. The player acknowledged my contribution to the social group in which we shared activity; the message embodied a small moment of amiable connection expressive of our common performative goals.

Players were required to come to raids with "consumables" such as elixirs and potions. As long as a player was raiding, there would be no end to farming. It was laborious gathering the materials for every raid, but again there was often a social payoff. Players exchanged potions, elixirs, food, and other enhancements to performance, developing exchange partners or becoming known for having unusual recipes or always being stocked up with appropriate consumables to share. The Fish Feast was a nicely communitarian expression of farming; players who fished and cooked could prepare a group meal, providing raid buffs, and a Fish Feast invariably appeared at appropriate moments during raids.[7] Behind each feast was a player who had spent time in one of the game's most repetitive, least challenging activities—fishing.

Repetitive actions in other domains rarely entail excitement and sociality; they tend toward boredom and isolation (housework, homework worksheets, bureaucratic paperwork). In *World of Warcraft*, the narrative and goals of the game world bound people in a shared fantasy in which repetitive actions could be generative of positive meanings and emotions. Within the magic circle, with its distinctive rules and stories not strictly accountable to everyday reality, the flax of boredom was spun into the gold of social capital and emotional wealth. The nuances of farming in *World of Warcraft* extended beyond the fact of its boredom (and a superficial appearance of being just like boredom at work) to its role as a resource deployed in performative development, the satisfaction of sharing in groups, and bonds of collective experience.

Miller (1973) noted that Freud believed fantasy to be "a tool for coping with the frustrating but uncontrollable events that are concomitants of life in society." Gaming may allow players to take up the challenges and disappointments of contemporary life that eat away at all of us, working through them in fantasy. Rather than "brainwashing," repetitive player activity suggests a process in which boredom is confronted and transformed in the hospitable environs of a game world. The game conserves socially valued qualities such as perseverance—which players must exhibit in order to undertake repetitive activities like farming—while at the same time suggesting the fundamental inadequacy of the typical rewards for such perseverance. The often disappointing results of sticking-with-it in real life are critiqued; a deflating end to long toil is eliminated, replaced with rewards that delight, enhance, and create social cohesion—bright, glowing things moving players forward in the logic of the game.

The Magic Circle

We have examined several ways in which game play articulates with other arenas of activity; it is not a sequestered activity walled up in a magic circle. But, from another perspective, we must revive Huizinga's notion of the magic circle in its fullness. The magic circle is expressive of one crucial aspect of play; the *meaningfulness* of play is bound within the activity of those who actually play. Miller (1973) observed:

> Someone who is left cold by baseball wonders what someone else can see in hitting a ball with a stick and running around in a circle to his starting point.

Every *WoW* player has had the experience of friends and family who do not understand why he or she gets so excited about a video game. From outside the magic circle, we see a person staring at a computer screen, perhaps clicking furiously. The enticements of the game are invisible. Within the magic circle, it's a different story. A player is developing a character, interacting with guildmates, descending into difficult dungeons, exploring new landscapes, watching the (virtual) starry night sky.

Huizinga (1950) observed that the magic circle entails a feeling of being "apart together"; it creates its own collective social order—one from which nonplayers are excluded. The meanings to do with game play are created *within* a play world and are legitimate and coherent only within that world.[8] Interpersonal "aggro" in one sense breaks down the magic circle by forcing players to attend to activity outside it, but in another sense such aggro is the very realization of the separation of players from those not-playing. Nonplayers are apart from the world in which a player's actions are sensible, interesting, compelling, meaningful. The non-sense of the game viewed

from outside sometimes generated agitation, annoyance, even anger. One
of my guildmates typed into guild chat:

> Bagdieb: i may be a tank, but i still can't handle gf aggro.

The ubiquitous use of the term "escape" to describe *WoW* play alluded to
its separateness. Players mentioned such escape in interviews, and I saw
it in chat. For example, a member of the U.S. Army with whom I played
remarked in party chat (not in response to an interview question):

> the game is escape, a great stress relief even my company commander plays
> lol he is a gm [guild master] for a guild on another server.

Salen and Zimmerman (2005) noted that entering the magic circle means
making a commitment to play; such commitment is intelligible only from
the player's point of view. "Without the magic circle, the actions of the
players would be meaningless," they observed.

The social order manifest in the magic circle is constituted in (at least)
three ways: through knowledge about structures and activities that occur
inside its enclosure; in specialized discourse; and in designated spaces of
play that mark and confine it. The following are some examples from *World
of Warcraft.*

At the "UI and Mods" session at BlizzCon, the user interface design
team assembled to discuss design philosophy and take audience questions.
The room was packed with hundreds of people. During the Q&A, a player
stood up and said:

> I'm a hunter and for the love of God can we get the quiver off the bag
> space?!

The audience erupted in raucous applause. Only *WoW* players would know
what the question meant, why a roomful of people would break into cheers
on hearing it, and the reasons why a player might invoke the love of God
with respect to a change in the user interface of *World of Warcraft.* (The
player referred to space taken up by the hunter's quiver, space normally used
to hold another bag.) Arcane knowledge is shared inside the magic circle; it
defines play activity and separates those who know from those who don't.

Collective order in the magic circle is expressed through knowledge of the rules of the game. In the previous chapter I argued that rules can be seen as a resource. Schechner (1977) described rules as another kind of resource, observing that the rules of a game are designed to defend the activity against encroachment from the outside. The rules in part establish a magic circle; they create a model world of permitted behaviors. To be part of the world, players must develop knowledge of the rules.

The collective social order is pervasively apparent in player discourse; semantic and syntactic conventions reflect the specialness of play inside the magic circle. (When I first started playing *WoW* I felt I was deciphering a code.) Here are some utterances I collected from *WoW* battlegrounds (contests in which teams play games such as capture the flag):

mage table plz
drood buff ftw!
help fc
omfg get out of mf!
f*ck st --- get bs
ZERG AS

Such utterances were meaningful to a *WoW* player; these particular requests expressed actions needed to move collective play forward in ways deemed desirable by the speakers. The utterances are incomprehensible to those who do not play and are, as Huizinga said, apart from the playing of the game.

A collective order is realized in enclosures within which play occurs. Huizinga (1950) noted that activity that involves repetition in a limited space, such as a playground, creates its own order, generating a logic comprehensible only within its boundaries (see also Garvey 1977). Of course physical enclosure is not always necessary; as Juul (2005) observed, people play chess by mail. But it is undeniable that we gravitate toward play spaces ranging from constructs such as dollhouses and model trains (carefully laid out in their own reserved space) to the grand swatches of natural land appropriated for golf in medieval Scotland.

Not only did *World of Warcraft* provide a large, highly elaborated game geography, but a particularly striking feature was "instanced" play—a magic circle within the magic circle. Instances, in which players entered zones inhabited only by a formal group (a party, raid, arena team, or battleground team) were distinctive enclosures productive of powerful play experience. Players encountered instances early in the game, and they were central to *WoW*'s design.[9] Raiding dungeons such as Serpentshrine Cavern were instanced; it was impossible to even enter them unless grouped.

One of my most frustrating early experiences was a quest in Teldrassil, island of the Night Elves, which required descent into a burrow inhabited by members of the ferocious Gnarlpine Tribe. The quest involved navigating a cave of narrow, twisting tunnels wherein lurked a bewildering number of closely spaced Gnarlpine furbolgs. Unlike the beautiful scenery outdoors, the Gnarlpines' dark, depressing den seemed broken down and shabby. Mushrooms sprouted, tree roots pierced the space from above, worn beams supported the dirt framing the den.

What was this abrupt shift from the lyrical landscape of Teldrassil to the damp darkness of the underground den? Over time I learned that such underground spaces were set-piece stages for critical encounters in *World of Warcraft*. The early quest with the Gnarlpine was not actually an instanced dungeon but an experience prefiguring instanced play, requiring descent into a confined, occult space. Later I would spend a good deal of time swimming to encounters in watery caverns, traversing the partially buried earthen remains of an ancient city, extinguishing fires within a sunken temple, battling orcs in the depths of a burning mountain, fending off death in crypts and tombs, and, of course, avoiding the elevator boss in Serpentshrine Cavern. Instances removed the group from others and sent them far away—usually downward—into private spaces. The descent underground (hence the term *dungeon*) cut raid members off from normal life aboveground and allowed a close visual encounter with a uniquely designed space different from that found everywhere else in the game.[10]

The inclusion of instances was consistent with *WoW*'s design as an arena of performance. Instances eliminated the presence of players who would certainly interfere with performative activity by ganking or otherwise harassing players engaged in the serious matter of downing difficult bosses. Whether intentional or not, cutting players off from all but those in the raid generated closeness and social cohesion; players depended on the group with which they faced the game's biggest challenges. Enclosure in a confined space unambiguously identified, in the context of guild raids, a player's closest partners. Raiding late at night with guild members and no one else, listening to their voices in voice chat, knowing how they played and tailoring performance in accordance, teasing, joking, and bantering within a small, known group—these actions were productive of considerable geniality and intimacy.

Taylor (2006) suggested that instancing might be less "interesting" than games designed to "facilitate large scale collective action." While not disagreeing that such action would be desirable in the context of some games, I think the special affordances of instancing were, within the logic of a game such as *World of Warcraft*, generative of an amazing level of amiability and positive sociality. Steinkuehler and Williams (2006) described *WoW* as a "third space."[11] Third spaces are not venues of large-scale collective action but deliberately small enclosures designed to encourage bonhomie and cordiality among peers. Moments such as first kills, a guild member finally getting a purple she has longed for, or a player managing a tricky maneuver (such as killing the demons in time), are moments of mutual celebration not to be tampered with by players (like the *Lineage* gankers) who would happily disrupt them. The magic circle, rightfully, keeps out as well as keeps in.

Contemporary theorizing suggests that the magic circle is partial. I have identified ways in which *World of Warcraft* interpenetrated real life. At the same time, the magic circle lives, bracketing meanings within an enclosure into which a player steps in order to play. Turner (1982) identified the *limen*, or threshold, as necessary to play and ritual. Players cross the threshold out of ordinary life to engage distinctive kinds of performative activity in a game space in which the rules are different, the culture unique, the rewards sensible only within the enclosure. It is no accident that game spaces delimit clear, identifiable geographies: the baseball field, the basketball court, the boxing ring, the casino, the arcade, the playground, the card table, the tree house, the game board, the golf course, the bowling alley, the *World of Warcraft*. These spaces take us away from work, away from school, away from the ordinary. We enter a smaller, more perfect universe in which satisfaction is not guaranteed, but we gain a pretty good chance of achieving moments of limited perfection.

PART THREE

Cultural Logics of *World of Warcraft*

CHAPTER SIX

Addiction

Having examined theoretical arguments about magic circles, performativity, and so on, this chapter, and the next two, take up broad themes of gaming that are part of academic discourse but also reach into wider arenas of conversation in the mass media and blogs and forums. I begin with the topic of addiction—a perennial favorite of the media and one which seems to crop up often when people ask me about video games.

Many readers will have encountered the notion of video game addiction in newspaper and magazine accounts. Some may know players they believe to be addicted. Players themselves speak of addiction. How exactly should we think about video game addiction? Dewey provides a useful perspective when he discusses the potential for aesthetic activity to become "overwhelming." I will use this notion, as well as the work of Seay and Kraut (2007) on "problematic use," to frame my analysis. I extend Seay and Kraut's work to encompass social aspects of problematic use.

As discussed in chapter 3, Dewey characterized active aesthetic activity as comprised of pleasurable means, successive phases of activity ending in satisfying completion, and collective expression. The final feature Dewey ascribed to aesthetic activity may help us understand why discourse around video gaming includes the term addiction. Dewey argued that aesthetic activity requires *balance and proportion*—qualities that in some circumstances may readily be lost. The passion that animates aesthetic activity contains within itself a dangerous seed; such passion can transmogrify to an extreme state in which it "overwhelms" us. Dewey (2005) wrote:

There is an element of passion in all aesthetic [activity] . . . [W]hen we are

123

overwhelmed by passion, as in extreme rage, fear, jealousy, the experience is . . . non-aesthetic . . . [T]he material of the experience lacks elements of balance and proportion. For these can be present only when . . . the act is controlled by an exquisite sense of the relations which the act sustains—*its fitness to the occasion and the situation.* (emphasis added)

Aesthetic activity may become overwhelming in circumstances of particular occasions and relations. The potential for aesthetic activity to devolve into a degenerate form of itself is not an inherent quality of any particular aesthetic activity (such as video gaming) but depends on the specificities of a subject's situation.

Obviously, millions of people play video games and are not addicted. We must reach beyond the artifact of the game itself as an explanation for why some people play to excess. It is easy to forget this simple logic under the influence of sensationalism in media accounts that deliver dispatches on the shocking nature of video games: this player sat at his computer too long and keeled over, that one dropped out of school because he could not concentrate on his studies, another abandoned friends and family for the game (see Chee and Smith 2005; Golub and Lingley 2008). Rettberg (2008) observed, tongue in cheek:

[T]he popular media have used the term [*addiction*] while terrifying us with stories of teenage *World of Warcraft* players (these stories are typically set in China, and like horror movies, the victims are always teens) literally *dying* because they *forgot to eat.*

In media accounts, the video game itself is the malefactor. The stories engender what Cohen (1973) called a "moral panic." As Cohen wrote in his study of Mods and Rockers in 1960s England:

Societies appear to be subject, every now and then, to periods of moral panic. A condition, episode, person, or group of persons, emerges to become defined as a threat to societal values and interests; its nature is presented in a stylised and stereotypical fashion by the mass media . . . Socially accredited experts pronounce their diagnoses and solutions.

The notion of video game addiction followed this pattern precisely. In addition to stories produced by journalists and promulgated by mass media, credentialed experts came forth to denounce video games. Orzack, a clinical psychologist at Harvard, said that she believed 40 percent of *World of Warcraft* players were addicted (quoted in Grohol 2006). Her declaration was widely reported in the media and contributed to the arousal of concern and disquiet about *World of Warcraft* and other video games.

To its credit, the American Medical Association's approach has been more measured. There is no entry for video game addiction in the *American Diagnostic and Statistical Manual of Mental Disorders*. For now, the AMA has stated that there is insufficient evidence to declare video gaming addictive (Addiction 2007). However, its members proposed that the American Psychiatric Association assess whether such a diagnosis should be included in the 2012 version of the Manual.

While this determination is being made, we can turn to Seay and Kraut's (2007) research. To avoid the baggage of the word "addiction," they deployed the term "problematic use." Seay and Kraut defined problematic use as game play that displaces important activities such as schoolwork, maintaining friendships, or family activities.

The authors found that players exhibiting problematic use scored low on measures of self-regulation. They argued that lack of self-regulation *precedes* problematic use of video games and that games themselves do not cause problematic use. In a longitudinal survey study of 499 video game users, the authors reported:

> [T]he overwhelming majority of those surveyed indicate no elevation in ... problematic use. This seems to indicate that ... online gaming is ... an enjoyable, or at least, benign activity.

This research supports the commonsense notion that problem players bring their problems to the game. As with most things that lead to addiction or problematic use (such as alcohol or overeating), generally the need precedes the object rather than the object creating the need.

"Addiction" is a cultural term in the game community as well as a clinical term used by psychiatrists and psychologists. What do players themselves say about addiction? The term is variably inflected in player discourse. Depending on context, it can be used humorously, to signal membership in an in-group of players (two related uses), or to denote problematic use.

In the following, Mark joked about the "addictive" qualities of *World of Warcraft:*

Mark: I have a really good friend in Germany who actually is another guy that I got into the game.

BN: You're an ambassador for the game.

Mark: Oh, I'm terrible. I'm like a pusher with crack on these things.

This post from the Scarlet Raven website included a joke about playing *WoW* at work. The word "Addict" was bolded and in blue:

Boss: "So Johnson, what did you accomplish today?"

Addict: "Well Sir, I killed over 60 Orc Shaman and Warriors, I got lucky and got a 'blue' off a random mob and I leveled! . . . Er . . . I mean, I answered over 60 phone calls, I got lucky and sent off a 'priority blue' email and I finished the TPS report."

Boss: "Very good Johnson! Keep up the good work."

For players, the term addiction was often used with a positive connotation. If players said they were addicted to *WoW,* it usually meant they had a deep connection to the game and were members of a group of people who understood its pleasures. A video gamer could claim to be an addict, deliberately choosing a strong term to connote enjoyment of the game and its separation from ordinary activities. One of my guildmates once remarked, "If only real life was this addicting." A college student said in an interview:

[*WoW*] is fun on many levels, and it's like a real world because you know you are playing with other real human beings rather than AI [artificial intelligence]. . . . It's addicting.

On the other hand, players recognized a pernicious side to excessive game play. They used the term addiction to describe players who spent too much time playing. Internet sites provided forums where players, or former players, could confess their addictions to "Warcrack." Posts on such sites tended to be somewhat uninformative, enumerating the number of hours spent at the game rather than analyzing why the game involved players so much. But some posters provided insights:

> If you make game friends, [playing *World of Warcraft*] is an easy way to waste hours. It's like hanging out on the corner or in a club, but on a really lazy level. There's no dressing up, spending money, etc. All of the human interaction for very low cost. And everyone looks so attractive and appealing. Real life is full of faults. The reality is real life can't compare. Real life is work, plain and simple. (Apadwe n.d.)

This player offered up the same theory as games researchers who describe multiplayer games as third spaces like tree houses or bars (Chee 2006; Steinkuehler and Williams 2006; Williams 2006; Williams et al. 2006). But the player suggested that playing video games was a "lazy" version of such forms of interaction characterized by the unreality of everyone looking "so attractive and appealing."

The following post satirized the addicted, lonely gamer stereotype:

> I'm 13 and im a girl and play wow about 12 hours a day and I also eat alot. It started with me not having any friends at school, so I got wow because I heard people on there were nice. When I made a bunch of friends I started skipping school to play and eventually failed school. My parents were always drinking and yelling at me and when they were drunk one day I got them to get me broadband. All I did is play wow and eat but I tried to stop. I am a guild leader and I have Six 70's and I raid every day with three diffrent guilds. I have also begun drinking alot while I play sometimes passing out at the keyboard. And I really want to get better with my life its just the game is so fun and really hard to quit. It's hard to go back to school because my parents have also started to do crack and usually cant take me, and when they can I am usually in a raid or doing PvP. someone on wow told me about this and suggested I share my story. I play a male character because guys dont like me and think im ugly. (Apadwe n.d.)

As with many stereotypes, there is a grain of truth informing the images and vocabulary the stereotype invokes—in this case the young person with huge problems who turns to a game for solace. I interviewed a clinical psychologist, Dr. Jane Kingston, who worked with clients whose use of video games fell into the problematic use category. She reported that problems with video games seem to be triggered by existing problems, as Seay and Kraut found, and that it can be difficult to break the cycle. She described a wife who came to her for help because her husband brought his laptop computer to the social events they attended and played games. He did not see anything wrong with his actions. She told me about a young child who resisted his parents' attempts to limit his use of console games. He brought the console to Kingston's office and threw it at his mother in a fit of anger. Kingston said the relationship between the two had been troubled. A high school student played *WoW* to the point of dropping out of school. Neither of his parents cared that he played *WoW* or that he had left school (shades of the satire). Kingston observed that she was not sure, in this case, whether playing *WoW* was the worst thing the teen could have done. He lived in an area in which marijuana was farmed and freely available, but he had not become a doper. She noted that the lack of services to help the young man, whose parents chose to neglect him, meant that he was at risk for activities potentially more destructive than playing *World of Warcraft*.

Problematic use of video games is sensible only in relation to other competing activities (since gaming does not have drastic physical effects). Addiction occurs when actions that produce a feeling of well-being and can be beneficial or benign under most circumstances (drinking alcohol, gambling, exercise, sports) supplant or threaten other vital human activities. A Chinese player said:

> Addiction is when you don't do anything else anymore. When you quit everything for the game. The person gives up other things. If you give up a lot of things for the game, then you are addicted.

The husband who took his computer to social outings, the boy who threw the console at his mother, the student who dropped out of school—all were clearly engaged in activities that lacked fitness for the occasion and situation. Dewey wrote of the *relations* sustained by an act, denoting its relationship to the larger context of related activities. It is this relation that must be examined in assessing whether a set of actions is aesthetic or has overwhelmed us.

As Dewey theorized, aesthetic activity is potentially dangerous because of the very quality of passion it carries. How do players manage this danger? I have encountered a few players who, in my opinion, played too much. It is undeniable that for some people *World of Warcraft* supplanted vital everyday activities. But more often I observed players self-regulating as Seay and Kraut described.

Building on the work of Bandura (1999) and other psychologists, Seay and Kraut identified three components of self-regulation: *self-monitoring,* that is, observing how much one is playing; *evaluation against perceived standards,* that is, assessing whether play is excessive in light of other responsibilities (similar to Dewey's notion of balance and proportion); and *self-consequation,* that is, self-administration of reward or punishment based on the outcome of self-monitoring and evaluation.

The following website post by Kel, a Scarlet Raven college student, depicts the three components of self-regulation in the player's own words:

> I suspended my account last night, since school has reared its ugly head. I have to focus everything on bringing up my grades over the next month or so. Hopefully I can get my act together and it won't be any longer than that. Good luck, and hope to see you all around the forums!

Kel observed that he was playing too much and it had affected his grades. The self-imposed consequence was suspension of his account. He identified reward and punishment: he would suspend the account and then reward himself in a month with renewed play if his grades improved.

To expand the notion of self-regulation, let us examine how it emerges in, and is shaped by, social activity. The very fact that Kel publicly posted this explanation of his actions is the first indication that his problems were not an isolated psychological phenomenon but an aspect of a shared community predicament. The community should be informed of, and involved in, his problems. The responses to his post demonstrated healthy community response, legitimating his actions and providing emotional support for the difficulties involved.

One guildmate responded:

> Gonna miss ya Kel, but School first. No doubt you'll have your grades back up in no time. Drop in and chat with us here when you can. /hug

Another wrote:

> Hopefully it all works out for you and you can get back asap!
>
> Aww, now I'm not gonna get my Belt of Blasting for a while.
>
> Hehe, regardless, good luck on your endeavors.

These players recognized and articulated that other activities should take precedence over game play. They provided moral endorsement of Kel's decision, as well as social support in encouraging him to prioritize activities to maintain an acceptable level of performance at school.

The responses were crafted with humor, as in the second poster's feigned regret at the postponement of the Belt of Blasting (an item Kel knew how to make), as well as affection ("/hug") and friendship ("gonna miss ya"). The responses likely eased, at least a little, the austerity Kel imposed on himself. While the invitations to return to the game, and to continue communicating through the website, might seem elements of temptation, they also tied Kel to a community that was clearly telling him to back off the game for awhile, making the admonitions more forceful.

A shared morality, which the first response succinctly expressed as "School first," ratified Kel's decision in the public space of the forum. Such open discussion of a player heading toward problematic use served to make visible to all who read the Scarlet Raven forums the possibility of problematic use, and the guild's moral stance. We may add to Seay and Kraut's formulation a social dimension in which players constructed, through discourse in guild websites, a morality regarding problematic use and a social space in which to express and enact moral principles. This is not to say that all guilds would respond as Scarlet Raven did, but to argue that problematic use finds expression in the collective activity of players and guilds.

Work may also preempt play. The following post by Templeton was offered in the context of several guild members having recently taken breaks from the game:

> Ok, ok, so I know that it is officially "against the rules" to have any more folks take a break, but I am afraid that it is time for me to take one. Got a lot of RL stuff going one, with a potential change in jobs, other things that

are taking (and need a lot of man hours) time to make sure that they are taken care of.

My account will stay active, because I do enjoy the game, and love raiding, but I have to spend about 3 weeks focusing on these things to make sure that my experience stays fun, and that I can get these things done.

Look for me in a little bit. I will still check the boards [forums], and feel free to PM [private message] me.

I'll be back soon.

Templeton

A guildmate responded:

Well we will be waiting for ya when you get back! GL [good luck] taking care of things, we do surely understand that RL always comes first. See ya soon!

Another said:

You better damn well be back soon!

-Val

PS. On a serious note, RL > WoW . . . take your time getting things worked out!

Pithy, unambiguous directives established a moral algebra: "RL always comes first" and "RL > WoW." The posts expressed friendship, the second in the form of a playful command to be back soon but with contrapuntal advice in the postscript to take time working things out.
Sapem wrote:

I need to start spending more time with my 16 month old son in the afternoons and weekends so ive decided to take a break from gaming for a while who knows I might come back in a month or so hopefully, I really enjoyed being with u guys

As with Kel and Templeton, guildmates' responses endorsed Sapem's action; for example, Pennit wrote, "Good decision on priorities. Have fun!"

Sapem, Kel, and Templeton were textbook cases of self-regulation—young adults with the maturity to back away. Younger players sometimes required more external support. Baalzamin, a high-school-age player, wrote the following (slightly incoherent) post:

see you later . . . much probably

yea. . . . lots of stuff going on right now, got in trouble for being truent that made me have bad grades (.38 grade point average) that i got in trouble for. just not going to be on wow for a while. . . . just letting you know.

it came so fast . . . my dad got home shut the internet off took my computer out of my room took my car keys took me down to my mom's and then took my phone. . . . it sucked.

One guildmate responded:

Take a break or quit if ya need, School is much more important than any game and if your grades are slipping then its time to focus on important RL stuff. See ya when you get back.

Another joked but sent a serious message:

I say drop out of school, sell drugs for a living, and play WoW full time . . . err No I dont. Quit screwing your self and get your grades up Bro! Its a video game lol

The responses to the three problematic users were written by different guildmates, but all expressed a common sensibility. All clearly denoted actions deemed appropriate for players spending too much time in *World of Warcraft*.

Problematic use may be mitigated by negotiation with those affected by a player's actions. Rowena, a graduate student I interviewed, described how her boyfriend would "flake out" on her when they had a dinner date, standing her up because he was playing *WoW*. She negotiated a rule in the relationship in which he would tell her when he would be playing, adding an additional hour to make sure he could fulfill his promise to spend time with her. He accepted this plan to manage game and girlfriend time, and it worked well. The couple later separated over other issues but remained on good terms.

One tank in Scarlet Raven left the game completely under pressure from his fiancée. Months later he returned, saying in guild chat, openly, and with no irony, that he had "my addiction under control." After the absence, he played less frequently and in a more moderate, less competitive way. Previously he had been a raid leader and had always sought the best equipment. Upon returning, his play was more casual.

Sometimes problematic use appeared to stem not from lack of self-regulation but from a vacancy in a player's life. Rowena recounted how her brother Bryce, uninterested in his high school studies, became immersed in *World of Warcraft*. The parents tried everything they could to separate him from the game. He became angry—it was the only time Rowena saw him throw "temper tantrums." She observed that his behavior was to be partially understood as a product of the game being "very motivating," invoking its Skinnerian aspects.

When Bryce went to college, he discovered a love of biology. He reduced his playtime dramatically, finding the balance of which Dewey spoke. Alienation from the high school curriculum created a vacuum in which the stimulation of the game became an attractive choice. Once he moved on to other interests, he had no difficulty regulating playtime.

Often self-regulation is simple; players just know when to stop. Many Chinese players discussed how their *WoW* play changed in response to the scheduling of exams or schoolwork. Typical comments were "Before my exams, I played a lot," "I played more when I did not have exams to study for," "I played a lot during summer vacation last year," and "Now school is going to start and I have nearly stopped playing to prepare."

Players sometimes used the word addicted to describe a playful relation to the game. Cultural terms such as addiction stretch, exaggerate, and distort what they express. But they are not random; they loop back on standard meanings of the words they playfully twist. Addiction in this context connoted not clinical illness but attachment to the game, the forgoing of activities that competed with *WoW* (such as television), and, ironically, freedom in choosing if, when, and how to play. When a player playfully said, "I'm addicted!" he declared his attachment to the game while at the same time signaling, through deliberate, ironic use of a loaded word, that he knew what he was doing. There was a kind of extreme autonomy in pretending to flirt with addiction—staying outside of it while engaging, with passion, an activity a player loved.

What kinds of activities did players forgo when devoting hours to *World of Warcraft?* One thing given up by some (though not all) *WoW* players was television. In the interviews, many players reported that they had stopped watching or had reduced viewing time:

> Mark: And, you know, my evenings. I clear time in my evenings. You know, I don't watch TV particularly.

> BN: So, have you stopped watching TV, or do you do that less?

> Mark: Not as a consequence of *WoW*, but as a consequence of gaming, yes.

On a Blizzard website in which players discussed how *WoW* affected their lives, one poster wrote:

> I've met quite a few couples who played together at night, which to me was better than TV together. It's certainly better than one partner viewing porn or entering Second Life. (Second Life n.d.)[1]

Some players reported that they had largely abandoned, or seriously curtailed, exposure to media such as television and books. More research is needed to establish the extent to which *WoW* displaces competing activities (see Bainbridge 2007). Careful investigation is necessary to discover the nuances of new behaviors. For example, players sometimes watched television while playing *WoW*, especially during activities that did not require much concentration (such as fishing).

Players often developed playlists, replacing *WoW*'s music. (I was always aghast when I heard this because I loved the *WoW* sound track.) In addition, many players drank alcohol and smoked marijuana while playing *World of*

Warcraft. I was alerted to this early on by my undergraduate students and began to notice guild and character names that clearly pointed to substance use. Players often spoke of drinking and smoking while playing. In guild or party chat they joked about the drinks they were mixing or how many beers they had had or talked about paraphernalia such as bongs. I mention these activities to propose that more research is needed. The level of escape or stimulation, or some other dimension, attained by immersion in a video game, layered with the altered consciousness of drugs or alcohol, suggests not necessarily addiction but the construction of a complex experience achieved by artful composition of a heterogeneous mix of technical and organic resources. This is not to say that drunken facerolling is a sophisticated form of play, but to indicate that the subtleties of the magic circles into which we propel ourselves are not yet understood.

Turkle (1984) spoke of the "holding power" of video games, observing (1998):

> The term addiction is most usefully saved for experiences with substances like heroin, which are always dangerous, always bad, always something to turn away from.

I think, though, that we must leave open the possibility that addiction, or problematic use, perplexes because it may arise when we are overwhelmed by the passion of activities we are deeply attached to, which, on their own, are not "always bad." It is precisely the regulation of such activities that engages public discourse, as well as private anxieties about friends and family members who appear to be overwhelmed. The potential for positive aesthetic experience to overreach itself into undesirable states of excess entails an ambiguousness with which we continually wrestle.

It seems important to question rhetorical moves that designate some activities as worthy of moral panic while leaving others aside, for example, calling out video games as addictive while giving obsessive sports fandom a free pass even though such fandom may affect marital or family life. Why do politicians (on a fairly regular schedule it seems) demonize rock music while ignoring elaborate supports for activities, such as gambling, which are, in some cases, ruinous to families?

Whether we entertain notions of problematic use or addiction, normative questions follow. Is playing *World of Warcraft* better than competing activities such as watching television or viewing movies or reading books? How does *WoW* compare to a steady diet of romance novels or frequenting the sleazier parts of *Second Life?* What if a player (like Bryce) has not developed other interests? Does *WoW* prevent people from getting dead drunk? Players need at least some cognitive capacity, so even though they may play and drink the game could provide a moderating influence. *WoW* might even have unusual redeeming social value; one member of my guild, a felon with several convictions for car theft, said that playing *WoW* kept him from returning to prison.

Just what should people be doing instead of playing games? The notion of video game addiction provokes as much moral as clinical inquiry. There is no normative answer my investigation can suggest, but I hope it brings forward discussion of what it is that people are giving up to play games, the vacancies in their lives they may be attempting to fill, levels of stimulation they appear to be seeking, and how we might think about ways to intelligently assess the impact of video gaming on the larger life of the culture.

CHAPTER SEVEN

Theorycraft and Mods

This chapter examines *WoW*'s capacity to stimulate participatory activity outside the game, using the materials of the game in novel, innovative ways. Arenas of such engagement include machinima production (Lowood 2008), fan art, fan fiction, and the development of knowledge bases such as Thottbot that compile game statistics and player commentary. These activities are not unique to *WoW*; they connect to a larger movement fostering user-generated content (see Kucklich 2004; Jenkins 2006; Pearce 2006; Yee 2006; Postigo 2007; Ito 2008; Kendall 2008). This chapter investigates two *WoW*-related activities I found particularly fascinating: theorycrafting and modding.

Theorycraft

The encoded rules of video games are known as "game mechanics."[1] Game mechanics specify outcomes as rules are invoked—what happens when you approach a monster many levels higher than your character, which elixirs can be taken in combination, how often Illidan drops the Twin Blades of Azzinoth. Some were discoverable through ordinary play, but others required systematic analysis. "Theorycrafting" is the discovery of rules that can not be determined through play. *WoW* came with almost no documentation, and while Blizzard employees sometimes answered questions on official forums, in general the absence of documentation left many juicy problems for theorycrafters to solve.

A well-known American website, Elitist Jerks, hosted theorycrafters' technical discussions of *WoW* game mechanics (elitistjerks.com). Interested players explored subtleties of game mechanics, plumbing the depths of *WoW* minutiae. The following is a theorycrafting analysis from the Elitist Jerks that investigated the mechanics of a small temporary helper (or "pet") called the Shadowfiend. Priests could summon a Shadowfiend, which lasted for only 15 seconds. The Shadowfiend did some damage and restored mana, a quantity necessary for spell casting that was depleted as spells were cast.

A poster wrote:

has anyone done a rigorous analysis of Shadow Fiend mechanics?

If so, can someone point me in the general direction?

Known:
(1) Pet does shadow dmg [damage] and is enhanced by shadow target debuffs
(2) Pet returns mana at 2.5x dmg done

Easy to figure out:
(1) How many "swings" per pet lifetime

Hard to figure out:
(1) How does pet dmg scale on target mobs from 68 thru 73?
(2) What percentage of player shadow damage benefits the pet?
(3) What is the crit pct?

The 5min cooldown on the spell makes it very difficult to exhaustively test by yourself.

Is there any interest out there in a group effort?

If we share enough data points (target level, min/max crit/non-crit, player +shadow) we should be able to figure it out . . .

Another poster responded:

I'd be happy to help out, as I'm curious myself . . . There's one thing that really annoys me about Shadowfiend: it seems to spend a significant amount of time moving when cast on a really big mob (Gruul). It seems to appear near the middle of Gruul's model, then move to the outside before it starts attacking. That's probably 500–800 mana lost while it moves.

And another added:

I guess we need a little more info:

Target Level
Target Debuffs: CoS, SW stack, Misery
Num Attacks
Num Crits
Min/Max for both Non-Crit and Crit
Player Shadow +Dmg

Am I missing anything?

Without worrying too much about the intricacies of the Shadowfiend, the posts demonstrate that players played a game about the game in which they attempted to figure out the game's own machinations. Technically oriented players designed quantitative experiments, performed tests, analyzed the results, published them online, and worked with one another to solve puzzles of game mechanics.

The Shadowfiend analysts were reflexively "remaking the material of experience," in Dewey's terms, by using observations about their own play (such as the movement of the Shadowfiend) to create new experience and understandings. This activity was conducted in a collective context through shared analysis of game mechanics. The first poster invited others to help him conceptualize the problem and collect data. Subsequent posters responded, validating that the first poster had raised an interesting issue, then expanding his formulation by enumerating further necessary variables. All agreed to collect and share data.

A softer form of theorycraft utilized game statistics to predict which gear would be most effective. Player-created websites analyzed and recommended gear for each class. At dwarfpriest.com, for example, the Dwarf Priest wrote:

I enjoy that *World of Warcraft* is a game with various dynamics and mechanics. It keeps the game from being too one-dimensional. However, I do regret that there is so much work that has to go in to truly understanding these mechanics. The most frustrating thing for me is how little information Blizzard actually gives us about certain things (such as threat and resistances). Our knowledge in many areas is the product of extensive player testing, and can change at any time, without notice. (Dwarfpriest.com)

The Dwarf Priest (who identified herself as a woman in her midtwenties), found hardcore theorycraft a bit taxing but enjoyed devising metrics with which to measure gear to predict its effectiveness for various priestly activities.

One of her accomplishments was a formula that weighted gear statistics. The formula was applied to each piece of gear to produce a rank ordering of all related gear: For example, the following is a partial list of rank-ordered priest-chest healing gear showing score, name, and where the gear was obtained.

Chest:
201.50 - Sympathy *Naxxramas - Sapphiron (heroic)*

201.20 - Valorous Robes of Faith *Naxxramas - Four Horsemen (heroic)*

196.52 - The Sanctum's Flowing Vestments Obsidian Sanctum – Sartharion (heroic)

194.58 - Blanketing Robes of Snow *Eye of Eternity - Malygos (heroic)*

193.66 - Robes of Mutation *Naxxramas - Noth (heroic)*

179.76 - Heroes' Robes of Faith *Naxxramas - Four Horsemen (heroic)*

169.34 - Spellweave Robe *Tailoring BoE*

167.43 - Digested Silken Robes?*Naxxramas - Maexxna (heroic)*

The Dwarf Priest explained:

This list was created using stat weights of all priest-healing stats and summing them to get the item scores. Items were then ranked according to their scores.

The stat weights used were:

0.74 Intellect
0.54 Spirit
0.35 Haste
0.15 Crit
1.00 MP5
0.60 Spellpower

(Dwarfpriest.com)

While players might disagree with certain stat weights (for example, I valued Crit more than the Dwarf Priest), the articulation of the formula enabled players to evaluate rankings and assess how items might work for their play style.

Theorycrafting is pretty serious analytical activity. With real math! Might it have pedagogical value? I have not seen research on this question, but it links to the work of education researchers Steinkuehler and Chmiel (2006). They studied the development of "scientific habits of mind" through game activities in *World of Warcraft*, examining discussion on a Blizzard forum devoted to customizing the druid character class. They found that the top three "habits" used to analyze customization were "social knowledge construction," "building on others' ideas," and the "use of counterarguments." While I see these practices as characteristic of broad critical thinking skills, and not as distinctively scientific, they do suggest ways in which gamers might engage skills very much like those we are supposed to learn in school.

Steinkuehler and Chmiel's list of habits also included "pragmatic understanding of theory," "theory-data coordination," "coordination of multiple results," and "reasoning through uncertainty"—that are indeed scientific.

The gamers in their study did not engage these particular scientific practices at all. But theorycrafters did. As we saw in the Shadowfiend experiments, theorycrafters conducted analyses in which they coordinated multiple results, used theory pragmatically, reasoned through uncertainty, and coordinated theory and data.

Claims about scientific reasoning in gaming raise the issue of where and how such reasoning is developed. While Steinkuehler and Chmiel (see also Steinkuehler and Duncan 2008) were optimistic about the potential of games to improve "science literacy" in educational contexts, the broad skills engaged by players on the druid forum, as well as theorycrafters' analytical and technical skills, were brought to gaming from other contexts, even if they were exercised, practiced, and sharpened through engagement with *World of Warcraft*. This is not to say that games do not have a role in a school curriculum but to ask whether a student who did not have a sense of, for example, how to use counterarguments, could develop that sense in a gaming-centric curriculum. Are such skills better learned in other arenas and then honed through gaming activity? Can they be directly induced by gaming? In order to establish curricular goals, it is critical to answer these and other questions opened by research on gaming and education.

Seed, a historian, included games in her undergraduate classroom to teach the history of European expansion in the fifteenth and sixteenth centuries. At first she deployed commercial games with historical themes, but subsequently moved to a method in which students designed their own games (Seed 2007). She particularly liked that game design enabled her to teach students that history is not a set of facts but an interpretive activity concerned with historical contingency. As she said:

> In order to teach students to design games, I had to teach them how to think about contingency, likely alternative outcomes of events. In this way, the students themselves were coming up with alternative paths that history might have taken had a particular path been followed.

Seed's pedagogy, as well as theorycrafters' deployment of scientific reasoning, suggests that at least some curricular uptake of gaming might center not on game play but on activities in and around games such as game design and analysis of complex game mechanics (see also Kafai 1995).

Modding

World of Warcraft is one of many games that allow players to create and install software modules—called modifications, mods, or addons—to add new functionality (Kucklich 2004; Postigo 2007; Whitehead et al. 2008). A famous video game mod evolved into the game *Counter-Strike,* the best-selling game of its genre. Originally a modification of the game *Half-Life, Counter-Strike* established that contemporary video games could and should enable modding.

Modding did not start with *Counter-Strike;* it goes back at least to 1961 when students MIT developed *Spacewar!* on the DEC PDP-1. Modding continued into the 1970s with games such as *Colossal Cave Adventure* (Jerz 2007) and may have even earlier roots in activities such as performance tuning PCs (turning up clock speed and the like) or the practices of automotive enthusiasts who rebuild vehicles in configurations such as lowriders or choppers (Willis 1978). Modding in games encompasses a range of activities, including the development of a whole new game (such as *Counter-Strike*); retexturing character models to change their appearance; and, as in the case of *World of Warcraft,* altering the user interface.

WoW modding was limited; the game provided a small hatch through which end user content penetrated the product. Players could not change game terrain, character appearance, the behavior of nonplayer characters, character class abilities, or quests (see Whitehead et al. 2008). But even with these limits thousands of *WoW* mods were available for free download on the Internet.[2] Mods were maintained by their developers, requiring updates as Blizzard issued patches. Most players did not write mods, but there was enough technical mastery in the player community to create mods propagated to millions of players. The black box was thus not wholly closed; it permitted entry of small but significant bits of player experience to be codified and incorporated into the game. Not all players used mods, but those who did had a wide choice; considerable customization was possible.

Mods were created by players who enjoyed games and generated ideas for customizing play. We interviewed Karl Isenberg, a founder of the Cosmos mod website, one of the earliest *WoW* modding sites.[3] He said that he created mods when he had "a good idea."

BN: So where do you get these good ideas?

Karl: I don't know. Either from the community—someone says, "Hey, I wish there was an addon that did this." Or, an addon where I look at it and say, "Oh, I wish it did this." And so either I modify it, or make my own addon that does it. Or just something off the top of my head.

Generally, modders wanted to explore new directions and deepen their connection to the game. Isenberg said that he started creating *WoW* modifications when he attained the first level cap of 60:

So after I hit 60, so after I hit the initial cap, I started looking for even more things to do with the game. And so I got into modding and my first addon was, like, a leet-speak translator [a translator for player-coded words].

Mod authors usually began modding for fun. Some then realized the economic potential of their labors and collected donations or developed "premium" versions of their mods. Sites that compiled and distributed mods generated revenue from advertising and might eventually be sold to larger companies.

Most mod authoring, however, was a labor of love—"an entertainment" in Isenberg's words. Isenberg described a modder he knew:

He's pretty stinking smart and he writes things just because he likes playing with new features. So he does theoretical tests like proof of concepts on various new features or things that haven't been done before.

The authors of some of the most popular *World of Warcraft* mods posted the following on their website.

If you would be interested in working on some of the most used projects in World of Warcraft, please feel free to contact us . . . Unfortunately this isn't a "job" for us, it's what we do in our free time, so we aren't able to offer monetary compensation. Our primary goal is to get the sites to a self-sustaining state, where they pay for themselves, and don't require us to pull out the checkbook. (ctmod.net)

CTMod claimed over 100 million downloads—an astonishing figure for any software.

Isenberg said that Cosmos generated only about a thousand dollars in the three years he was affiliated with it, which was used for server costs and related expenses. He explained:

> There's a group that is sort of mod-centric and theoretical and analytical about perfect mods and what's the best way to write things. And then there's people that are trying to make money . . . And they are not entirely separate, but sometimes you go from one to another.

Modders sometimes felt ambivalent about users of their mods, finding many woefully unsophisticated. Isenberg said:

> So there is a learning curve to using mods, and if you can't figure that out then I don't really want to let you use them. Like, I'd rather you don't use them because it saves me work . . . My care meter has gone down over the years.

However, he admitted that part of the reason to distribute mods on the Internet, and not just write them for a few friends, was "fame." He began:

> You share because I mean, the same reason the Open Source community shares. You share because you either think it's the right thing to do, or some people liked your mods so instead of responding to a bajillion emails about them, you post it so they can just download them.

After a pause, he said, with perfect comic timing:

> Do you like watching download counts? I love watching download counts.

We laughed about the anonymous "fame" measured in download counts. Many modders cared about the size of their audience and used quantitative tools to count downloads. Isenberg said watching download counts was "a fulfilling thing." (See Scacchi 2004; and Kelty 2008 on similar Open Source dynamics.)

Mods are protected by copyright but not software patents (an expensive, complex process beyond the resources of modders). Blizzard was thus free to incorporate features based on mods, and indeed *WoW* contained many features that first appeared as player-created mods.

We asked modders how they felt about the uptake of their mods directly into the commercial software (Kow and Nardi 2009). On the one hand, modders were deeply flattered, but on the other they no longer had their mods to care for. We did not speak with anyone who felt ripped off or exploited. They simply missed their babies.

What exactly did *World of Warcraft* mods do? Their primary functions were to reduce player effort, make visible invisible parts of the game, enable information sharing, aid players in coordinating with one another, and capture aspects of play history. As discussed in chapter 4, mods did not, in every case, improve player experience. But many mods filled obvious gaps in *WoW's* design and allowed players freedom to customize the game as they wished.

Mods were useful in part because *World of Warcraft* was so information intensive. Players improved performance through knowledge of tiny but numerous facts about the game, the management of multiple character and equipment statistics, and attention to rapid state changes during battle.

Mods enhanced these abilities by displaying information about facts and variables not visible in *WoW's* standard user interface. One of the first mods many players downloaded showed the coordinates of the game geography. Because the geography was huge, it was often difficult to know where to find a particular NPC or an item required to complete a quest.

Mods helped players keep their gear and materials organized, revealing how many empty slots were available in the bags that contained a player's equipment and other paraphernalia. Mods showed how soon equipment would have to be repaired. They allowed players to switch equipment with a single key press (it was common to have multiple sets of equipment for different game activities).

Mods enabled players to redesign the user interface to reflect personal preferences. Some players constructed interfaces with the complexity of airplane cockpits while others chose a minimalist style with a few simple windows and buttons. One player I met described a setup with four monitors that he used to display the output of dozens of mods. (He was playing the interface!)

During challenging encounters, players tracked rapid state changes in multiple variables related to players and monsters. Mods showed the state of variables, such as the duration of temporary magic spells or curses, or the amount of aggro a character was generating. A popular mod displayed the characters that were the current target of a set of monsters in group play—functionality that Blizzard eventually incorporated into the game. Some mods triggered visual or auditory alarms, useful in fast-paced group play.

One heavily used mod, Gatherer, remembered where a player had collected herbs and mineral ores, marking the player's world map so he could return to the same spots on future gathering expeditions. Another popular mod, Auctioneer, collected data about Auction House transactions, allowing players to quickly scan prices, suggesting which items were under- or overpriced and proposing reasonable minimum bids and buyout prices. I did not use this mod, but I usually knew when I had underpriced something as it sold immediately, almost certainly to someone using Auctioneer. Mods, then, affected not only players who used them but players who did not.

Auctioneer software supported collaborative information practices; its information was partially accessible to all players in a guild, even those who did not have Auctioneer downloaded. A player could type, for example:

? Mystical Mantle of the Whale

into the guild chat window and Auctioneer would scan guildmates' Auctioneer databases and whisper information on the pricing of the item. If a player needed only pricing information (and not the other services Auctioneer provided), he could take advantage of collective information without having to download, troubleshoot, and reinstall the mod after a patch. Guild use of Auctioneer generated an efficient collective resource, removing the necessity for reduplication of software management effort.

This innovation strikes me as potentially valuable in many contexts, a possible adaptive potentiation, in Sutton-Smith's terms, that may prove useful outside the arena of play. Small increases in productivity scale—across employees or members of an organization—to measurable effects. Labor is divided so that instead of every individual managing many software modules each manages a few, sharing the information they produce. The labor of software management is stretched across the collectivity, resulting in time savings.

Auctioneer was not an isolated instance of such information sharing. Gatherer had an option to mark the player's map with the locations of minerals and herbs collected by others in the player's guild. In this case the player needed to have Gatherer downloaded but did not need to actually visit each of the nodes to mark their locations.

Gatherer announced when a guildmate visited a node—an interesting form of mutual activity awareness. Awareness mechanisms have been identified as critical for effective collaboration (see, e.g., Heath and Luff 1991; Gutwin and Greenberg 1998; Tang et al. 2001; Begole et al. 2002). Gatherer offered occasions for light conversation ("Illy is stealing my flowers!"); such moments engendered social bonding and supported collaborative work (see Nardi 2005).

Certain *WoW* mods, then, were distinctively communitarian, ideologically shaped to assert the primacy of information sharing, making available information logged into databases, and opening group members' activities to the gaze of others. While the discussion of certain mods in chapter 4 was somewhat critical, the communitarian mods seemed to move the player community toward generous sharing.

As players added mods, a feeling of empowerment grew, a sense of styling the game to personal tastes. Zaq and Jacquii, both rogues, conversed in guild chat:

> Zaq: Jacquii, LazyRogue is a Mod i use. U can write ur own script to attack certain ways and react to certain situations. I use it because i find it fun to tweak my script and troubleshoot what doesnt work and what works for me. I dont have much script writing skills, so this is a fun way to learn something and understand how things work.
>
> Jacquii: cool ty [thank you]

In everyday life, Zaq was a bartender. He learned to write simple scripts that he could "tweak" and "troubleshoot," gaining a sense of the possibilities of computational technology in a way that he described as "fun." Zaq modified his play experience according to his own personality, discovering how he liked to play his character through experiments with LazyRogue. He shared his knowledge and enthusiasm with Jacquii, enabling her to learn more about how to customize and empower her character.

When I discovered mods, I was surprised that Blizzard allowed such experimentation with its software. Wouldn't it break? Wouldn't players be able to hack *World of Warcraft*? How could such a complex software system be opened to absolutely anyone who wanted to write a mod?

The game was opened through a narrow, regulated channel.[4] Mods did not include programs working outside the *WoW* folder in which they were installed, nor did they run on their own outside the folder. Human governance was also in effect; Blizzard monitored mods, assessing whether they were consistent with its philosophy of play. Such oversight enabled players to freely experiment without altering the game in ways that would distort player experience as Blizzard had codified it.

An instance of oversight occurred on December 6, 2006, when Blizzard issued a patch that disabled many mods to which *World of Warcraft* players had become accustomed. One such mod was Decursive, used by certain classes to remove "debuffs" including curses, diseases, and disempowering magic spells. Decursive automatically looped through afflicted players, requiring only a single key press to cure everyone in a party. Blizzard felt this made decursing too easy and that such mods were changing the nature of *World of Warcraft*, improperly diminishing its challenge.

After the patch, Decursive no longer worked. But the author rewrote it so that, while it could not remove debuffs with one key press, it was still easier than *WoW*'s standard user interface which required players to select each affected player with the mouse and then click on the appropriate decursing spell. The new Decursive cut this work in half, combining selection and removal of the debuff.[5]

With Decursive, the modding community had disrupted *World of Warcraft*, taking it in directions Blizzard deemed unsuitable. Blizzard responded to protect the core gaming experience in conformance with its vision, eliminating mods that failed to preserve what it conceived as desirable play experience. Such a model of governance arguably calibrated diverse elements, taking account of user experience while at the same time forestalling potential difficulties of more sweepingly democratic approaches. The very term "addon" suggests the relative contributions of player community and designed product; mods were "added to" an existing world. Both Blizzard and modders used, and accepted, this term.[6]

Having a vibrant modding community was an asset for Blizzard. Over time, Blizzard acknowledged and appeared to appreciate the modding community. However, initially there was little support for modding, although mods were permitted (Kow and Nardi 2009). In 2004 the Blizzard website contained a post that read:

> There is no official support for modifying the *WoW* interface. If you break it, you get to keep both pieces :)

This lack of support suggests that Blizzard did not view modding as a source of free labor (see Postigo 2007). Blizzard slowly warmed to the modding community, in part due to the efforts of an employee named Sam Lantinga (better known by his alias, Slouken), who took it upon himself to participate in the IRC channel inhabited by *WoW* modders (Kow and Nardi 2009). In 2004, modders were told they could "keep both pieces," but by the time of BlizzCon 2008 Blizzard and the modding community enjoyed cordial relations. At the "UI and Mods" session, a panelist addressed modders in the audience, saying:

> This is a really great community that you guys are part of.

He commended the contributions of modders in extending the game in ways that Blizzard could not:

> We can't make hundreds of options, but you can.

Another panelist said:

> We'd like to thank the addon community for everything they've done.

Modding is part of a larger movement of participant production on the Internet in which people create content simply because they want to. Ito (2008) detailed the activities of amateurs, including the production of online comics, music, videos, and anime. Like modders, purveyors of these arts sometimes transformed their efforts into paid work, although generally their activities centered on creativity and sharing as end rewards (Ito 2008).

Modding establishes an ethos that allows for a more open relationship between people and technology. While sustained by a great many technological features and processes beyond the reach of players, *World of Warcraft* represents a family of technological artifacts that open the black box at least partially, trying out alternative principles of human engagement with technology that enable the incorporation of direct user experience. *World of Warcraft,* and, more broadly, a range of video games, allow players to intervene and modify some of the ways games are played. In this respect, games such as *WoW* are to some degree reflexive, allowing the experience of playing to feed back on the game and aspects of the software through which it is enacted.

Theorycrafters and modders approached *World of Warcraft* as an occasion for opening up new play experiences, for moving beyond reproducing play in predictable ways. They discovered the freedom to alter play, to dwell in what Dewey called "an attitude of freedom." Mods were reshaped as players responded creatively, engaging a readiness to "look at an addon and say, 'Oh, I wish it did this.'" Theorycrafters were roused to action when pondering such enigmas as the puzzling movement of the Shadowfiend. Remaking the material of experience began with an idea for a mod that occurred to a player or a theory question that piqued interest. It blossomed in a social context as discussions took place in chat channels and Web forums. The invitation to enrich and deepen experience through reflections on play enabled players to find satisfactions in doing "even more things with the game." Theorycrafting and modding are embodiments of Dewey's articulation of aesthetic experience as recursively generating new aesthetic experience:

> Works of art that are not remote from common life . . . are . . . marvelous aids in the creation of such a life.

The game itself is the "work of art not remote from common life"; its rules ensure that overall artistic excellence is not compromised while at the same time the capacity to alter rules in controlled ways is designed into the system.

CHAPTER EIGHT

Gender

From the moment one creates a character and must choose its gender, gender is always present, in varying ways, in *World of Warcraft*. This chapter examines how gendered experience in *World of Warcraft* was constructed in two distinctive ways: through patterns of discourse and through the design of the game. I argue that discourse practices created a "boys' tree house" but that the game itself countered with surprisingly feminine, domestic nuances.

The discussion is based on my participation in several guilds on North American servers. I believe my data are descriptive of gendered practice in most North American guilds. However, specialized guilds such as Christian guilds, gay guilds, guilds of professional colleagues, and so on, may enforce different rules of discourse. I eagerly await future analyses of gendered practice in such guilds, as well as those from other parts of the world. My observations on discourse in battlegrounds, general chat, and other public chat channels were consistent across the servers on which I played.

The Boys' Tree House

[13:53] Dan: So how did you get into this game?
[13:54] Mrs. Pain: my husband
[13:54] Dan: How old are you by the way?
[13:54] Mrs. Pain: 39
[13:54] Mrs. Pain: I am a mother of 2 girls
[13:54] Mrs. Pain: and a wife of 21 yrs

Many female players, such as Mrs. Pain (interviewed by an undergraduate in instant messaging), found their way to *World of Warcraft* through husband, boyfriend, brother, cousin, or male friend. Other female gamers had been playing competitive video games for years and played *WoW* as one of many games. A few female players were introduced to *WoW* by female friends or relatives.

What did female players find when they stepped into *World of Warcraft*? Competitive video gaming is typically associated with males, and *World of Warcraft*, despite the presence of a healthy minority of females, was a male-dominated space. It was not an unfriendly dominance; female players were talked to, listened to, included, and aided, just as male players were. But the social space was maintained as one in which males set the rhetorical tone. Sexualized, homophobic language was normalized in text and voice chat (although stopping short of what would probably take place in a men's locker room). Male players casually mentioned things like blow jobs and buttsex. They spoke of raping, or being raped by, mobs or players in battlegrounds and arenas. They used words such as douche bag, pussy, cunt, and pimp. The term gay was a generically derisive (and liberally invoked) adjective. Males called players fag, faggot, or homo if displeased or as a joke. Male players sometimes taunted other males by referring to them as "little girls."[1] I label this discourse "male" because it was primarily (though not exclusively) males who engaged it.[2]

Female players, numerically a minority, and more conservative in speech, were, I argue, a presence in a boys' tree house.[3] Discourse was led by males; they used sexualized and homophobic language more often than females and language that female players nearly universally avoided such as mentions of rape and the use of words like cunt and homo. However, the boys' tree house in *WoW*, while male oriented, was a complex space; males maintained control through the use of aggressive language, but the tree house allowed females more latitude in speech and action than everyday life typically does—latitude they often leveraged and enjoyed.

My observations on male rhetorical practice in *WoW* are consistent with those of Golub (2007) who studied a North American raiding guild. He reported a typical incident of sexualized language:

At one point, one [raider's] microphone sent some noise across the channel. The [male] raid leader asked . . . "John . . . is that a dick in your mouth?"

Golub (2007) was quite clear on the use of masculinist talk in *World of Warcraft* and that such talk was "transgressive" with respect to the larger culture. Apart from this work I have found few analyses that highlight the casualness and prevalence of this style of discourse which I encountered everywhere in *WoW.*

Kavetsky (2008) studied gendered language in a raiding guild. She reported:

> [T]he guild's leadership emphasizes a "family-friendly" atmosphere—a trait noted by virtually all those interviewed. This does not mean that there are no off-color jokes (these are predominantly men in their twenties and thirties, after all), but rather reflects an attempt to create an environment where a variety of people feel comfortable.

Kavetsky did not explain what kinds of language the guild accepted from "men in their twenties and thirties." She reported that males used language that females did not use but was silent on the nature of the language and its impact, naturalizing it with the parenthetical "men in their twenties and thirties, after all." Her topic was gendered language in *World of Warcraft,* so we might expect analysis of how male joking was handled within the "family-friendly atmosphere."[4]

Discourse inhabited its own sphere in *World of Warcraft* in text and voice chat. The free expression permitted in these channels enabled males to establish rhetorical practice as they liked. Voice chat was, of course, completely outside any means of official discipline, and while game masters took action when racial slurs in text chat in public channels were reported (which happened rarely), there was little they could (or wanted?) to do given the much higher prevalence of sexualized, homophobic terms.

The following is an anecdote that I believe captures the way in which rhetorical practice was deployed to position women in the tree house.

One evening I was playing in a 25-man pug composed of a core of players from one guild and an assortment from other guilds, including me, to make up a late-night run. After a wipe, as we were regrouping, the raid leader asked in voice chat if there were any real life females present apart from the one he knew. Though it was clearly a setup, I answered (for Science of course) "Ya, me, Innikka, I'm female." The raid leader said he had gotten a fortune cookie at lunch in which he was promised a wish. "Innikka, would you please immediately email me naked pictures of yourself?" he asked. I replied, very truthfully, "I'm pretty sure you don't want pictures of me." He said, with mock sadness, "Ah, I knew I would not get the wish the fortune cookie promised."

No one commented on this little exchange or laughed. Females were implicitly asked to agree to the condition that they were participating in an activity in which males were the dominant gender. The other woman in the raid was in my guild. She was a skilled player and had been accepted as a member of the late-night group. I was being tested and put on notice that the guys were in charge.

When such an event occurs, there are two choices. The player can play along and continue to play the game or she can leave. There is no opportunity for reasoned discourse or a way to win through humor. No matter how clever a response a player might come up with, the mere asking of the question and her presence as a small minority ensure that she has been called out as the exception.[5]

And anyway, it was just a joke! Vandenberg (1998) observed of play that "The ease with which the real can be rendered not real, by the simple signal, 'This is play,' reveals the contingency and fluidity of the social construction of reality." Such fluidity is a means by which behaviors in which one group acts out at the expense of another can be rendered unaccountable.

Mrs. Pain reported that her daughter refused to play:

[13:56] Mrs. Pain: my daughter tried playing but she thought the players were too rude
[13:56] Mrs. Pain: I have certain ppl [people] I play with
[13:56] Mrs. Pain: and being an adult I could handle myself

Mrs. Pain accommodated to "rudeness" by cultivating an in-game social network and through the resource of her maturity. Her daughter made the decision to not play.

In the workplace or classroom, in family activities, and in many mixed-gender venues, the kind of masculine discourse that was utterly normal in *World of Warcraft* would not be permitted. Everyday life is rife with male dominance, but it is generally hidden under a welter of coded language, polite niceties, and superficial civility. In-game, such dominance was embraced, exaggerated, and given free expression in coarse masculine language.[6] Vandenberg (1998) noted that in play:

> It is thrilling to transform the real to the not real, to journey into forbidden areas of darkness behind the public mask of conventionality, and to become aware of the freedom to do so in the process.

This discussion raises many questions for which I do not have answers. Why did males find it amusing to engage in sexualized, homophobic talk? Why was calling someone a "little girl"—not a "little boy"—so derisive? Golub (2007) reported that such discourse realized "intense camaraderie." However, this is something to be explained rather than asserted.

Was *World of Warcraft* a social environment in which "a woman today can do everything as long as she does it in relative subordination to a man" (Haavind, quoted in Corneliussen 2008)? Was *WoW* discourse the result of the suppression of certain kinds of masculine discourse in ordinary life in favor of the politically correct? Was such discourse the acting out of young males? Pearce (2008) reported that baby boomer age men in the game *Uru* were less inclined to speak in the ways common to *WoW*. However, I observed men in their thirties, forties, and fifties regularly engaging in masculinist talk in *WoW*, so I am not so sure.

Women sometimes used terms for females such as bitch, slut, whore, and hooker (an apparent acceptance, on the part of the less powerful, of the logics of the powerful; see Freire 2000). They flirted and engaged frequently, and with enjoyment, in explicit sexual banter. I do not want to represent female *WoW* players as shrinking violets because they were not. For some, the boys' tree house was a space in which they were welcome to speak any way they wanted.

But female players generally avoided hardcore masculinist rhetoric. They did not belittle other players by calling them "little girl" (or "little boy" for that matter). They sometimes used "gay" to disparage (much less often than males), but I never heard a female call anyone "homo." Female players avoided the language of what one player referred to as "the female denigrations," by which she meant words such as cunt or slang terms for genitalia such as clit (see Thelwall 2008). Female players did not joke about rape.

It is unclear how female players felt about such language. Since they did not typically employ it themselves, at some level it was rejected. One evening a female player, Karlin—herself given to very colorful language—said in voice chat, with dismay, "Sahm just called us cunts." Sahm had used the word in text chat. He made a joking apology. Having been called out by a popular female member of the guild, I did not hear him use the word again (although others did).

Sometimes it seemed that male players sustained the atmosphere of the tree house simply by invoking masculinist terms. As a male player, Barbarino, came online, the following comments were made by male players with no rancor:

Jene: barbarino is a slut.

Popzikal: he is gay and faggot

Barbarino did not respond, nor did anyone say anything. It was as though the ether of the chat channel must be regularly refreshed with the recitation of sexualized, homophobic words.

WoW was an arena in which males set the tone for the use of language prohibited in many everyday settings (notably school and work). However, the magic circle may also invite women to "forbidden areas of darkness." In the private chat channel for healers opened during raids in Scarlet Raven, women sometimes discussed sexual methodologies in humorous detail. There were usually a few males present in the channel, but they said nothing. Having a gender majority and a silenced male population seemed to provide a space in which women took the lead in subversive talk because they could control the terms of the conversation. However, this was largely an invisible, private channel seen by only a few in the guild. In guildwide chat, as well as *WoW*'s other chat channels, males established the dominant rhetorical practice.[7] Golub (2007) suggested that raiding activity, and its associated rhetorical practice, was "deeply tied to [players'] sense of masculine self-competence and control." He did not elaborate on this theme, but his comment points to the need for more research to understand how a sense of male self-competence and control plays out in a competitive game world in which females are also present.

The Interactive Gendered Landscape

Despite all the sexualized talk, possibilities for actual flirtation and romance in *World of Warcraft* were complicated by the real life gender imbalance of players. The Internet is, of course, a great sexual shopping mall, so I was curious about the ways in which males and females negotiated a space in which sex was an entrenched part of the discourse, many young, unattached people were present, and anonymity provided cover for explorations difficult or impossible in real life.

I will argue that *WoW* players evolved two interactive planes in which gendered practice occurred. The dominant plane dampened heterosexuality, creating a relaxed space in which males did not have to worry about heterosexual activity. A secondary plane sustained heterosexual flirtation and romance. The dominant plane, produced and reproduced through the repetition of several practices which I will describe, yielded a stable, predictable backdrop tailored to the desires of many male players. The secondary plane, episodic and erratic, was more likely to entail rupture and tension while at the same time offering possibilities for pleasurable intimacies for both genders.[8]

The Dominant Plane

The first plane was constructed in part through the practice of male players playing female characters. In a North American sample of *WoW* players, Yee (2005) found that 23 percent of real life males' characters were female characters. This choice—to play a female character—precluded a player from presenting as a male who might engage the interests of a female player through a (virtual) male body. Male players playing female characters erased the possibility of flirtations deploying the character as a resource, choosing instead a female fantasy character at which to gaze. Not only did the female character serve its own player's desires, at the same time, it made provision for the gaze of other males. Male players came together for "girl watching," an activity stereotypically characteristic of all-male groups and consistent with the boys' tree house.

Males getting together to watch girls would be likely to choose attractive female characters at which to gaze, and—no surprise—they did so (see Yee 2005; DiGiuseppe and Nardi 2007). The servers were full of alluring female Night Elves and Blood Elves, while the homely ladies of the Dwarf and Orc races were rarely seen. Distribution of male characters across the races was more even (Yee 2005). Gazing at female characters was, for males, a significant aspect of the visual experience of play.

When we interviewed males about why they chose female characters, they said two things. "Why not?" and "If I have to look at a someone's ass for three hours, it's going to be a girl's." (Recall that the character is typically seen in third-person perspective.) The latter comment was a *WoW* cliché and was mentioned in several interviews.

I supervised four undergraduate male players who conducted independent studies on various aspects of *World of Warcraft*. I asked them if I should believe men who said they just liked looking at female characters—was that really the reason they chose them? Was there something deeper? Was an identity workshop (Turkle 1995) taking place in *WoW?* Were males finding their inner female? The students said of males who said they liked looking at their female characters, "Believe them!"

My in-game experience supported this view. Both male and female players acknowledged that males liked looking at attractive female characters. One evening when I had just joined a new guild, I was talking in voice chat and a male player said, "A Night Elf who's really a girl!" A female player rejoined, "Guys just like Night Elves because of their boobs."

When one of my guildmates changed his male character to a female (something players could do for a fee), the guild teased him mercilessly about his "sex change operation."[9] In defense, he typed into the guild chat window, "i didn't wanna keeping looking at a guy character." This logic was taken to be transparent and obvious, and no one questioned it.

Through the design of certain of the female characters, *WoW* provided a resource to reproduce a standard gender dynamic, the male gaze (see Mulvey 1975). However, visually, things were pretty tame. While the male gaze was sustained in *WoW,* in particular through the design of the Human, Night Elf, and Blood Elf racials, as well as some of the NPCs, and a few items of "kombat lingerie" (Fron et al. 2007b), for the most part, female characters were relatively modest. Other video games contain far more egregious body and costume designs (see Taylor 2003a; Hayes 2005; Fron et al. 2007b). And though males tended to like Blood Elves and Night Elves, *WoW* offered a range of female character types of varying attractiveness, again unlike many games (see Corneliussen 2008).

Further shaping of the gendered landscape ensued from the common rhetorical practice of males calling each other slut, hooker, whore, or bitch, terms typically associated with women. This discourse had the effect of deleting sexual difference among males and females—such difference being a precondition for heterosexuality—in the first plane, as anyone could be called anything by anyone.

Players usually assumed that other players were male. In pugs, players often addressed me as "man," "dude" or "bro" or referred to me as "he," for example, "Ask the priest if he has any mage food on him." No one that I observed pretended to be a girl when he had a female character; there was no "gender bending" (see Yee 2005).[10]

The salience of possible heterosexual encounters further receded in the first plane through the way in which players used flirtatious emotes. Emotes were one-word commands that caused the character to animate and/or voice actions and which output a text message in the chat window. If, for example, Innikka selected another player with the mouse and typed /sexy, the command generated the text "Innikka thinks Zeke is a sexy devil."

Just as with the terms hooker-whore-slut-bitch, the emotes were used within and across real life genders, blunting heterosexual impact. Common emotes for flirting included /hug, /kiss, /lick, /moan, /whistle, /love, /wink, /grin, /cuddle, /flirt. Players' habit of invoking emotes between and within genders rendered them "safe," reducing the risk of making a move that might be rejected; a player could select a player at whom to direct an emote without feeling as though he or she had made a declaration of interest.

For male players, retrenching to the boys' tree house to watch girls and engage in the activities of the game created a space in which pressure to compete for females was reduced or simply deleted. By flattening the interactive sexual landscape, males established the choice for themselves of focusing on performance, and kicking back to enjoy rough talk, without the need for the sometimes vexing activities of heterosexuality. It took work on their part to make this happen: choosing female characters, using gendered words across genders, and "flirting" with their own gender. The regularity with which these actions were engaged, to the point where they sometimes appeared to be random (as with the comments about Barbarino), suggests that males had considerable interest in undertaking actions to ensure the sustenance of the dynamics of the tree house.

Another practice suggesting a male desire to retrench from heterosexuality, within the confines of *WoW,* occurred during late-night runs. Players sometimes announced in chat that they might be forced to depart in order to attend to their wives' sexual needs ("damn it, she's horny" "my wife, um, needs me"). Although attentive to their wives' needs (possibly to avoid serious aggro), these players were attempting to delay freely offered sexual activity in favor of playing *World of Warcraft.* Sometimes a player left for a short while, presumably to negotiate the timing of the necessary activities. One player returned and deadpanned, "no problem. she's out cold."

The dominant plane was shaped by and for males. How did females fit in? The first plane was not maintained to shield females from the risks of heterosexual interaction as it was for males; female players squeezed into its interstices. Hayes (2005) observed, "Women have different interpretations of and responses to overtly gendered practices within video games." Some females teased males about their proclivities toward Elves. Some ignored the machinations of the tree house and just played the game. Others negotiated the rhetorical space. For example, occasionally male utterances elicited a heartfelt female "ewww" in the chat window, indicating that the grossness of a comment was too much. Such negotiations were relatively uncommon, but when they occurred the impact could be significant, such as Karlin's reaction to Sahm's name-calling—a clear statement of her personal limits.

It is also possible that the actions that comprised the first plane bespoke complex gender dynamics such as males' confused feelings about other males, and fears of homosexuality. I do not have data with which to explore such possibilities, though they are worth pursuing and not inconsistent with my interpretations of the actions of the first plane, which probably operated at multiple levels. Following Bakhtin (1982), we should consider "any written discourse an unfinished social dialogue," and it is my hope that this discussion will stimulate further research analyzing the complexities of gendered rhetorical practice in games such as *World of Warcraft,* a topic oddly missing from the literature.

The Secondary Plane

The secondary plane of gendered activity, a counterpoint to the first, incorporated cross-gender intimacy. In any space with males and females, boy will meet girl. Entangled with the mutations and transfigurations of cross-gender characters, rhetorical practices, and exaggerated gender norms,

were the simple desires of ordinary people for interaction with the opposite sex. It is easy to overlook this pervasive, fundamental reality in academic discussions of "constructing gender" and the like. The flattening of
the sexual landscape in the first plane did not eliminate possibilities for
flirtation and romance; it merely offered the choice not to worry about
them. Flirtatious and romantic activities were, however, definitely present
in *World of Warcraft*. For those who engaged them, whether married or
not, they offered an aspect of play considerably more difficult to maneuver in real life where such activities are more likely to be taken seriously,
leading to the possibility of rejection, aggro on the part of significant others, grievous misconstruals, disciplinary measures at work, or complex love
affairs. In *WoW*, people could play at flirting—no/few strings attached. As
Vandenberg (1998) observed, play has a built-in escape hatch:

> [In play] the real can be rendered not real, by the simple signal, "This is
> play."

This is not to say that real romance did not blossom out of playing-at-
flirting in *World of Warcraft* or that flirting did not sometimes have serious
in-game consequences. Occasionally, in the midst of a thousand ephemeral
little flirtations, more serious developments lay ahead.

Early in the interview cycle, I interviewed (separately) a young player
and her mother, both players. The young woman, who was married, had
met, in-game, a player with whom she had fallen in love. She came to
the brink of divorce, planning a trip to meet her *WoW* lover in the foreign
country in which he resided. The mother intervened, urging her daughter
to stop playing *World of Warcraft* and mend her marriage. The daughter
complied and gave up *WoW*. In the interview, she was wistful about the
pleasures of the game, into which memories of romance were woven with
remembrance of game elements she described having loved.

Other instances of flirtatious activity entailed perils that played out in
relation to performative dimensions of *World of Warcraft*.

Sean participated in a raiding guild of undergraduates. Trouble erupted
in his guild when a group of male "e-pimps" and their female "e-hos" who
"talked dirty" to them, became a source of tension. During raids, the e-hos
directed their talk to the e-pimps, ignoring the other males. The neglected
males were livid at their exclusion from the lively sexual banter.

The situation was intolerable for them, and discord grew until guild officers threw the e-pimps and e-hos out of the guild. Tellingly, the sexy guildmates were removed not under the auspices of talking dirty, but by being cast as incompetent players who could not raid properly. The gender issues, though obvious to everyone and unmistakably inscribed in the sexualized terms of the conversation, were not brought to bear as reasons for what Sean called the "purge." Instead, a performative argument was constructed and accepted, legitimizing the purge as a performative deficiency rather than a dispute among the males.

Serena, a young player I interviewed, was forced to call on personal forbearance to accommodate a female-unfriendly practice in her guild of players in their twenties. Women were not allowed to speak on voice chat during raids. It was considered too disconcerting for the males, whose attentional focus, and thus performative excellence, might be disrupted by the sound of feminine voices. Serena was real life friends with many in the guild and enjoyed raiding with them. She accepted the guild policy but felt it was unnecessary.

A top European raiding guild, Nihilum, was rumored to refuse membership to women. A female blogger/player reported (WorldofWarcraft.com 2007a):

According to GM [guild master] Kungen, there are a lot of reasons they don't recruit females, but the one he highlights is the need for recruits to have a "high abuse tolerance." And a bit later in the thread, poster Awake adds that female applicants are avoided because of drama.

The construction of drama as a reason for excluding females was consistent with the experiences of Sean's guild, and the rumor was widely believed. However, a member of Nihilum posted, on an official Blizzard forum, that the putative exclusion of women was a false rumor stemming from an "internal joke" within the guild (WorldofWarcraft.com 2007b). The guild member went on to say that although Nihilum in fact had no women, women were free to apply.

The idea of the ban was believed (I first heard mention of it in Terror Nova, where it was taken seriously) and generated considerable discussion on blogs and forums. Opinions varied, but some posters endorsed exclusionary practice. One wrote:

It's not a misogynistic ideal for Nihilum to be a guys-only guild; in fact, it's exactly like most sports: there's women's hockey and men's hockey.

In the secondary plane of gendered activity, the tensions of heterosexuality sometimes brought with them old cultural logics even when they distorted conditions under which men and women might share joint performative activity. Physical differences between male and female bodies are presumably the reason for women's and men's hockey. Such differences are not relevant to activity that involves no feats of strength, yet the same argument was made.

That excluding women was a "joke" in Nihilum indicates that the notion of such exclusion was taken to be, on some level, "funny." Would Nihilum have joked about excluding an ethnic or racial group? The guild could not muster a single female player, suggesting de facto exclusionary practice.

Despite the disruptions and tensions occurring in the secondary plane, there was also a good deal of friendly flirtation and real romance. For example, two players, Juli and Nino, whom I had known in Scarlet Raven when they were both single, coincidentally ended up in my new guild, during which time they married. (Although in keeping with the disruptive potentialities of the second plane, an Irish player whom Juli had declared, before her marriage, to have "the sexiest accent," continued to flirt egregiously with her. That she was married seemed to make the flirtation more interesting to him, and I cannot say she discouraged him.)

Much romantic activity undoubtedly occurred in whispers, and of course I have no record of others' whispers. Through my own experiences, it was apparent how casual interactions might move to requests for personal information and expressions of interest. In one somewhat farcical encounter, I inadvertently activated the attentions of a man who was engaged to a woman in the guild whose mother was one of my in-game friends. Let me explain the progression of events (which occurred in the post–Scarlet Raven guild).

Flirtation in *World of Warcraft* often begins with the deployment of emotionally safe, impersonal emotes.[11] Although I was known as the guild "goody-goody," and teased as "pure" and in danger of corruption by the sexualized and scatalogical talk that dominated late-night voice chat, I used the impersonal flirting emotes widely and frequently because I found them funny and everyone enjoyed them. There was one player with whom

I always seemed to trade a long string of emotes; we liked throwing in some of the less common commands such as /ruffle ("Zeke ruffles Innikka's hair") and /charm ("Innikka thinks Zeke is charming").

The guild ran both 10- and 25-man dungeons frequently. I noticed that Zeke engaged Innikka in flirty emoting only in the less challenging 10-man runs. I attributed this to the need for greater concentration in 25-man. One evening, in a 10-man, we needed a character with higher damage abilities for a particular boss. Zeke, a tank, said he would switch to Malore, a mage with high damage. (During a raid, it was possible for a player to leave the raid and the raid to bring in another player.) I whispered to him that I didn't know Malore was his character. He whispered, "she's not, i have access to a lot of accounts." I had played with Malore a few months previously, but she had not logged in recently.

Some time later, Zeke's whispers grew more personal. I had not seen that there might be anything other than emoting going on, and told him I was married. Zeke then revealed that he was engaged to Malore (whom he had met in *World of Warcraft*) but that the relationship was not going well. The emoting was restricted to the 10-man runs because Mianna, Malore's mother, attended the 25-man runs. Though things were difficult with Malore, Zeke still felt restraint in the presence of a potential mother-in-law. He had access to Malore's account because she was his fiancée, and had been vague in answering my question regarding the switch to avoid embarrassment.

Once things were out in the open, we laughed about the comedy of the situation and continued friends. Zeke was not exactly my age, but was older—divorced with a 12-year-old child. On my part, I liked him because he was a good player and always helpful to guildmates (and he was better at the emote game than anyone else). For his part, he said that his feelings were raw from his troubles, and any kind of female approval was a small comfort.

The secondary plane of gendered activity, then, engaged intimacies sometimes no different than those of any online space, affording communicative potentialities from which flirtatious or romantic activities might spring (see, e.g., boyd and Ellison 2007; Bardzell and Bardzell 2008; Toma et al. 2008). At other times, the particularities of the performative contours of *World of Warcraft* shaped expressions of intimacy and the complexities they entailed in the context of game performance. At still other times, conventional cross-gender confusions played out in misreadings schematized by the particularities of social structures (such as guilds and raids) and practices (e.g., sharing accounts) peculiar to *World of Warcraft*.

In sum, what I have called the dominant and secondary planes of gendered interaction in *World of Warcraft* constructed two distinctive orientations. In the first plane, heterosexuality was devitalized in favor of the comforts of the tree house. In the second plane, heterosexuality was engaged, sometimes in relations of tension and discord, and other times in mutually pleasurable interactions between male and female players.

Gender Participation and Game Design

Chapter 4 inquired into the power of software artifacts to direct human activity. This chapter has discussed the effects of the design of female characters on gendered practice in *World of Warcraft*. Most analysis of low rates of female participation in competitive video games focuses on the design of the games themselves. Many studies note that competitive games often include gendered elements unappealing to women (Cassell and Jenkins 1998; Taylor 2003a; Graner Ray 2005; Hayes 2005; Mortensen and Corneliussen 2005; Fron et al. 2007b; Kafai et al. 2008). These analyses highlight issues such as the kombat lingerie (Fron et al. 2007a) female characters may wear, and hypersexualized female body types (Taylor 2003a; Hayes 2005; Fron et al. 2007b). The harsh masculinity of environments depicted in game spaces is seen as off-putting to women (Fullerton et al. 2007). The studies point out that game designers are nearly all male (Graner Ray 2005; Fron et al. 2007b; Consalvo 2008) and that advertising at trade shows is often designed around the girl-watching theme (Fron et al. 2003a). Some games contain elements particularly disturbing to women, e.g., in *EverQuest* there are moments at which a player must run around acquiring gear to cover nakedness (Klastrup 2004, cited in Mortensen and Corneliussen 2005). Other design elements reinforce a surly masculinity—such as *Neverwinter Nights'* brothels (Mortensen and Corneliussen 2005).

What about *World of Warcraft*? Did its design discourage female players? About 20 percent of the North American *WoW* population was female (Yee 2005)—a higher proportion than in many competitive video games such as first-person shooters (Kennedy 2005). But still, nowhere near 50 percent.

This middling number—20 percent—says that something was happening in *World of Warcraft* that fostered a higher than usual number of females. But it also says that something else was happening that kept the figure well under that expected in a random distribution. I believe that *World of Warcraft*'s design contained elements of strong appeal to women (and, in interesting ways, men), but that the gender conventions of the boys' tree house forestalled some female players. In addition, the sheer amount of time it took to play *World of Warcraft* may have affected female participation.

I will never forget how enthralled I was when I first approached Darnassus, capital city of the Night Elves. Outside its walls were beautiful meadows colored emerald green and a particularly striking purple-violet. I hadn't expected to find my favorite colors in *World of Warcraft*, especially in such exquisitely complementary shades. I felt at home. I felt dazzled, I felt that the game was designed for me. While appreciating that men may also like these colors, I consider them feminine—they appear in female clothing, jewelry, and upholstery and curtain fabrics; they are not typically associated with the material world of males.

Rather than being expressive of stereotypical masculinist sensibilities, *WoW* was more nuanced, introducing elements appealing to women (and many men) in both game activities and the presentation of the game space. Fullerton et al.'s (2007) description of masculinist games establishes a baseline with which we can compare *World of Warcraft*. They wrote of masculinist games:

> Thematically, these games revolve around narratives of warfare, antiterrorism, invading aliens, zombies, science fiction, combat with robots. Aesthetically, their settings tend to be highly rectilinear, typically manmade spaces, often the bruised and embattled remains of an urban environment, warehouse, office building, space ship, space colony, or high tech laboratory gone horribly wrong. They are typically constructed of hard materials: cinder block, metal grid work, HVAC infrastructure, with heavily mechanical components, reinforced by the sound effects of footsteps echoing on metal or concrete floors. They are often bleak, militaristic, post apocalyptic or futuristic. Spaces are dimly lit and color palettes are dark and monochromatic.

Few women and girls are attracted to game spaces depicting disorder, terror, and violence. Nothing about *World of Warcraft* matched this description (with the exception of some dark lighting, and that was polychromatic).[12] On the contrary, varying palettes of tertiary colors, the sounds of water or frogs croaking, beautiful night skies, the use of curves and soft shapes, and snug inns, shops, and storefronts, constructed a visual experience congenial to most female players. Although *WoW*'s audio could be cacophonous during battle, it was also the case that in Karazhan harpsichord music was heard. Medieval tunes played in the cozy inns of the capital cities (where one could seat one's character before a roaring fire). Symphonic music in many parts of the game geography was reminiscent of the scoring of feature films, creating a cultured atmosphere—in contrast to the desolation of the games Fullerton et al. describe.

A favorite *WoW* activity was the acquisition of small cuddly pets such as piglets or baby elephants. Such pets would be unthinkable in masculinist games. Seasonal changes in *WoW* graphics included decidedly feminine elements: season-appropriate wreaths, candles, and garlands of flowers festooned the capital cities. Artistically, *WoW* was a long way from menacing footsteps echoing on a concrete floor.

A feminine element of domesticity suffused *WoW;* it was especially evident in the capital cities, which provided a *home.* After bruising battles, a player returned to the safety of, say, Ironforge or Orgrimmar to replenish supplies, auction off loot, bump into friends, watch duels, admire the rare mounts of lucky players. These spaces were the staging ground for seasonal decorations and activities such as the Lunar Festival (around the time of Chinese New Year), Halloween, Christmas, and the Midsummer Fire Festival. The capital cities were clean, orderly, and in perfect repair. They exuded stability and good governance. The masculinist spaces described by Fullerton et al. (2007) were, by contrast, always on the verge of chaos and destruction—hardly places in which to find the colorful decorations beautifying capital cities during holiday events in *World of Warcraft.*

WoW was populated by powerful male and female NPCs. Some of the biggest bosses were female. Corneliussen (2008) observed, "The relatively large number of female NPCs indicates a willingness by Blizzard to break with traditional ways of gendering computer game universes." Male and female characters deployed the same powers, delimited by class not gender. There were neither princesses to be rescued nor dashing male heroes saving the day. Despite *WoW*'s medieval accents, standard gendered fairy tale tropes were turned on their head. Princess Theradras, for example, was a wonderfully hideous, misshapen gal who put up a tough fight and whose desirable loot made her fun to kill—the opposite of a damsel in distress safe inside a tower awaiting her prince. The male Blood Elves, about as close as *WoW* got to handsome princes, were not the manly studs of fairy tales but amusingly effeminate boy-guys, animated by feminine gestures.[13]

In a popular Web comedy series, *The Guild,* produced by actress, writer, and gamer Felicia Day, the following dialogue (season 2, episode 10) dramatized the opening for female players created by *WoW*'s feminine elements. (The game in the series is a *WoW* knockoff, and the characters play together in a guild called The Knights of Good.)

Codex, the main character, is having a party at her apartment. She is infatuated with a neighbor, Wade. Wade shows up with a tall, self-confident girl, Riley, who makes Codex feel even more insecure than usual. (Codex and her friends refer to Riley as Stupid Tall Hot Girl.)

Riley: Wade said you were a gamer. That's bitchen! It's so hot to meet another girl who games. It's tight. What games do you play?

Codex: Uh, you know, role playing games mostly.

Riley: Oh (sneers). I'm an FPS girl. Halo, boom, headshots! I'm ranked and stuff.

Codex: Well, I kill stuff too, it's just I wear prettier outfits.

Codex references *WoW*'s feminine aspects through her invocation of "prettier outfits." She's been owned in the interaction by the competitive girl ranked in a masculine game but manages to point out that she "kills stuff too." Codex's comment exemplifies the truly disparate elements that come together in *World of Warcraft:* killing stuff and pretty outfits (as well as the other feminine elements they stand in for). The outfits Codex referred to were not male-fantasy kombat lingerie; *WoW* gear included, among many lovely designs, beautifully flowing robes for mages and priests and elegant pants and tunics for rogues and druids.

Game activities, especially crafting and gathering, were cross-gendered. Ducheneaut et al. (2006) reported that 30 to 40 percent of players' time was spent in formal groups, a reasonable proxy for competitive play. When

A *Halo* character

A *World of Warcraft*
Blood Elf

not in the formal grouping of a party, raid, arena, or battleground, and thus engaged in competition, players were busy in varied activities, including buying and selling at the Auction House, crafting gear, collecting materials, brewing potions, cooking, making bandages, fishing, and farming.

In ordinary life, many of these activities are associated primarily with one gender, such as cooking (female) or blacksmithing (male). In *WoW*, both genders engaged in them. It was notable to see grown men (or rather, their characters) sitting before virtual fires frying up fish or baking chocolate cake. Or to come upon the character of a female player smelting metal or heaving a mining pick. Male players tailored elaborate colorful robes for themselves while female players stood before forges pounding out swords. Cooking, sewing, and collecting herbs are traditionally feminine activities while engineering, blacksmithing, and mining are typically masculine. *WoW* offered players the chance to *play at* these gendered activities, allowing them to move back and forth across boundaries of male and female. Players chose activities because they made sense for the development of their characters, contributing to their performative abilities. This motivation obscured and downplayed, but did not remove, gender attributions (see also Corneliussen 2008).[14]

Just as male players got down with cooking and making jewelry, with picking flowers and working at handicrafts, so female players enjoyed the chance to be tough, to talk about, and engage in, killing and pwning. Taylor (2003b) reported of her *EverQuest* study participants:

> I have been struck by how often women remark on enjoying jumping into the fray of fights, taking on difficult monsters, and, as one user put it, "kicking ass."

I questioned a female rogue in Scarlet Raven, an older woman who called herself the "Guild Grandma":

> To Jacquii: how come you chose rogue?

> Jacquii whispers: don't like being so squishy and I lov being in the middle of the fight. and I can take shit down easy on rogue!

WoW subverted gender norms by offering activities with traditional gender connotations that were presented as simply things to do to improve your character, or merely to play, like Jacquii taking shit down. Players ran back and forth across invisible gender boundaries unselfconsciously engaging transgressive practice—not *qua* transgression, but in conformance with the logic of the game—to enhance performance. Corneliussen (2008) remarked, "Gender is present in *World of Warcraft* in many ways, but it is not necessarily insistent or obvious."

By contrast, masculinist shooter games such as *Quake* overtly reinforce hyperreal gender norms (Fullerton et al. 2007). Any female player is by definition a visible rebel. Kennedy (2005) studied female *Quake* players. One of her study participants said:

> Next time we played together over a LAN [local area network] connection I held up my end and I could see that the blokes were really surprised and even a bit fed up that I was "fragging" them so successfully . . . I LOVED IT! (Amanda/Xena)

Kennedy observed:

> These female players—who take pleasure in the mastery of the game which is seen as requiring skills which are clearly demarcated as masculine—are aware of the transgressive nature of their pleasure.

Amanda's character Xena developed "masculine" skills that she deliberately showed off in the public arena of LAN play. The skills were unambiguously perceived as masculine. In *WoW*, collecting herbs, cooking, and so on were not gender marked. Nor was killing things.

WoW players had no need to form opinions about gendered game activities or even think about them; they simply assumed the activities as being necessary to play. Within the game, the activities were an aspect of the gender-neutral performative activity of improving a character. The covertness of the gender inflections released players from obvious reflections on gender while allowing them to perform, in play, cross-gender activities. *WoW* was, then, quietly subversive in its gender dynamics, enabling the unremarked enactment of cross-gender activities as an aspect of character development.

Females nearly always chose female characters in *World of Warcraft* (Yee

2005; Kavetsky 2008). The reasons were unclear. Female players said they wanted a character who represented "who I am." They were vague in their answers while men gave simple, crisp responses to questions about character choice. Graner Ray (2004) received the same vague answers from female players she interviewed, e.g., "Playing a male character just doesn't feel right" (see also Taylor 2003a).

It seems, then, that *WoW* enabled males to get a kick out of cooking or picking flowers and, at the same time, to indulge in masculinist language far beyond that permissible in many everyday settings. Females reinscribed conventional female preoccupations in choosing female characters, but they simultaneously participated in a social order in which they could talk about killing and pwning and engage in over-the-top flirtation and sexualized talk.

These juxtapositions seem like contradictions. But play permits us to abandon acquiescence to a consistency demanded in everyday life. In play we move to a space in which we can be more than one thing, however opposed those things might be in the logics of ordinary existence. When inhabiting the magic circle, we thrust out in both directions, engaging, in exaggerated form, quotidian conventions, while at the same time crossing over to "forbidden areas of darkness."

The complexly gendered game space of *World of Warcraft* offered something out of the ordinary for both males and females. Given the huge popularity (and presumed profitability) of *World of Warcraft*, we can endorse the rightness of Fron et al.'s (2003a) argument:

> Far from being a commercial death knell to the video game industry, [designing beyond the standard male stereotypes] can actually serve to expand the game market to be more diverse, inclusive, and welcoming across a broader demographic range.

World of Warcraft—with its candles and flowers, its domestic coziness, provisions for safe flirtation, and topsy-turvy accountings of traditionally gendered folk tales—seemed to move toward a play space of the kind envisioned by Fullerton et al. (2007), a space "where everyone can feel included, inspired, enlivened, and entertained." Hayes (2005) observed that "games that combine elements associated with more stereotypically masculine and feminine pleasures and strengths may ultimately be the most stimulating and . . . valuable games." It seems that *WoW* has realized such a space, combining masculine and feminine elements in its design, appealing to women more than most competitive video games.

Why, then, aren't even more women playing *World of Warcraft?* While female gamers are visible and their presence should not be ignored (see Bryce and Rutter 2005; Taylor 2006), in *WoW,* they are still a minority.

I do not have a ready answer to this question and can only say that it requires more research. The answer is likely to be found in a tangle of gendered practices and ideations, including the fact that women feel they do not have enough time to devote to a game like *WoW.* Systematic research is essential for looking into this question, but in describing my research in casual conversations women often responded that they did not have time for such a game. Female disinterest in competitive gaming is also likely part of the story—an aspect of deep, little-understood cultural predicaments. The need to accommodate males' sexualized, homophobic rhetoric was surely a constraint for many females. In battlegrounds when (probably young male) players were typing vagina, pussy, and faggot into the chat window just because they could, I was reminded of Mrs. Pain's daughter.

We must also ask why women themselves have not created games that meet the requirements delineated by Fullerton et al. and Hayes (see also Flanagan and Nissenbaum 2007; and Flanagan et al. 2008). It is not up to men to do this for us. "Girl games," such as *Purple Moon,* essentialized stereotypical female elements. This strategy proved a failure, and "Today, there is no pink aisle at most local games stores," as Jenkins and Cassell (2008) pointed out.

Perhaps as women come to see themselves more boldly, as they acknowledge a need for fun and permit themselves the recreational time men take as a given, they will come to competitive gaming as Mrs. Pain did:

[14:03] Mrs. Pain: alot of the players I play with are guys
[14:03] Mrs. Pain: and are alot younger then me
[14:03] Mrs. Pain: but I have formed a friendship with them
[14:03] Dan: Do you think age matters in games?
[14:03] Mrs. Pain: NO
[14:04] Mrs. Pain: I think ppl who don't know me have a certain stereo type of me
[14:04] Mrs. Pain: they think A. I am not a woman

[14:04] Mrs. Pain: just pretending to be one

[14:04] Mrs. Pain: or B

[14:05] Mrs. Pain: Iam big, fat and ugly

[14:05] Mrs. Pain: it is impossible to think that a woman and mother could enjoy herself?

[14:05] Mrs. Pain: what once you hit a certain age the fun stops?

[14:06] Mrs. Pain: and you cant juggle your life to fit in games

[14:06] Mrs. Pain: once they get to know me

[14:06] Mrs. Pain: they love me

[14:06] Mrs. Pain: well most

[14:06] Mrs. Pain: lol

CHAPTER NINE

Culture: *WoW* in China . . . and North America

In an Internet cafe in Shanghai, a nurse, age 22, has just completed a boss kill. Other characters are nearby, some dancing, some running around. The nurse, who plays a warlock, auctions off the boss's loot to the raid members, counting down 4 3 2 1, before the final price is set and typed into the chat window. Those who won an auction pay her, and take receipt of their new armor, weapon, recipe, or pattern. Everyone in the raid receives a cut of the gold collected in the auction.

In North America, if one says "China" and "*World of Warcraft*" in the same sentence, the immediate free association is typically "Chinese gold farmer." I am puzzled by the fascination with Chinese gold farming—in our world of global capitalism, anyone can make money selling anything, so why not in a virtual game? The meme belies an inchoate sense of disturbance; far away, Chinese people have found a way to intrude into the North American economy by slipping into a virtual world (see Nakamura 2009).

The single biggest national group of *WoW* players was Chinese (Blizzard Press Release 2008). Chinese players were an overwhelmingly important market for Blizzard and a critical part of the global gaming community. Chinese people played *World of Warcraft* for the same reasons as North Americans or Europeans or Koreans, and they were employed elsewhere to make a living. There were gold farmers in China, but they were a tiny minority of players, as were their North American and European counterparts.

In the vignette, the player conducted what the Chinese called "gold raids." She was not raiding for real money but was directing a practice I did not observe in North America—running raids with auctions to raise game gold for individuals or guilds who needed it to purchase better equipment. Chinese players participating in gold raids were after high-end "purple" loot (loot was color coded) to empower their characters for raiding. One player explained:

> When I got to level 60, my equipment was not good. I participated in some gold raids for better equipment. At that time I was covered in greens [low-end gear] so it was certain the raid team in the guild would not accept me. I joined gold raiding activities and gradually gained the purple gear.

Gold raids allowed players with sufficient gold to acquire items they wanted without having to be lucky or raid a lot. Normally, a player would have to win the roll of the dice in a raid or accumulate points for raid participation using "DKP" (Dragon Kill Points) (see Thott n.d.). The Chinese used DKP, but came up with gold raids as an alternative, adding another solution to the ever-present problem of improving performance through better gear. With gold raids, a player merely needed to have gold, and the game offered many ways to earn gold without the rigors of regular raiding.

I went to China to try to understand something of the roughly half of all *World of Warcraft* players. With my research assistants, I talked to players in Internet cafes, dormitories, and apartments. We interviewed 40 people, 34 male and 6 female. Study participants included students, a factory worker, a middle school teacher, a bank employee, a marketing supervisor, a vice president of design for a Chinese game company, and a venture capital broker. The players we spoke to ranged in age from 18 to 37, although most were in their twenties.

Study participants were acquired through the social networks of the Chinese research assistants, and by requesting interviews in Internet cafes. When possible, we asked the cafe owner or manager if it was okay for us to interview. We were never refused and were always treated cordially. We approached players in the cafes and asked if they would have time for an interview. Most said yes. We sometimes sat beside study participants and watched them play, as we did with the nurse in the gold raid. In some cases we took study participants to dinner or to a nearby restaurant for soft drinks or a snack. Interviews were audiotaped. They were transcribed and translated by the native speakers on the team.

Playing games in an Internet cafe, Beijing, Summer 2007

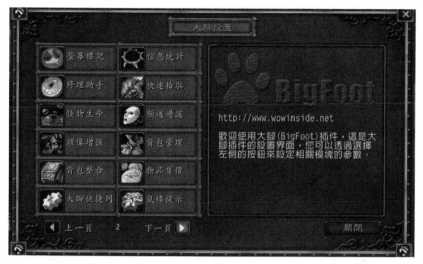

Bigfoot, one of two of the major mod compilation sites in China

My biggest finding in China was that, overall, Chinese players were remarkably like the North American players I studied. They liked the sociability of *WoW,* the competitive challenge, the graphics, the color. They extended the game through the use of mods. They played with friends and family.

The major difference in play between China and North America was the setting in which the game was often played—the *wang ba* or Internet cafe. In *wang ba,* players were surrounded by other players; it was a "mixed reality" of virtual and physical social interaction (Lindtner et al. 2008). *Wang ba* are the second most frequent site of computer usage in China after the workplace (CNNIC 2007), providing places to access digital technologies for millions of people. Internet cafes are popular not only in China but in Korea (Stewart and Choi 2003; Chee 2006; Rea 2009), Australia (Beavis et al. 2005), the United Kingdom (Wakeford 2003), Canada (Powell n.d.), and elsewhere.

In China, and wherever they are found, Internet cafes go a long way toward solving problems of the so-called digital divide; they offer quality computer hardware in accessible public spaces. Chinese players reported choosing *wang ba* either because they did not own personal computers or because they had low Internet bandwidth and/or low-end computer equip-

Close quarters in a dorm room in Beijing, Summer 2007

ment. *Wang ba* provided high-end equipment and bandwidth that made game play more enjoyable.[1]

Qiu and Liuning (2005) observed that Chinese players frequented Internet cafes not only because of the computer equipment but to meet friends and peers. We observed this social practice and also found that tight living spaces and family dynamics affected decisions about where to play. The rooms in student dormitories we visited were shared by four to eight people and could accommodate no more than a small desk and bed for each student, an area that was also used as a work space. Many young professionals in China live at home with their parents until they are married.

Small living spaces, as well as parental disapproval of game play, drew players to Internet cafes. A worker at a trading company in Shanghai explained why he played in an Internet cafe:

> First, my house is tiny and it affects my parents. Second, the computer hardware at home is not as good.

These findings are consistent with those of Thomas and Lang (2007) who reported that *wang ba* "have emerged as the place for urban Chinese youth to be youth, [and], as one of the few places young urban Chinese can escape the pressures of schooling, work, and their parents."

The social atmosphere of the *wang ba* was crucial to players' experience. A young business professional with good equipment at home explained that he nonetheless went to *wang ba* because:

> Home has no atmosphere.

Another player said:

> I enjoy playing at the café because there are more people, it's more exciting. Most of the guild activities are at night, so the people all show up late in the Internet café. I enjoy the atmosphere of people playing around me.

A bank employee said:

> Sometimes, when I come to play at the Internet cafe, I meet people here. So these people, I would get their QQ [Chinese instant messaging system] ID to stay in touch. People who sit next to you in the cafe or I know from real life, we are more inclined to keep in touch.

Guild members sometimes met face-to-face in *wang ba* to play together. One player told us that his whole guild had developed, and played together, in a cafe. Often guild members living in the same city knew each others' phone numbers and coordinated playtimes on the phone. Our first interview in China was with a group of five young men who had assembled in an Internet cafe to play *WoW* after work and were then planning to go to dinner together.

The interplay of the physical and the virtual was apparent when players sat next to each other engaging in both face-to-face and digital interaction. Chinese players moved between visual and social immersion online, and the social and physical context of the *wang ba*. Given the global prevalence of Internet cafes, it seems we are redefining, and reshaping, "virtual" experience into a hybrid, mixed reality of the virtual and the physical (see Crabtree and Rodden 2007; Lindtner et al. 2008).

The same dynamic was at play in North America and Europe in more limited settings. In student dormitories where LAN parties are held, and social networking software such as Facebook is utilized to organize dorm social life (Ellison et al. 2007; Lampe 2007), a merge of the physical and digital takes place. One of my first interviews for the *WoW* research took me to San Diego to visit three students who played together in their apartment. It was a shocking mess, with old pizza boxes strewn around, dirty clothes dumped in the most unlikely places, and serious grunge everywhere. Each student sat in his own room at his own computer, but they called out to one another and occasionally jumped up to go look at one another's screens.

In everyday social contexts, family members and friends may play together in the same physical space, talking and laughing while they play (Peterson 2007). So while the *wang ba* is a kind of public space not widely found in North America, some of its sociability is replicated in other settings.

Shared interest in a game provides a means by which people collaborate and socialize. In *wang ba,* players sat next to each other to talk and play:

> If there is an empty seat next to a *WoW* player I go over there to sit next to him—even though it is in a really crowded area. We look at each other's equipment and have a conversation about it. Sometimes we exchange seats with other people so that we [*WoW* players] can sit closer to each other. If I am playing by myself I am bored and leave the Internet café. The people here are nice, we play together, they all live around here. We know each other from playing the game.

Notions of "cyberspace" or "metaverse" situate activity solely within the virtual context, missing the more complex experience in which a merge of virtual and real occurs. In *wang ba,* players drew on face-to-face interaction in the physical space of the cafe, as well as the content of the virtual world of the game to shape experience.

Although the *wang ba* had a positive social energy, we observed a somewhat higher level of wariness on the part of Chinese players than was common in North America. Every economic transaction in and around the game contained within it the potential for abuse, a potential of which Chinese players were constantly aware. In particular, the system of payment for the game presented an opportunity for cheating that probably contributed to Chinese players' more common experience of being defrauded.

In North America, most players paid for *WoW* by credit card. In China, "point cards," which provided a certain number of hours of play, were used. Often players exchanged game gold for point cards. Sometimes the transaction went bad (in either direction). Having been cheated in a point card transaction was a common experience and came up in the interviews repeatedly. (Initially we did not know enough to ask about it; players themselves raised the topic in the open-ended interviews.)

Many players had had their characters stolen through keylogging or by other means. While North Americans also lost characters, it seemed more of a risk in China. A survey conducted by the China *WoW* Developers' Group reported that half of nearly 400 respondents had had their accounts stolen at least once (Kow and Nardi 2009). One Chinese modder facetiously remarked, "If you have not had your account stolen, you are not a real *WoW* player."

Gold raids sometimes became "black gold" raids in which a guild would recruit players from outside the guild to participate in the raid and then keep all the gold for itself. Promising to distribute the gold at the end of the raid, the raid leaders would instead immediately logoff, leaving the nonguild players empty-handed. Or an individual player would organize a pug and keep all the gold.

Chinese players fought these practices by using the General chat channel to broadcast the names of guilds and individuals who conducted black gold raids. They would also broadcast the names of players who had cheated them individually when selling point cards. After an incident in which he did not receive a point card he had paid for, one player explained:

> I reported in the General chat that the person is a liar and is ripping people off. Then he [the perpetrator] logged off. I added him to my Friends List so that I can see every time he comes online and I can tell other people he is not trustworthy.

This player went on to say that if you have had a character stolen you should "go online and warn other people." He suggested creating a low-level character for this purpose.

I never saw the General chat channel on North American servers used to report cheaters. But guild websites posted stories about players to avoid. For example, a player on the Scarlet Raven website alerted the guild about someone whose paladin character often organized pugs and rolled on gear he did not need. A second player responded to the post, saying that he had also had a bad experience with the miscreant:

> I will certainly agree/confirm all of this. I ran heroic SH [a dungeon] with him and several other instances in the past. He is an amazing pally tank, but a gigantic dick.

> He need rolled a piece of gear I wanted for my shaman and won, then sharded it and hearthed.

The paladin ninja-ed the shaman gear which he could not use except to transform to a shard (a component in enchantments). The gear the shaman wanted was a rare drop, not something he could hope to obtain without probably running the instance again many times. A shard, on the other hand, could be made from any piece of gear. After inappropriately taking the gear, the paladin disappeared, just as his Chinese counterparts had.

Chinese players went public in denouncing swindlers, while North Americans tended to warn guild members, suggesting the somewhat higher sense of alertness developed on the part of Chinese players.

Some players felt there was considerable cheating because of China's rapid transition to a new economy. One said:

> [There is more cheating in China] right now with the quality of life, definitely more than in Europe or America. This is going on in China because Chinese people find money very important because it's just becoming industrialized. It's a little more chaotic.

While North American players bought and sold *WoW* accounts on the Internet, and there were plenty of gold-selling and power-leveling services, there appeared to be more real money/game transactions in China or at least more kinds of such transactions. For example, one guild paid for its voice chat server with gold raised by the guild, which was then sold for RMB (Chinese currency). To economize, many players earned all their play by buying point cards with game gold. Point cards generally sold for 300 to 550 gold, although prices fluctuated and varied by server. One player said:

> I got a lot of gold with my hunter character. I used it to buy point cards. For example, 400 gold for a point card. I look at it as a free game, because I exchange game gold for point cards.

Another said:

> If you are clever, you can earn a point card one day in-game.

Just as *World of Warcraft* drew together and mingled real and in-game economies, it also became entangled in Chinese political realities:

> Horde have a race Undead. In the past it had only bones with no flesh. Now all Undead grow flesh on their bodies which is not good-looking.

Just before we arrived in China, the Chinese government declared that the Undead race, presented as skeletal creatures, would have to be redrawn with "flesh on their bodies," as the player noted. In addition to fleshing out the images of Undead, images of skeletons that remained after player death were replaced with large, apparently freshly dug graves heaped with brown dirt. The government action was part of an effort to "purify the Internet of anything that might affect national cultural information security or undermine the attempt to promote a harmonious society" (Dicki 2007; see also Golub and Lingley 2008).

Skeletons have no particular traditional meaning in Chinese culture, and pictures of them did not violate cultural sensibilities (although it would be disrespectful to fail to attend to the remains of a parent or close relative). The prominent graves were far more realistic and noticeable. A player who was an employee at a consulting firm said:

> I am not quite clear about the reason [for the action]. Perhaps it is China's political situation. In the past when you died [in the game] there were bones and skeletons, but now graves are used instead. What we were told is that the skeletons frustrate and scare people. But I feel graves are actually scarier.

The government's action appeared to be a reminder that its censors were monitoring the game and could alter game design to conform to a value pervasively promoted by the Chinese government: "harmony." One player explained:

> It's a grave, which didn't exist before. Before . . . there used to be a skeleton. It . . . is part of the government project to introduce harmony.

Another player was more critical:

> We dislike the harmony such as the disappearance of skeletons . . . It is feudal and introduced as part of the whole cultural environment in China.

It is perhaps alarming that a government would intrude into a video game to change something as innocuous to Western eyes as a skeleton. But video games seem to attract the attention of moral arbiters. Bainbridge and Bainbridge (2007) analyzed the video game monitoring activities of fundamentalist Christian organizations in the United States. Such groups cannot force Blizzard to redraw game graphics, but their critical gaze and directives to their adherents share some similarities with the Chinese government's attempts to shape game content to reflect cultural ideations such as harmony.

Bainbridge and Bainbridge (2007) reported that a website called Christian Answers evaluated video games according to a quantitative scheme. Games were rated on a scale of 1 (worst) to 5 (best) in the following way:

> Christian Rating ("Is the game anti-Christian and immoral in any way?"), Violence ("Is it violent? Does it encourage violent behavior?"), Adult Content ("Sexual encounters, nudity, or suggestive or sexually immoral material?"), and Game Play ("Is the game fun to play? High quality?")

Apart from the dubiousness of scoring games with such quantitative scales (how many body parts need appear to get the dreaded score of 1 for Adult Content?), Bainbridge and Bainbridge observed that the ratings appeared in reviews whose texts criticized games for positively valuing non-Christian traditions and which attempted to create fear around themes such as "witchcraft" and "sorcery." They reported the following reviews, which give a sense of the logics and rhetoric Christian critics employed to discourage adherents from playing video games.

For example, witchcraft raised red flags for Christian reviewers:

> Perhaps reminded of Exodus 22:18, "Thou shalt not suffer a witch to live," reviewers are offended by thirty-eight games involving magic and witchcraft. Even the popular Pokémon games for young children, in which the player trains cute little animals, come in for criticism: "To gain the competitive edge, a trainer must use magic potions to heal and strengthen his Pokémon, and wear magic badges to control the stronger Pokémon. In addition, the really powerful Pokémon have psychic powers and can throw curses. This bears disturbing similarities to witchcraft."

Reincarnation was also feared. One reviewer wrote sadly that:

> In *Final Fantasy VII,* instead of actually dying, characters in this world diffuse into the planet—into the "Lifestream," where their consciousness lives on.

The suspicion with which games were viewed by those who found their appeal threatening was expressed in different institutions in China and North America, but the disapproving gaze transcended national boundaries. The activity of watching and judging was sustained in China by government officials and in North America by functionaries of conservative religious traditions. Around 40 percent of Americans identify as born-again Christians (Barna Group 2008); Christian monitoring of games is a culturally significant activity.

Players themselves may gaze with disapproval at the practices of other players. In China, many male players avoided playing female characters. They feared being called "ladyboy"—a term that connotes transvestite or transsexual. One player said:

> I hate such ladyboy characters.

Another said he always played males. We asked why.

I don't know. I just dislike turning into a ladyboy. Although the game is a virtual one, a boy is supposed to be a boy and a girl is supposed to be a girl ...Before this game, I played a Chinese game in which boys and girls could get married. If the two are both boys, I would feel disgusted.

Players repeated this theme:

Dai: My characters are all male. If I picked a female character, they would call me a ladyboy.

Guang: If you are a boy but you play a female character, others will call you ladyboy. I don't want to be called that.

Jian: It's strange to play a female. I do not like the way people look at you if you play a female character. I don't like people mistaking me for a female.

Quan: I don't like the way it feels to play a female character. It doesn't feel comfortable. I don't like the way other players look at me and talk to me then.

One male player began with a female character because he liked the way it looked. But he soon gave up:

When I was first developing my character, the female one, it was always really troublesome to explain that I am a guy in real life. The male is more natural.

A female player who played a female character said:

Sometimes people mistake me for a man and they call me ladyboy. But I don't care.

Despite the disapproval of ladyboys, some Chinese males did choose and enjoy female characters because the female characters were "prettier."
    One male player said:

Sometimes I choose a female character, if it looks pretty.

He favored Night Elves.

Another player agreed:

> The female Elf is the most beautiful.

Another said:

> I never played a female character before. I wanted to see it. The movement is prettier.

We asked male players who played females if they sought a new kind of experience or identity. They answered as American males had.

> BN: Is playing a female also a kind of experience change?

> Chen: No, it is not. I am a male myself and it is not interesting if there is a male in front of me and I have to face him every day. If your character is a female, it will be more pleasing to both the eye and the mind.

Another player said that playing a female was not a problem for him because it was obvious in chat that he was male:

> BN: Do people approach you differently because you are a female character?

> Bao: No. They usually can figure it out by the way you chat.

Another said:

> If I play a female character, I would say that I am a guy. If they ask me, I tell them.

As in North America, there appeared to be no effort to engage in gender-bending in the sense of males presenting as females. Playing a female character was simply a positive visual experience for males willing to risk being called ladyboy.

While gender-bending was no more a part of the Chinese than the North American *WoW* experience, I sensed a more sober ethos among Chinese than among North Americans. In China, ladyboys were met with moral disapproval. North American chat was full of sexual fun up to and including sexual predation. For example:

> [14:32] Mrs. Pain: I do know we have fun with the new players
> [14:32] Mrs. Pain: that dont want to believe I am a woman
> [14:33] Mrs. Pain: one of the guys I have known for awhile
> [14:33] Mrs. Pain: tells them I am a sexual prediditor
> [14:33] Mrs. Pain: looking for young boys
> [14:33] Mrs. Pain: lol
> [14:33] Dan: lol
> [14:33] Mrs. Pain: and I am a man
> [14:33] Mrs. Pain: and dont believe me
> [14:33] Mrs. Pain: lol
> [14:34] Mrs. Pain: and chippie [a player] tells new ppl we are lizbian lovers

Understanding cross-cultural differences in expressions in sexually themed chat requires much more research, although it seems that discourse such as Mrs. Pain's, invoking homosexuality as a joke, would have been unlikely in China.

It is difficult to know the percentage of female *WoW* players in China. In a large Internet cafe in Beijing, we did a count. About 10 percent were female (6 out of 57). While there are undoubtedly many reasons for such a low rate of female participation, we were told that female players were less skilled at *WoW* and in particular they were poor at PvP play.

Why Chinese female players were less skilled at PvP play is a complex cultural question.

Wenjing Liang, one of my research assistants, suggested that traditional gender roles are still strong in China and displays of strength and competition are not traditionally feminine. In her words:

> In Chinese traditional morality and culture, males are supposed to be active and be breadwinners, while females are supposed to be quiet and live at home. Additionally, females are more sensitive to feelings and

emotions, and they like activities such as watching movies, chatting, and shopping.

There was a marked preference for PvP among the players we talked to. Since most players appeared to be playing on PvP servers, it seems possible that *WoW* in China has been established as a masculine space in part because of its association with PvP, the more competitive, masculine form of the game. We counted the local servers available in Beijing (servers were divided regionally in China). There were 127 PvP servers and 20 PvE. We were only able to find one player on a PvE server out of the 40 we interviewed (he was visiting Beijing from Inner Mongolia). In North America, about half the servers were PvP. I have no data on whether women tended to choose them less often; further research is needed on this question.

It should be noted that there were many women in Chinese Internet cafes; the cafes themselves were not masculine spaces. Women were watching movies or instant messaging or engaged in other digital activities.

In addition to the vastly larger number of PvP servers, PvP was marked linguistically in China, referred to with the English "PK" or "player kill."[2] Players reported that they enjoyed PK because of its performative challenge and interest. PvE was "boring," a word used repeatedly in the interviews.

A male player remarked:

I think playing against computer characters is far less interesting than playing with the human brain. The competition between living players attracts me.

Another said:

One of the unique things about this game is that you can do PK, you can fight against somebody else.

Both male and female players told us that females were less skilled at PK and did not enjoy it. Qing, Mei, and Luli were female players:

Qing: In general girls don't like PK.

Mei: For girls playing PK, it is easy for them to lose a fight and be killed because the skills of girls are really not good. My PK abilities are weak and I lose often.

Luli: Girls seldom PK with each other.

Male players in China also posited female players' generally lower level of skill at the game as a whole. A 25-year-old software engineer said:

There are some complicated controls in *WoW* so girls don't play as often.

Another said:

You can tell the difference between a male and female player by their play-ing style. There are probably about 10 percent that are women. Being a woman in the game, they are getting taken advantage of, because they are weaker.

A male player said, rather dubiously, of his girlfriend who played:

For female players, it is certain she is a good player, compared with other girls.

In China, the prevalence of PvP play, and its association with mascu-linity (akin to the masculinity of first-person shooter games reported by Kennedy, as well as Codex and Stupid Tall Hot Girl), seemed to render *WoW* less desirable to female players. Female players themselves agreed that they were less skilled at PK, and they declared less interest in it. Males felt that PvE was boring; their choice of PK was not intended to exclude women, although it may have had that effect. In North America, the greater pres-ence of PvE servers possibly creates an opening for women since it appears that many women start playing *WoW* with a boyfriend, husband, or other family member. If more men begin to play in spaces more comfortable for women, women may be more likely to participate. This empirical question requires further data and analysis.

Of course it is not only women who come to *WoW* through members of their personal social networks. Men do, too. In China, the social experi-ence of play seemed even more important than in North America for many players. Thomas and Lang (2007) remarked on the unique role of *wang ba* in China, observing that the Internet cafe is one of the only places to "escape" parents and the rigors of the Chinese educational system. There seemed to be fewer opportunities for young people to socialize outside of school and home. In North America, starting in elementary school, myriad venues support such social life: sports associations and clubs (such as AYSO soccer or swim teams), church groups, after-school clubs, and even garage bands (which require garages, something absent in China). A Chinese player observed with approval that *WoW* was engineered to require collaboration:

> The game requires collaboration, so we might say, why don't we go out to play together?

Another Chinese player noted that without collaboration the game cannot be played as successfully:[3]

> In *WoW*, people who don't fit in with a group cannot get good equipment easily.

Several noted that collaboration and the competition of PK went together:

> Chen: After I played *WoW* for awhile, I realized it's more meaningful than other games because of the collaboration. Even PK requires collaboration.

> Liu: I like the team cooperation in battlegrounds.

> Feng: I can play with other players. Anything can happen in the game. The Alliance might come in and attack you. It's exciting. I like the fact that you fight against real people and not the computer. Everyone controls his own character. You compete with each other.

A player who enjoyed raiding observed:

> When raiding, there are so many people doing something together, which is very enjoyable.

One player compared Chinese games to *WoW:*

> Individual heroism is more common in Chinese online games than in *WoW.* Many Chinese games focus more on the fighting between players. In *WoW,* players play together in raids and can fight against the monsters together.

Several players emphasized the team aspect of guilds, e.g.:

> When joining a guild, you are not a single person but a team.

WoW enlivened out-of-game social life as well. One player said that he and his colleagues from work played together in the evening and that during the day at work, "We always have something to talk about." A player in Shanghai reported:

> One of the people from the guild came to Shanghai recently. We all went out to dinner together and hosted him.

The sociability of *World of Warcraft* amplified the sociability of the *wang ba,* extending and reshaping it. Players shared not just the congenial social atmosphere of the cafe but an engaging virtual space that formed the basis of lively conversations and absorbing joint activity.

Game Design and Cultural Borders

The popularity of a game designed in Southern California in a country like China, with its radically different history and culture, foregrounds the question of the power of a software artifact to organize human activity. In fundamental ways, *WoW* is *WoW* wherever it is. Were it not for language barriers, any *WoW* player could sit down and play on any server anywhere in the world. There appears to be a common core of participatory aesthetic experience that transcends national and cultural borders. The broad themes of performance, competition, visual immersion, and sociability that emerged in North America were also evident in China.

The appealing aesthetic experience of game play excited similar concerns in both cultures on the part of authorities who attempted to impose

Any *WoW* player would recognize this scene and the player controls. Screenshot taken in an Internet cafe, Beijing, Summer 2007.

disciplines to register their disapproval. Whether invoking "harmony" in China or "Christian values" in North America, the response of authoritarian elements in both societies was to intrude a watchful eye into the game space, to create a presence in order to continually make visible and reinforce certain cultural values.

The similarities in player and societal responses to *World of Warcraft* reposition exotic activities like Chinese gold farming as less remarkable than the qualities of an artifact capable of producing aesthetic experience that is cross-culturally "absorbing," "compelling," or "pleasurable," in the words of our play theorists. The similarities suggest new questions: Just how far can *WoW* stretch: to what cultures and across which boundaries? And why is *WoW* relatively weaker at crossing gender boundaries in both China and North America? Are there historical causes or is there something fundamentally masculine about the kind of visual-performative medium *WoW* is? And what is it about video games that attracts the attention of conservative cultural authorities?

At the same time that we examine cross-cultural similarities in *WoW* play, we should be alert to variable cultural inflections in player experience. Such variability indicates that assumptions about virtual worlds as sites of gender-bending and flexible identities must be scrutinized with careful empirical data. There is no North American analog to the ladyboy meme in Chinese *WoW* play, with its tendency to suppress males playing female characters however much they would like to look at them. Chinese in-game economic innovations such as gold raids (and their degenerate form, black gold raids) demonstrate differential local cultural solutions to certain universal problems of the game. The Chinese "town crier" practice of denouncing unethical players in the General chat channel suggests the more pervasive fear of being cheated in China compared to North American practice, which located such matters as internal to guilds. The overwhelming choice for PvP play on the Chinese servers we examined was striking, possibly impacting female participation in *World of Warcraft* and linking to complex themes of competition, masculinity, and femininity.

In an article in *Science*, Bainbridge (2007) observed:

> The present moment marks a major historical transition. Video games and computer games are in the process of evolving into something much richer, namely virtual worlds, at the same time that electronic games are surpassing the motion picture industry in dollar terms and beginning to cut into television.

WoW, and other social games, are emerging as global artifacts that appear to sustain, in vastly different cultural contexts, alternatives to, or displacements of, traditional media. The narcotized populace passively immersed in a spectacle of images seems to have given way, in part at least, to activity in digital worlds that create their own playful problems to be solved with cultural imaginings such as gold raids and Dragon Kill Point systems. That people behave badly in virtual game worlds, requiring player-developed social controls, is perhaps nothing more than an indication of the worlds' status as, and footing in, real human social activity—both East and West.

Coda

"Are you still studying *World of Warcraft*?" one of my colleagues at a conference questioned me rather sharply. He was not an anthropologist (who would not ask such a question, at least not in that tone), and his query reminded me of anthropology's commitment to the long haul, and of my allegiance to activity theory and Dewey's work grounded, as they are, in a belief in the fullness of time. Taking the long view has informed much of what I have written about *WoW* in this book: examining players' own commitments to staying with the game to improve their characters; the development of activities like theorycrafting and modding that, over time, moved players into new relations with the game; understanding actions such as interpretation and construction in the context of larger moments of activity; seeing *WoW*'s Skinnerian rewards as thrilling in their own right but also aspects of a player's bigger plans to move ahead in the game; investigating trajectories of "addiction" in which players reflexively shifted their activities, informed in part by community response to their predicaments; and considering national cultures and gender as they intersected the game at this particular time in history.

Part of my wholly unexpected enthusiasm for *World of Warcraft* arose from long-standing frustration with the passivity encouraged by our society, from television to high culture. I enjoy both but feel they are not "attributed their right proportion" to use Kallinkos's phrase. Video games, at least good ones, engage and stimulate visual, cognitive, and social capacities. The visual-performative medium captures, in cheap commodity form, some of the satisfactions of exciting real life activities such as Burning Man or ballroom dancing—activities that require resources of time, money, and access to engage. Many of the babysitting parents, soldiers, soldiers' wives, students with little money, and chronically ill whom I met in-game were ace players; they had mastered a difficult game and worked it into lives which would not, at least in the immediate future, accommodate similarly engaging real life activities.

I see *World of Warcraft* as a work of art. Can a medium be an artistic production? I think it can, and that is just what Dewey was arguing with respect to "active aesthetic experience." Dewey spoke against the cordoning of art in cultural fortresses, a protocol requiring people to trudge, periodically, to museums, to pay homage in respectful, passive silence, to art such as paintings hanging on walls. While it is true that the black box may sometimes seal off game designs that can be altered only slightly more than famous paintings, the defining difference between the orderings of a museum and a video game is the game's production of active, performative experience. The beautifully arranged pixels on my *World of Warcraft* screen served as a backdrop for *my* activity. The pixels demanded no obeisance; they were, on the contrary, there to showcase me. The artwork in *WoW* exuded a touching humility; even in the far corners of the geography where play activity was light, the designs were often superb. I sometimes went fishing in the outermost areas of the Borean Tundra in part to see wonderfully rendered Viking boats plying their way to harbor. The boats were not only well drawn, but animated with a swiftness and distinctive movement that provided visual delight.

The rules in the black box are sometimes viewed as inducing quasi-fascistic dominance for which appropriate response is celebration of those who act in defiance of their power, or of those who move on the margins to smooth the dislocations that rules inevitably generate. While not denying the importance of the rebels hacking round the rules, and the game masters and guild leaders striving to assuage player dissatisfaction, these participants have submitted, in a sense, to the game and its rules, which orient their activity. The legitimacy of the rules is endorsed through the very engagement of these actors even as they probe for ways to exploit weaknesses or labor to relieve disappointments.

The supremacy of rules can be a good thing. Digital rules, in the context of excellent design, nurture us by providing reliable experience preserved through mechanical encapsulation and execution. Changes in rules must be handled carefully; we are still working through issues of governance and management of virtual worlds, finding ways to incorporate the many, varied voices of participants, as well as the corporate interests that bring us the worlds in the first place.

At the same time that digital rules powerfully direct and orient experience, there is significant participant contribution to experience in virtual worlds. In *World of Warcraft*, this contribution was particularly apparent in gender relations. The game itself was surprisingly feminist, but player culture masculinist. There was something really good for female players with the pretty outfits and baby pets and exquisite color palettes, but from the point of view of actual play activity, I would not call *WoW* "a playground for feminism" as Corneliussen (2008) did. There was far too much talk of rape and reference to players as fags and homos for that.[1]

At the same time, the focal concern with performance in *World of Warcraft* meant that female players had opportunities to unambiguously display mastery on a level playing field (see Wine 2008). Without the intrusion of the physical body suggesting a logic of segregation as in sports, video games offer opportunities for gender-neutral skilled play. Such play was not always the outcome, but there were many, many fine moments in *World of Warcraft* when it was.

Games are cultural entities, but they do not come to life until actually played. Games are things with formal rules and spaces; game play is the activity of playing. The two are different, and we must be aware of the subjective dispositions of those playing which determine whether a set of actions—even actions involving a cultural construct we define as a game— is play or not-play. Thus I developed a somewhat complicated notion of game play incorporating the work of several theorists that emphasized subjective disposition toward gaming activity as critical to understanding what it means to play a game.

Of course we are not searching for categorical purity (a sterile exercise bound to end in failure). Some game play, such as gambling in Crete (Malaby 2003) or cockfighting in Bali (Geertz 1977), seems playful in varying degrees; according to Malaby and Geertz, the displays of masculinity entangled in these activities drew on deep anxieties, and the need to constantly reassert masculine identity verged on a kind of social obligation. But the research also identified the deep pleasures of gambling and cockfighting, and these activities remind us that no activity is always manifest in its purest form. Analytical categories are intended to slice into the chaos of something as complex as game play, not to suggest that activity can be pristinely realized in each instance.

Encountering *World of Warcraft* caused me to reexamine cultural categories of work and play. From my earliest *WoW* research, I saw that they were extremely salient categories for players. Nonetheless, the concepts are slippery. Is farming for six hours to obtain one set of gear really play? When you look closely, work and play are troublesome concepts; proposals to abandon them as analytical categories are tempting. But I think it useful to have ways to distinguish between, on the one hand, Ito's amateur anime producers, Steinkuehler's overachieving druids, eggheaded *WoW* theory-crafters, and players staying up late with their guild to finish off a difficult boss—and most of what we do in school and at work. School and work need not be activities we would rather just get through without performing the actions if we could—but they are. Most of the time. In explaining resistance to the adoption of gamelike environments at work (such as *Second Life*) one study participant said:

> And some of the resistance is the fear that it looks like a game and therefore people are scared that it looks like they are messing around . . . You should have boring flat text and a spreadsheet in front of you, otherwise it's not work. They view work as a task placed in front of them—usually an onerous one. And usually in text or with some numbers. And anything else is obviously playing and playing is bad because it's not work.

Work is boring partly because we design it that way out of a belief that it *should* be boring.

Although the theories of Huizinga, Callois, and Dewey are from the last century (and Tom's fence two centuries ago), their thoughtful understandings continue to inform us of why players happily do "homework" and "research" on *World of Warcraft* but describe work and school as boring and soul crushing. The actions required do not satisfy in themselves, nor do they end in moments of limited perfection. Perhaps it is a dream to suggest that they might, but the research of education theorists studying games, as well as pioneers such as Bainbridge, who holds conferences in *World of Warcraft* (see Bohannon 2008) and *Second Life,* indicate that we are not yet finished defining what work and school might be.

There is much more to say about *World of Warcraft*—about guild politics, player forums, identity formation, hax and exploits, twinks, surveillance, game lingo, learning to play, knowledge management, *WoW* trading cards, and dozens of other *WoW*-related subjects. But as Borges's cartographers learned, the perfect map is perfectly useless. Lest "succeeding generations come to judge a map of such magnitude cumbersome, and . . . abandon it to the rigors of sun and rain," my labor draws to a close. I inscribe a few more marks, small moments of the research about which I felt "absurdly pleased," to borrow a phrase from one of Tolkien's creatures:

> [14:07] Dan: What do you like about the games you play, you already said you like making friends and what else?
> [14:07] Mrs. Pain: hmmm
> [14:08] Mrs. Pain: and its not just about making friends cause I do have a very busy social life and many friends
> [14:08] Mrs. Pain: I think its kinda an excape
> [14:08] Mrs. Pain: escape
> [14:09] Dan: escape from what?
> [14:09] Mrs. Pain: time to relax and have fun
> [14:09] Mrs. Pain: from the kids
> [14:09] Mrs. Pain: my busy life
> [14:09] Dan: So kind of like a stress release?
> [14:09] Mrs. Pain: I actually game unstead of watching tv
> [14:09] Mrs. Pain: ya
> [14:09] Mrs. Pain: away to get away and have fun with some friends
> [14:09] Mrs. Pain: but I am still home for my kids
> [14:10] Mrs. Pain: and I am in the same room with my husband who is a gamer

Multiplayer video games have pushed "cyberspace," "hyperreality," "virtuality," the "metaverse," and "life on the screen" smack back into real life, generating hybrid physical-digital spaces of visual-performative activity. This blend is most obvious in the Internet cafes of China and elsewhere, but also present in dorms and homes in North America and Europe. Mrs. Pain explained the lure of the virtual in its manifestations as "fun" and "escape" while observing that she was "still home for my kids" and "in the same room with my husband." For her, games supplanted television, another mode of escape, enabling an active engagement with friends and spouse. Dewey hoped that aesthetic experience would permeate ordinary life. Mrs. Pain's gaming is perhaps an exemplar of the kind of active aesthetic experience situated in an everyday environment that Dewey spoke for.

A young female warlock who regularly topped the damage charts in battlegrounds wrote of a possible future for video games. She produced the following abstract for a paper for her MBA program (Ly 2008):

> The popular massively multiplayer online role-playing game (MMORPG), World of Warcraft, is used as a tool to discuss new developments concerning computers in human behavior. MMORPGs are relatively a new breed of computer games. Some critics may be skeptical of how computer games relate to real-life situations in business and work environments. However, this paper demonstrates that by examining MMORPGs, insightful considerations can be revealed involving computers in human behavior in the following two areas: 1) how virtual scenarios can be applicable as the best kind of job training for managers and employees and 2) how human behavior and interaction can be studied through MMORPGs. World of Warcraft incorporates aspects that exist in the realities of business and work environments. These aspects include hierarchical organizational structures, the specific duties each player is expected to perform, the management of teams to accomplish common goals, and the development of interpersonal skills as well as relationships.

A generation schooled in navigating the social hierarchies of guilds, meeting the challenges of pulling remote players together for coordinated teamwork, taking seriously the need for individual competence, and learning to make friends in cyberspace is positioning itself for a world in which work becomes increasingly global, travel is restricted by the disappearance of fossil fuels, and people are happy to have a good-looking avatar stand in for them in colorful virtual spaces more stimulating than the visually dead cubicles of many corporate work spaces.

And from China:

> Chen: I learned several things about the West. *WoW* has a Western story, which is different from Eastern stories and history . . . The game belongs to the whole Western culture. Mages, druids, and so on originate from

Western myths, and are relevant to the whole Western myth of the story. Some *WoW* races like gnomes, dwarves, and elves, and also dragons, are described in European myths.

BN: Doesn't China have dragons?

Chen: Dragons are different with us. Western dragons are evil while Chinese dragons stand for happiness.

Games are venues for unselfconscious cross-cultural encounters afforded by software artifacts that embody but at the same time transcend culture. Just as Chen found interest in encountering European dragons and the novelty of gnomes and dwarves, so may we in the West delight in knowing of happy Chinese dragons. They may come to us as future commodities in video games, just as mythological creatures of the West have made their way to China through *World of Warcraft*.

Language travels in games, too. Rea taught children English in Korea in 2006–7. He reported the appearance of an English gaming term in *Sudden Attack*, a first-person shooter produced by GameHi, a Korean entertainment company, and its subsequent deployment in quite a different context (Rea 2009):

[I was] surprised . . . when one of my third-grade students yelled "fire in the hole!" before launching a ball of paper across the room at one of his classmates, mimicking the tossing of a grenade in *Sudden Attack*.

Finally there is the need to remember the sharp edge of play against ordinary life—its improbability, even absurdity. Much academic scholarship on play is so serious, so removed from the lightness of play, as to render the phenomenon under study nearly unrecognizable. When reading learned treatises that treat multiplayer video games as objects of study (such as this one), it is good to keep in mind that no matter how much we analyze games as spaces in which to create new work relations, as possible platforms for education, or as encounters with other cultures, contemporary multiplayer video games captivate because they are the site of a great deal of good old-fashioned frolic and tomfoolery.

Such as the following.

My son Anthony, his fiancée Jackie, and some of their friends started playing *World of Warcraft*. My son emailed me:

> Jackie was jealous that our friend Duke's character Kwimbae has more gold than our elves (Kurhah and Zaurak), so she sent him this message via WoW mail . . .

> Dear good sir

> I am Princess Wanamoni, the only daugther of the late King Itake Yomoni of Ashenvale. My father was poisoned to death by a rival Horde prince while on a business outing in Orgrimmar. My father thought Me so special took good care, but now I have no one and no money. Please Help me good sir send 50 Gold to my associate, Kurhah. she will invest the money in a special account in stormwind and you will receive 1063%.

Such silliness is delightful, original, and productive of what Dewey called "remaking the material of experience."

Let me end with the lunacy of playing *WoW*, its comfortable, goofy, intimate, jokey, unserious, informal surface. An early morning exchange, as I logged my priest for a moment before work, made me smile. I was greeted by Gilarye, a young player who had me on his friends list:

> Gilarye whispers: help! i'm dieing

> To Gilarye: hey gil

> Gilarye whispers: come save me!

> To Gilarye: i'm just on for a sec camping a vendor

> Gilarye whispers: *gasp*

> Gilarye whispers: *slap* yr mean!

> To Gilarye: laters gil, have a good day :D

Notes

Chapter One

1. *WoW* had 70 levels of play during the period of research reported here. To avoid confusion for those who do not play and might talk to others who do, I mention that there are 80 levels of play, the state of the game at the time of writing.

2. See Damer 2009 for an account of the coinage of the term *virtual world*.

3. Copy for an online ad for the first-person shooter *Combat Arms* read, "Head shots are tough, but nut shots are harder." The ad included an animated visual.

4. If you look closely, you may find a few small, cartoony blood drips but very few. The comparison here is to games in which such elements are an important part of the gut-level visual stimulation of the game. *WoW* has plenty of weapons, including guns; I don't find them scary, although it could be argued that some of the larger ones are quite noticeable. Often weapons are "enchanted," lending them sparkles or glows, diminishing realism, and rendering them visually benign. Imagine a machine gun in a first-person shooter with colorful sparkles!

Chapter Four

1. I discuss raiding quite a lot because I was in a raiding guild and I found it fascinating. But player forums were replete with discussions of how to handle performative challenges in all *WoW* contexts, including soloing. For example, the following is a portion of a lengthy post on thottbot.com explaining how to solo the quest Stranglethorn Fever. It indicates the precision with which players analyzed (and wrote about) performance:

> After several failed attempts, I managed to complete this quest solo as a level 48 hunter. It was not easy, but I'll share some tips that I have learned (the hard way . . .). I went with my wolf pet. His dps is a bit less than an offense-centric pet, but he seems

to hold focus better, as bite only fires once every 10 seconds. This seems to give him more focus available for the all-vital growl. He has a few more HP and AC than my cat, so I thought that he might hold up a bit better on this quest.

First, and perhaps key to the quest, is that you HAVE to keep the witch doctor alive and chanting through TWO waves of gorillas. It is on the third wave that Mokk spawns. There is a named gorilla in the second wave, but the heart is dropped on the third phase. You do NOT need an alive-and-well witchdoctor after Mokk spawns. All you need to do is loot the heart for the completion of the quest.

The first wave wasn't too bad. They spawn outside the cave and come rushing in. I put my pet on them as soon as they appeared, trying to make sure he pulled as much aggro as possible. I kept assisting him until he needed to be healed. That, of course, produced some aggro on to me which was handled via feign death. I managed to clear the first wave with a healthy pet, but almost no mana remaining . . .

This page, with detailed screenshots and player commentary, repays study. It can be found at http://thottbot.com/?qu=348.

2. An analysis of arena play would be very interesting. Arena was pure performance. In short matches players fought in teams of two, three, or five. Most players did not do arenas (which required collecting yet another set of gear and were extremely challenging), but those that did enjoyed high-voltage competition. I played arenas for a while (pretty casually) until my arena partner left the game.

3. There were metrics galore in *WoW*. In battlegrounds where players engaged in games such as capture the flag, a table that players could access any time during a match showed how much damage and healing each player contributed, as well as who accomplished key game actions such as capturing a base or flag. Similar metrics were available after arena matches.

4. *World of Warcraft* included timed contests. In one, a mob named Patchwerk had to be defeated in less than three minutes. In my post–Scarlet Raven guild, we were sure we had brought Patches down in under three minutes but did not get the award. We petitioned a game master who said we were .001 second away. In some contexts, it conceivably would not matter that we had missed by a hair's breadth, but the rule was reliably followed by the software and we did not get the award. I wondered if the GM actually had this data; no matter what, the system had followed its own clock and rules.

5. There were other mechanisms for feedback, such as the public test realms, and data collected by game masters in response to player questions, comments, and problems. I expect Blizzard also data mined key websites, used focus groups, and so on. The point is that Blizzard developed mechanisms for soliciting player opinion.

6. Of course not all players were happy with all changes. The game grew slowly easier in many ways, to the dismay of some who had been playing a long time and preferred more challenge. For example, the Stranglethorn Fever quest was "nerfed"; it no longer

required the efforts described by the hunter. One player commented on the thottbot webpage with the hunter's post, "As stated, this quest is a joke now. Bliz has made it so easy for the people leveling up nowadays compared to us old schoolers."

7. An enterprise resource planning system is a organizationwide software system that coordinates all the organization's information and resources.

8. I have direct experience of mangles. My mother had one—the mechanical kind—with which she ironed our sheets and pillowcases. The linens were utterly flat after the stress of the rollers passing over the fibers. In metaphorical usage, this flatness disturbs me; it smooths away important prominences to which we should attend.

9. Fron et al. (2007b) and Jordan (2007) made the same argument about the flexibilities of board games. I personally remember deciding only how to deal with Free Parking in Monopoly and then slavishly playing for hours exactly as the game was designed. Although I didn't like board games, I played a lot of them with my friends and siblings. I do not recall changing the rules of checkers, Chinese checkers, the Game of Life, Candyland (yes I played it!), Risk, or card games such as poker, euchre, hearts, war, Tripoli, gin rummy, or other games we played. (I liked card games.)

10. Scarlet Raven did not use a point system (alternating between dice rolls and Suicide Kings), but the guild I joined afterward used DKP, and my experiences of DKP were from that guild.

11. I do not mean cheating the system through clever maneuvers (see Consalvo 2007) but cheating fellow players. *WoW* made no effort to prevent such cheating with respect to the loot scenarios I describe.

12. *WoW* contained several loot distribution mechanisms; I have given a few examples for purposes of my argument.

13. In research I conducted at IBM on virtual worlds in the workplace, this theme was echoed by the managers I spoke to. For example, one manager said the team chose another virtual worlds platform because "You never know what's around the corner in *Second Life*. That's very scary for some people." His work centered on the development of a "safe, business-oriented, friendly" platform.

14. In healing the main tank I was standing in a spot in which the south wall created a lot of lag on my computer, so my timing had to be split second to keep the tank healed and run at the right moment. That kind of challenge was fun and would have been dampened with a mod.

15. For those familiar with the game, at the time of this writing Innikka was healing as discipline. Since this spec did not show the effects of shields and other mitigation in the most commonly used mods, she enjoyed a happy freedom from meters. She kept Recount tuned to the dps to see how they were doing since it measured their contributions more accurately and helped her prioritize where to throw shields when the tanks appeared safe. Even the priest forums, which normally counseled that priests adjust to the realities of meters (see Wine 2008), vigorously argued that the contributions of discipline priests were not recorded by meters and that proper education of raid leaders was essential.

16. Videogamesblogger headlined a post "*World of Warcraft* hits 11 million users world-wide! Making it the 75th biggest country in the world." The population of *WoW* was considerably larger than that of Denmark or Dubai, as well as a great many other countries. See http://www.videogamesblogger.com/2008/10/28/world-of-warcraft-hits-11-million-users-worldwide-making-it-the-75th-biggest-country-in-the-world.htm. Last accessed March 2009. (See also Bainbridge 2007.)

17. For those familiar with the game, during 3.0, when my post–Scarlet Raven guild had done everything but Sarth +3, we went to Sunwell and wiped repeatedly with a full 25-man raid because we had not studied the strategies.

18. Those familiar with the game will recall that nostalgia runs began well before the Achievements system made it instrumental to go back to old dungeons.

19. Ducheneaut et al. (2006) described *WoW* as a spectacle, but they referred to players watching other players. I refer to the game itself.

20. *Hawt* is a playful spelling of "hot," a term connoting approval of the visual design of the gear in this context.

21. Brecht and others of course attempted to unify audience and performers; perhaps *WoW* is a populist realization of that impulse made possible through the affordability of digital technology.

22. Even professional architects gave *World of Warcraft* high marks for the visual design of its buildings. One architect wrote: "The stunning diversity of buildings of Azeroth secures it the top spot [in a competition for best architectural design in video games]. Towering Gothic structures recall the 'dreaming spires' of Oxford given a subversive geometrical revamp. The architecture of the Blood Elves, on the other hand, has softer, more organic influences. Similar to Gaudi's Parc Guell or Sagrada Familia, nature is expressed in stylised form—the very essence of Art Nouveau." See http://www.fastcompany.com/blog/cliff-kuang/design-innovation/architecture-video-games-top-10.

23. Fan culture is vibrant, but in assessing the impact of television, it is undeniable that most people just sit in front of the TV. Television is appealing in part because it is passive, demanding little of us—a comfort when we are tired, depressed, or in need of downtime. Although we may worry about those who seem to need too much such time, it is puritanical to insist that television be active and social when what it is good at is helping us let go.

Chapter Five

1. "Lol" is an acronym for "laugh out loud" and is a common chat term. It does not actually mean "laugh out loud" but rather connotes a smile, or friendliness, or irony, depending on the context. If someone is actually laughing out loud they would more likely type "rofl," which stands for "roll on the floor laughing." I am not sure what they would type if they were actually rolling on the floor laughing.

2. Huizinga (1950) has been critiqued for his claim that play "has no material interest, and no profit can be gained by it" (see Stevens 1978). Some theorists throw out the

baby (Huizinga's good work) with the bathwater (this particular claim). His good work should be recognized, but Huizinga was clearly wrong on this issue; it has been shown that even animals deprived of play suffer (see Stevens 1978).

3. Turner (1982) observed that the word *entertainment* shares a notion of separateness, being derived from the Old French *entretenir,* "to hold apart."

4. Notions such as the Protestant work ethic rankle a bit; in our global economy, work ethics are as likely to have arisen in a village in Mexico or an urban center in Asia as anywhere else. Suggesting that player activity arises from such constructs seems problematic even when used metonymically.

5. Golub (2007) recounted the incensed reactions of players to a reduction in the size of shoulder armor worn by the Draenei race. Three hundred forty-one messages of protest were posted to an official Blizzard player forum. One player wrote, "[Y]ou can no longer pretend you are surprised when we are unhappy . . . This matter is . . . purely cosmetic, but it makes us regret our choices at character creation. We work very hard for the items that you are ruining and we do not appreciate it."

6. Not all players farmed; it was an activity for serious players. I am responding to the dialogue introduced by Yee, Poole, and Rettberg, which identified farming (and related video game activities) as in need of explanation.

7. Players complained about the need for too many raid consumables—it was massively time consuming to prepare them—and, in the cycle of feedback/change discussed in chapter 4, Blizzard eventually reduced the quantities needed. I thought it was a good decision, preserving social capital and the investment in professions such as alchemy many players had made but reducing the time needed for farming.

8. Ducheneaut et al. (2006) used the phrase "alone together" to describe *World of Warcraft* sociality. Though the phrase appears to play off Huizinga, it is about something else altogether, denoting a statistic Ducheneaut et al. generated showing that players are in formal groupings 30 to 40 percent of the time (being "alone" the rest of the time). "Alone together" does not, as I understand it, engage arguments about the magic circle.

9. Instances are part of the design of other games as well.

10. Not all raiding dungeons were belowground. But a lot of them were, including such *WoW* archetypes as Deadmines, Scholomance (how I loved Scholo; I remember the descent well because I had to shackle the ghost at the bottom of the stairs), Molten Core, and the Coilfang instances. Many instances were designed around vaults, sanctums, and lairs.

11. I.e., a space away from home and work. Third spaces in RL include bars, beauty salons, and bingo nights.

Chapter Six

1. Although I do not know for sure, I interpret this player's comment on *Second Life* as a reference to its reputation for being dominated by adult-themed activity (see Bardzell and Odom 2008).

Chapter Seven

1. There are various ways to define game mechanics (see Sicart 2008), but for purposes of this chapter I am interested in the ways in which game rules produce outcomes.

2. Over 4,000 mods were available at curse.com and wowinterface.com (mod distribution sites) according to a count we did on December 8, 2008 (see Kow and Nardi 2009).

3. Karl Isenberg's real name is used with permission.

4. Mods comprised scripted programming files written in XML and Lua. Lua was used to specify functions. XML specified user interface elements. Mod users downloaded the files into a folder in the game directory where they were read when the game began. See Takhteyev (2009) on Lua.

5. Decursing was burdensome when many players were afflicted. Instead of seeing players' health restored after issuing a healing spell (the payoff for healers), the healer saw only the removal of the debuff—less satisfying. Members of damage classes that could decurse, such as mages, were forced to stop doing what they loved—damage—in order to remove debuffs.

6. Although outside the study period, in April 2009, Blizzard established firmer guidelines for mod authors, partly in response to the appearance of advertising in some mods. The commercial aspects of modding remind us that "community participation" is complex; participants have variable motives (see http://forums.worldofwarcraft.com/thread.html?topicId=15864747207&sid=1).

Chapter Eight

1. I searched for sociolinguistic analyses of gendered talk in video games and found little. Wright et al. (2002) constructed a typology of talk in *Counter-Strike* that included "Explicit gendered, racialized or homophobic talk," but they gave no examples and did not discuss or analyze the talk.

2. I want to reiterate that I knew the gender of guildmates through voice chat.

3. Williams et al. (2006) used the metaphor of the tree house to describe social life in *World of Warcraft*. I build on their notion but am focused here on gendered aspects of sociality which are perhaps not so benign as those of generic tree houses.

4. Wine (2008) discussed male rhetorical practice on a *WoW* forum, observing the aggressive-submissive postures of male posters.

5. My son agreed that being made the exception rendered this exchange one of fundamental inequality, but he observed that I could have scored some points by replying with something like, "Yeah, send me a picture of your balls, and then I'll have your email address." This rejoinder did not occur to me at the time.

6. I am indebted to Celia Pearce for her insight on the exaggeration present in masculinist discourse in games such as *WoW*.

7. Thelwall (2008) studied MySpace users and found that in the United States males used stronger language than females. This is consistent with my findings. But in the

United Kingdom, younger males and females exhibited similar patterns of language use, possibly due to the development of a female "ladette" culture involving heavy drinking.

8. My data concern activities in heterosexual guilds and my general observations of gendered activity in *WoW*, which were of heterosexual activity.

9. The "sex change operation" happened in my post–Scarlet Raven guild, but I report the incident as it was so apropos.

10. I am referring to dynamics in guilds and pickup groups; it is possible that some newbie male players pretended to be real life females. I don't have any data on that.

11. I use the term "safe" in an emotional sense; see Taylor (2003a) for a discussion of females' sense of freedom and safety in roaming anywhere in a video game without fear of physical harm, something they could not do in real life. Such roaming puts males and females at the same risk of in-game dangers, again a departure from real life.

12. Games such as *Lineage* and *Ragnarock* have lighter color palettes than *World of Warcraft*, although *WoW* is bright compared to the games described by Fullerton et al. (2007).

13. As a Blizzard product, *WoW*'s gendered elements are particular to *WoW*. Blizzard also produces masculinist games such as *Starcraft*. I have not played *Starcraft* but watched the video trailer several times during my two days at BlizzCon. It was both funny and sad. Funny because the two main characters managed to package up every imaginable hypermasculine stereotype dredged from the bowels of popular culture, and sad because so many men must identify at some level with the characters. Of course that's funny, too.

14. The feminine robes of the male mage provoked humor and even inspired a satirical player video, *Big Blue Dress*. The vocal of an original song laments the sorry state of affairs faced by male mages, asking why "A man of my stature should have to wear a dress" (http://www.youtube.com/watch?v=vqO7zEWu0W0).

Chapter Nine

1. The Internet cafe speaks to the continuing importance of the large-screen format. Despite the affordability, and hence ubiquity, of cell phones, it is enjoyable to watch movies, play video games, and interact with multiple applications on a bigger screen— exactly the activities we observed in Internet cafes in China.

2. At an art gallery in Beijing, we met a Chinese artist, Caixiaoxiao, who used "PK" as a theme in his art. One of his works was a large picture in which a headshot of Mu'ammar al-Gadhafi was juxtaposed with one of the artist, both images of the same size. It was titled, in English, *PK PK, Caixiaoxiao's Political PK*. We asked the artist how to interpret the picture. He told us that interpretation was up to the viewer, but that he saw himself in a kind of competition with al-Gadhafi. In the picture, both men are wearing hats with the Communist star, al-Gadhafi the traditional ethnic hat he is often photographed in, and the artist a Mao cap. The young Chinese research assistants who had taken me to the gallery did not recognize al-Gadhafi, so the work had a greater impact on me. The artist appeared to be in his late thirties.

3. This sentiment on the need to collaborate was common to both Chinese and North American players. Dreadlock, a young player I interviewed, connected the fun of *WoW* to opportunities for meeting people. (The :D icon means grin.)

> To Dreadlock: what do you like about the game?
> Dreadlock whispers: its fun :D
> To Dreadlock: right! but why?
> Dreadlock whispers: cant feal lonly while playing it!
> Dreadlock whispers: to meet people, etcw
> Dreadlock whispers: i love instances
> To Dreadlock: why do you love them?
> Dreadlock whispers: because they make it so you MUST group
> Dreadlock whispers: its not an option
> To Dreadlock: how do you find people to group with?
> Dreadlock whispers: advertising in the chat channels, guild and asking my friends
> Dreadlock whispers: also instances are an oppertuniy to meet people

Coda

1. Corneliussen played on a European server; things may be much different there. More research is needed.

References

Aarseth, E. 1997. *Cybertext: Perspectives on Ergodic Literature*. Baltimore: Johns Hopkins University Press.

AMA. 2007. Too Much Video Gaming Not Addiction, Yet. *Washington Post,* June 27. http://www.washingtonpost.com/wp-dyn/content/article/2007/06/27/AR20070 62700995.html. Last accessed January 2009.

Ang, C. S., and P. Zaphiris. 2008. Social Learning in MMOGs: An Activity Theoretical Perspective. *Interactive Technology and Smart Education* 5:84–102.

Apadwe. n.d. Are a Lot of People Really Addicted to World of Warcraft? http://www. askapadwe.com/81/are-a-lot-of-people-really-addicted-to-world-of-warcraft/. Last accessed October 2007.

Ashby, R. 1956. *An Introduction to Cybernetics*. London: Chapman & Hall.

Bainbridge, W. 2007. The Scientific Research Potential of Virtual Worlds. *Science* 317: 472–76.

Bainbridge, W., and W. Bainbridge. 2007. Electronic Game Research Methodologies: Studying Religious Implications. *Review of Religious Research* 46:35–53.

Bakhtin, M. 1982. *The Dialogic Imagination: Four Essays*. Austin: University of Texas Press.

Bandura, A. 1999. A Sociocognitive Analysis of Substance Abuse: An Agentic Perspective. *Psychological Science* 10:214–17.

Barab, S., S. Zuiker, S. Warren, D. Hickey, A. Ingram-Goble, E.-J. Kwon, I. Kouper, and S. C. Herring. 2007. *Situationally Embodied Curriculum: Relating Formalisms and Contexts*. WileyInterScience Online Periodicals. www.interscience.wiley.com.

Bardzell, J., and S. Bardzell. 2008. Intimate Interactions: Online Representation and Software of the Self. *interactions magazine,* October, 11–15.

Bardzell, S., and W. Odom. 2008. The Experience of Embodied Space in Virtual Worlds: An Ethnography of a *Second Life* Community. *Space and Culture* 11:239–59.

Barma Group. 2008. Born Again Christians. http://www.barma.org/FlexPage.aspx?Page= Topic&TopicID=8. Last accessed July 2008.

Baudrillard, J. 1983. *In the Shadow of the Silent Majorities.* New York: Semiotext(e).

Beavis, C., H. Nixon, and S. Atkinson. 2005. LAN Cafes. *Education, Communication, Information* 5:41–60.

Begole, B., J. Tang, R. Smith, and N. Yankelovich. 2002. Work Rhythms: Analyzing Visualization of Awareness Histories of Distributed Groups. In *Proceedings of the 2002 ACM Conference on Computer-Supported Cooperative Work,* 334–43. New York: ACM Press.

Blizzard Entertainment. 2008. *World of Warcraft* Reaches New Milestone: 10 Million Subscribers. Press release. http://www.blizzard.com/us/press/080122.html. Last accessed July 2008.

Boellstorff, T. 2006. A Ludicrous Discipline? Ethnography and Game Studies. *Games and Culture* 1:29–35.

Boellstorff, T. 2007. *Coming of Age in Second Life.* Princeton: Princeton University Press.

Bohannon, J. 2008. Slaying Monsters for Science. *Science* 20. http://www.sciencemag.org/cgi/content/full/320/5883/1592c.

boyd, d., and N. Ellison. 2007. Social Network Sites: Definition, History, and Scholarship. *Journal of Computer-Mediated Communication* 13 (1).

Brown, B., and M. Bell. 2004. CSCW at Play: "There" as a Collaborative Virtual Environment. In *CSCW 2004: Computer Supported Cooperative Work—Conference Proceedings,* 350–59. New York: ACM Press.

Butler, J. 1990. Performative Acts and Gender Constitution: An Essay in Phenomenology and Feminist Theory. In *Performing Feminisms: Feminist Critical Theory and Theatre,* ed. S. Case, 121–40. Baltimore: Johns Hopkins University Press.

Callois, R. 1961. *Man, Play, and Games.* New York: Free Press.

Callon, M. 1991. Techno-economic Networks and Irreversibility. In *Sociology of Monsters: Essays on Power, Technology, and Domination,* ed. J. Law, 79–93. London: Routledge.

Castronova, E. 2005. *Synthetic Worlds.* Chicago: University of Chicago Press.

Cefkin, M., S. Stucky, and W. Ark. 2009. The Grand Diversion: Play, Work, and Virtual Worlds. *Artifact* 2.

CGAlliance. n.d. http://www.cgalliance.org/forums/showthread.php?t=15533. Last accessed August 2008.

Chee, F. 2006. The Games We Play Online and Offline: Making *Wang-Tta* in Korea. *Popular Communication* 4:225–39.

Chee, F., and R. Smith. 2005. Is Electronic Community an Addictive Substance? In *Interactive Convergence: Critical Issues in Multimedia,* ed. S. Schaffer and M. Price, 137–55. Oxford: Inter-Disciplinary Press.

Chen, M. 2009. Communication, Coordination, and Camaraderie in *World of Warcraft. Games and Culture* 4:47–73.

Cherny, L. 1991. *Conversation and Community: Chat in a Virtual World.* Stanford: Center for the Study of Language and Information.

Choontanom, T. 2008. Build Theory in Guild Wars and World of Warcraft. Honors thesis, University of California, Irvine.

CNNIC. 2007. The 20th China Internet Report. http://www.cnnic.cn/uploadfiles/pdf/2007/7/18/113918.pdf. Last accessed April 2008.

Cohen, S. 1973. *Folk Devils and Moral Panics.* London: St. Albans.

Consalvo, M. 2007. *Cheating: Gaining Advantage in Videogames.* Cambridge: MIT Press.

Consalvo, M. 2008. Crunched by Passion: Women Game Developers and Workplace Challenges. In *Beyond Barbie and Mortal Kombat: New Perspectives on Gender and Gaming,* ed. Y. Kafai, C. Heeter, J. Denner, and J. Sun, 214–33. Cambridge: MIT Press.

Corneliussen, H. 2008. *World of Warcraft* as a Playground for Feminism. In *Digital Culture, Play, and Identity: A World of Warcraft Reader,* ed. H. Corneliussen and J. Rettberg, 135–53. Cambridge: MIT Press.

Corneliussen, H., and J. Rettberg, eds. 2008. *Digital Culture, Play, and Identity: A World of Warcraft Reader.* Cambridge: MIT Press.

Crabtree, A., and T. Rodden. 2007. Hybrid Ecologies: Understanding Cooperative Interaction in Emerging Physical-Digital Environments. *Personal and Ubiquitous Computing* 4:1–38.

Csikszentmihalyi, M. 1997. *Creativity: Flow and the Psychology of Discovery and Invention.* New York: HarperCollins.

Damer, B. 1998. *Avatars!* Berkeley: Peachpit Press.

Damer, B. 2009. Meeting in the Ether: A Brief History of Virtual Worlds as a Medium for User-Created Events. *Artifact* 2.

Delwiche, A. 2007. From the Green Berets to America's Army: Video Games as a Vehicle for Political Propaganda. In *The Players' Realm: Studies on the Culture of Video Games and Gaming,* ed. J. Williams and J. Smith, 104–19. London: McFarland.

De Souza, A. 2006. From Cyber to Hybrid: Mobile Technologies as Interfaces of Hybrid Spaces. *Space and Culture* 9:261–78.

Dewey, J. 2005. *Art as Experience.* New York: Perigee. First published 1934.

Dibbell, J. 2006. *Play Money.* New York: Basic Books.

Dibbell, J. 2007. The Life of the Chinese Gold Farmer. *New York Times Magazine,* June.

Dicki, M. 2007. Censorship Reaches Internet Skeletons. http://archive.gulfnews.com/articles/07/07/03/10136373.html. Last accessed April 2008.

DiGiuseppe, N., and B. Nardi. 2007. Real Gender Choose Fantasy Characters: Class Choice in World of Warcraft. *First Monday,* April.

Ducheneaut, N., and R. Moore. 2004. The Social Side of Gaming: A Study of Interaction Patterns in a Massively Multiplayer Online Game. In *CSCW 2004: Computer Supported Cooperative Work—Conference Proceedings,* 360–69. New York: ACM Press.

Ducheneaut, N., M. Wen, N. Yee, and G. Wadley. 2009. Body and Mind: A Study of Avatar Personalization in Three Virtual Worlds. In *Proceedings Conference on Human-Computer Interaction,* 1151–60, New York: ACM Press.

Ducheneaut, N., N. Yee, E. Nickell, and R. Moore. 2006. "Alone Together?" Exploring the Social Dynamics of Massively Multiplayer Online Games. In *Proceedings CHI06*, 407–16. New York: ACM Press.

Dutton, W. 2008. Social Movements Shaping the Internet: The Outcomes of an Ecology of Games. In *Computerization Movements and Technology Diffusion*, ed. M. Elliott and K. Kraemer, 499–517. Medford, NJ: Information Today.

Dwarfpriest.com. 2008. The Best Holy Priest Healing Gear. http://dwarfpriest.com/2008/12/02/the-best-holy-priest-healing-gear/. Last accessed February 2009.

Ellison, N., C. Steinfield, and C. Lampe. 2007. The Benefits of Facebook "Friends": Exploring the Relationship between College Students' Use of Online Social Networks and Social Capital. *Journal of Computer-Mediated Communication* 12.

Ellul, J. 1964. *The Technological Society*. New York: Vintage. First published in French in 1950.

Engeström, Y. 1987. *Learning by Expanding: An Activity-Theoretical Approach to Developmental Research*. Helsinki: Orienta-Konsultit Oy.

Fawcett, B. 2006. *The Battle for Azeroth*. Dallas: Benbella Books.

Fields, D., and Y. Kafai. 2007. Tracing Insider Knowledge across Time and Spaces: A Comparative Ethnography in a Teen Online Game World. In *Proceedings of Conference on Computer-Supported Collaborative Learning*, 230–39. New York: ACM Press.

Flanagan, M., D. Howe, and H. Nissenbaum. 2008. Values in Design: Theory and Practice. In *Information Technology and Moral Philosophy*, ed. J. van den Hoven and J. Weckert, 63–87. Cambridge: Cambridge University Press.

Flanagan, M., and H. Nissenbaum. 2007. A Game Design Methodology to Incorporate Activist Themes. In *Proceedings of the Conference on Human-Computer Interaction*, 155–63. New York: ACM Press.

Fron, J., T. Fullerton, J. Morie, and C. Pearce. 2007a. Playing Dress-up: Costume, Role Play, and Imagination. In *Philosophy of Computer Games Online Proceedings*.

Fron, J., T. Fullerton, J. Morie, and C. Pearce. 2007b. The Hegemony of Play. In *Proceedings Digra Conference*, 309–81.

Fujimoto, T. 2005. Social Interactions Experienced in the Massively Multiplayer Online Game Environment: Implications in the Design of Online Learning Courses. Paper presented at the Annual Conference of the Association for Educational Communications and Technology, October 20, 2005. http://www.personal.psu.edu/tuf105/archive/SocialInteractionsInTheOnlineGame-Fujimoto.pdf.

Fullerton, T., J. Morie, and C. Pearce. 2007. A Game of One's Own: Towards a New Gendered Poetics of Digital Space. In *Proceedings DAC*. Perth.

Freire, P. 2000. *Pedagogy of the Oppressed*. New York: Continuum International Publishing Group.

Garvey, C. 1977. *The Nature of Children's Play*. Cambridge: Harvard University Press.

Gee, J. 2003. *What Video Games Have to Teach Us about Learning and Literacy*. New York: Palgrave Macmillan.

Geertz, C. 1977. Deep Play: Notes on the Balinese Cockfight. In *The Interpretation of Culture*, ed. C. Geertz, 21–40. New York: Basic Books.

Golub, A. 2007. Being in the *World (of Warcraft)*: Raiding, Care, and Digital Subjectivity. Paper presented at the American Anthropological Association Meetings, December 2007, Washington DC.

Golub, A. 2009. Being in the *World (of Warcraft)*: Raiding, Realism, and Knowledge Production in a Massively Multiplayer Online Game. *Anthropological Quarterly*. (Based on, but substantially different from, the paper presented at the American Anthropological Association Meetings, December 2007, Washington DC.)

Golub, A., and K. Lingley. 2008. "Just Like the Qing Empire": Addiction, MMOGs, and Moral Crisis in Contemporary China. *Games and Culture* 3:59–75.

Graner Ray, S. 2004. *Gender Inclusive Game Design. Expanding the Market.* Hingham, MA: Charles River Media.

Grohol, J. M. 2006. Expert: 40 Percent of World of Warcraft Players Addicted. http://psychcentral.com/blog/archives/2006/08/10/expert-40-percent-of-world-of-warcraft-players-addicted/. Last accessed January 2009.

Groleau, C., C. Demers, and M. Barros. 2009. From Waltzing to Breakdancing: Introducing Contradiction in Practice-Based Studies of Innovation and Change. In *Proceedings EGOS.* Vienna.

Gutwin, C., and S. Greenberg. 1998. Effects of Awareness Support on Group Usability. In *Proceedings CHI'98,* 511–18. New York: ACM Press.

Hansen, S., N. Berente, J. Pike, and P. Bateman. 2009. Of Productivity and Play in Organizations: The Real-World Organizational Value of Immersive Virtual Environments. *Artifact 2.*

Hayes, E. 2005. Women and Video Gaming: Gendered Identities at Play. Paper presented at the Games, Learning, and Society Conference, Madison, WI.

Hayes, E., and I. Games. 2008. Making Computer Games and Design Thinking: A Review of Current Software and Strategies. *Games and Culture* 3:309–32.

Heath, C., and P. Luff. 1991. Disembodied Conduct: Communication through Video in a Multimedia Environment. In *Proceedings of the SIGCHI Conference on Human Factors in Computing Systems: Reaching through Technology,* 93–103. New York: ACM Press.

Hobart, M. 1987. Summer's Days and Salad Days: The Coming of Age of Anthropology. In *Comparative Anthropology,* ed. L. Holy, 45–68. Oxford: Basil Blackwell.

Hook, S. 1995. *John Dewey: An Intellectual Portrait.* Amherst, NY: Prometheus Books. First published 1939 by the John Day Co.

Huhtamo, E. 2005. Slots of Fun, Slots of Trouble: An Archaeology of Arcade Gaming. In *Handbook of Computer Game Studies,* ed. J. Raessens and J. Goldstein, 3–21. Cambridge: MIT Press.

Huisman, J.-W., and H. Marckmann. 2005. I Am What I Play: Participation and Reality as Content. In *Handbook of Computer Game Studies,* ed. J. Raessens and J. Goldstein, 389–404. Cambridge: MIT Press.

Huizinga, J. 1950. *Homo Ludens: A Study of the Play Element in Culture.* Boston: Beacon Press.

Hurwitz, B. 2000. Cardiovascular Reactivity as an Indicator of Risk for Future Hypertension. In *Stress, Coping, and Cardiovascular Disease,* ed. P. McCabe, N. Schneiderman, T. Field, and A. Wellens, 181–202. Mahwah, NJ: Erlbaum.

Ito, M. 2008. *Digital Youth Research. Final Report: Work.* http://digitalyouth.ischool.berkeley.edu/book-work. Last accessed February 2009.

Jackson, P. 1998. *John Dewey and the Lessons of Art.* New Haven, CT: Yale University Press.

Jenkins, H. 2006. *Fans, Bloggers, and Gamers: Exploring Participatory Culture.* New York: New York University Press.

Jenkins, H., and J. Cassell. 2008. From Quake Grrls to Desperate Housewives: A Decade of Gender and Computer Games. In *Beyond Barbie and Mortal Kombat: New Perspectives on Gender and Gaming,* ed. Y. Kafai, C. Heeter, J. Denner, and J. Sun, 48–62. Cambridge: MIT Press.

Jerz, D. 2007. Somewhere Nearby Is Colossal Cave: Examining Will Crowther's Original Adventure in Code and in Kentucky. *Digital Humanities Quarterly* 1 (Summer).

Jha, P., R. Peto, W. Zatonski, J. Boreham, M. Jarvis, and A. Lopez. 2006. Social Inequalities in Male Mortality and in Male Mortality from Smoking: Indirect Estimation from National Death Rates in England and Wales, Poland, and North America. *Lancet Online.* http://cghr.org/publications/Lancet_SocialInequalities_Jul2006.pdf. Last accessed July 2008.

Jordan, W. 2007. From Rule-Breaking to ROM-Hacking: Theorizing the Computer Game-as-Commodity. In *Proceedings DiGRA Conference,* 708–13.

Juul, J. 2005. *Half-Real.* Cambridge: MIT Press.

Kafai, Y. 1995. Gender Differences in Children's Constructions of Video Games. In *Interacting with Video,* ed. P. Greenfield and R. Cocking, 39–52. New York: Ablex Publishing.

Kafai, Y., C. Heeter, J. Denner, and J. Sun, eds. 2008. *Beyond Barbie and Mortal Kombat: New Perspectives on Gender and Gaming.* Cambridge: MIT Press.

Kallinikos, J. 2004. Farewell to Constructivism: Technology and Context-Embedded Action. In *The Social Study of Information and Communication Technology: Innovation, Actors, and Contexts,* ed. C. Avgerou, C. Ciborra, and F. Land, 140–61. Oxford: Oxford University Press.

Kallinikos, J. 2006. *The Consequences of Information: Institutional Implications of Technological Change.* Cheltenham: Edward Elgar.

Kallinikos, J. 2009. On Design and Molecules: Rethinking Technology and Materiality. Unpublished paper. London School of Economics.

Kaptelinin, V., and B. Nardi. 2006. *Acting with Technology: Activity Theory and Interaction Design.* Cambridge: MIT Press.

Kavetsky, J. 2008. Men Behaving (Not So) Badly: Interplayer Communication in World of Warcraft. Masters thesis, Bowling Green State University, Bowling Green, OH. http://www.ohiolink.edu/etd/view.cgi?acc_num=bgsu1213989105. Last accessed April 2009.

Kelty, C. 2008. *Two Bits: The Cultural Significance of Free Software.* Durham: Duke University Press.

Kendall, L. 2008. 'Noobs' and 'Chicks' on Animutation Portal: Power and Status in a Community of Practice. *International Journal of Web Based Communities* 4.

Kennedy, H. 2005. Illegitimate, Monstrous, and Out There: Female Quake Players and Inappropriate Pleasures. In *Feminism in Popular Culture*, ed. J. Hallows and R. Mosley, 214–30. London: Berg.

Kensing, F., and B. Blomberg. 1998. Participatory Design: Issues and Challenges. *Computer Supported Cooperative Work* 7:167–85.

Klastrup, L. 2004. En ny tids fiction. In *Digitale Verdener—de nye mediers Æstetik og design*, ed. I. Engholm and L. Klastrup, 89–115. København: Gyldendal.

Klastrup, L. 2008. What Makes *World of Warcraft* a World? A Note on Death and Dying. In *Digital Culture, Play, and Identity: A World of Warcraft Reader*, ed. H. Corneliussen and J. Rettberg, 117–36. Cambridge: MIT Press.

Kline, S., N. Dyer-Witheford, and G. De Peuter. 2003. *The Interaction of Technology, Culture, and Marketing.* Ontario: McGill-Queen's University.

Kow, Y. M., and B. Nardi. 2009. Culture and Creativity: *World of Warcraft* Modding in China and the U.S. In *Online Worlds: Convergence of the Real and the Virtual*, ed. B. Bainbridge. Springer.

Kucklich, J. 2004. Precarious Playbour: Modders and the Digital Games Industry. *Fiberculture.*

Kuutti, K. 1998. Making the Object of a Work Activity Accessible. In *Proceedings of the Workshop on Understanding Work and Designing Artefacts*, 1–12. London.

Lampe, C., N. Ellison, and C. Steinfield. 2007. A Familiar Face(book): Profile Elements as Signals in an Online Social Network. In *Proceedings of the SIGCHI Conference on Human Factors in Computing Systems*, 435–44. New York: ACM Press.

LandoverBaptist. n.d. Winning Souls to Christ in *The World of Warcraft.* http://www.landoverbaptist.org/news0105/wow.html. Last accessed August 2008.

Lastowka, F., and D. Hunter. 2004. The Laws of Virtual Worlds. *California Law Review* 92:1–72.

Latour, B. 1994. On Technical Mediation: Philosophy, Genealogy, and Sociology. *Common Knowledge* 3:29–64.

Leontiev, A. 1974. The Problem of Activity in Psychology. *Soviet Psychology* 13:4–33.

Li, Z. 2004. The Potential of America's Army the Video Game as Civilian-Military Public Sphere. Masters of Science in Comparative Media Studies. Massachusetts Institute of Technology.

Lin, H., and C. Sun. 2007. Cash Trade within the Magic Circle: Free-to-Play Game Challenges and Massively Multiplayer Online Game Player Responses. In *Proceedings DIGRA Conference*, . 337–43.

Lindtner, S., B. Nardi, W. Yang, S. Mainwaring, H. Jing, and W. Liang. 2008. A Hybrid Cultural Ecology: *World of Warcraft* in China. In *Proceedings on Computer-Supported Cooperative Work*, 371–82. New York: ACM Press.

Lowood, H. 2008. Game Capture: The Machinima Archive and the History of Digital Games. *Mediascape* (Spring).

Ly, S. 2008. How Computer Games Can Enhance Organizational Effectiveness. Unpublished paper, MBA class, University of California, Irvine.

Lyotard, J.-F. 1984. *The Postmodern Condition.* Manchester: Manchester University Press.

Malaby, T. 2003. *The Gambling Life.* Urbana: University of Illinois Press.

Malaby, T. 2006. Coding Control: Governance and Contingency in the Production of Online Worlds. *First Monday,* September. http://firstmonday.org/issues/special11_9/malaby/index.html. Last accessed January 2009.

Malaby, T. 2007. Beyond Play: A New Approach to Games. *Games and Culture* 2:95–113.

Malaby, T. 2009. *Making Virtual Worlds: Linden Lab and Second Life.* Ithaca: Cornell University Press.

Malliet, S., and G. De Meyer. 2005. The History of the Video Game. In *Handbook of Computer Game Studies,* ed. J. Raessens and J. Goldstein, 23–46. Cambridge: MIT Press.

Malone, K.-L. 2007. Dragon Kill Points: The Economics of Power Gamers. Masters thesis, University of Wisconsin–Milwaukee.

Mankekar, P. 1999. *Screening Culture, Viewing Politics: An Ethnography of Television, Womanhood, and Nation in Postcolonial India.* Durham: Duke University Press.

Miller, S. 1971. Ends, Means, and Galumphing: Some Leitmotifs of Play. *American Anthropologist* 75:87–98.

Miller, D., and D. Slater. 2000. *The Internet: An Ethnographic Approach.* New York: Berg.

Mnookin, J. 1996. Virtual(ly) Law: The Emergence of Law in *LambdaMOO. Journal of Computer-Mediated Communication* 2.

Morningstar, C., and R. Farmer. 1991. The Lessons of Lucasfilm's *Habitat.* In *Cyberspace: First Steps,* ed. M. Benedikt, 42–57. Cambridge: MIT Press.

Mortensen, T., and H. Corneliussen. 2005. The Non-sense of Gender in *NeverWinter Nights.* In *Proceedings Women in Games Conference.*

Mulvey, L. 1975. Visual Pleasure and Narrative Cinema. *Screen* 16:6–18.

Mumford, L. 1934. *Technics and Civilization.* New York: Harcourt, Brace, and World.

Murray, J. 1997. *Hamlet on the Holodeck: The Future of Narrative in Cyberspace.* New York: Free Press.

Nakamura, L. 2009. Don't Hate the Player, Hate the Game: The Racialization of Labor in *World of Warcraft. Critical Studies in Media Communication* 26:128–44.

Nardi, B. 2005. Beyond Bandwidth: Dimensions of Connection in Interpersonal Interaction. *Journal of Computer-Supported Cooperative Work* 14:91–30.

Nardi, B., and J. Harris. 2006. Strangers and Friends: Collaborative Play in *World of Warcraft.* In *Proceedings Conference on Computer-Supported Cooperative Work,* 149–58. New York: ACM Press.

Nardi, B., S. Ly, and J. Harris. 2007. Learning Conversations in *World of Warcraft*. In *Proceedings Hawaii International Conference on Systems Science*, 1–10.

Nardi, B., C. Pearce, and J. Ellis. 2009. Productive Play: Beyond Binaries. *Artifact* 2:1–9.

Nardi, B., D. Schiano, and M. Gumbrecht. 2004. Blogging as Social Activity, or, Would You Let 900 Million People Read Your Diary? In *CSCW 2004: Computer Supported Cooperative Work—Conference Proceedings*, 222–28. New York: ACM Press.

Nardi, B., D. Schiano, M. Gumbrecht, and L. Swartz. 2004. Why We Blog. *Communications of the American Association for Computing Machinery* 47:41–46.

Noël, S., S. Dumoulin, and G. Lindgaard. 2009. Interpreting Human and Avatar Facial Expressions. In *Proceedings Interact*, 207–20. Uppsala, Sweden.

Orlikowski, W. 1992. The Duality of Technology: Rethinking the Concept of Technology in Organizations. *Organization Science* 3:398–427.

"Parents Set to Sue Blizzard after World of Warcraft Player Dies." 2005. http://www.gamesindustry.biz/articles/parents-set-to-sue-blizzard-after-world-of-warcraft-player-dies. Last accessed January 2009.

Pearce, C. 2006. Productive Play: Game Culture from the Bottom Up. *Games and Culture* 1:17–24.

Pearce, C. 2008. The Truth about Baby Boomer Gamers: A Study of Over-Forty Computer Game Players. *Games and Culture* 3:142–74.

Pearce, C. 2009. *Communities of Play: Emergent Cultures in Online Games and Virtual Worlds*. Cambridge: MIT Press.

Perkins, C., and A. Cacioppo. 1950. The Effect of Intermittent Reinforcement on the Change in Extinction Rate following Successive Reconditionings. *Journal of Experimental Psychology* 40:794–801.

Peterson, H. 2007. The Game of (Family) Life: Intra-family Play in World of Warcraft. Ph.D. diss., London School of Economics.

Pickering, A. 1995. *The Mangle of Practice: Time, Agency, and Science*. Chicago: University of Chicago Press.

Polin, L. 2008. Graduate Professional Education from a Community of Practice Perspective: The Role of Social and Technical Networking. In *Communities of Practice: Creating Learning Environments for Educators*, ed. C. Kimble, P. Hildreth, and I. Bourdon, 159–82. Charlotte, NC: Information Age Publishing.

Poole, S. 2008. Working for the Man: Against the Employment Paradigm in Videogames. Keynote presentation, Future and Reality of Games Conference. http://stevenpoole.net/trigger-happy/working-for-the-man/. Last accessed February 2009.

Postigo, H. 2007. Of Mods and Modders. *Games and Culture* 2:300–313.

Powell, A. n.d. Space, Place, Reality, and Virtuality in Urban Internet Cafes. http://www.culturalstudies.ca/proceedings04/pdfs/powell.pdf. Last accessed August 2008.

Qiu, J., and Z. Liuning. 2005. Through the Prism of the Internet Café: Managing Access in an Ecology of Games. *China Information* 19:261–97.

Raessens, J., and J. Goldstein, eds. 2005. *Handbook of Computer Game Studies*. Cambridge: MIT Press.

Rea, S. 2009. Playing the Citizen. Unpublished paper. University of California, Irvine.

Reeves, B., T. Malone, and T. O'Driscoll. 2008. Leadership's Online Labs. *Harvard Business Review Online*. www.hbr.org. Last accessed August 2008.

Rettberg, S. 2008. Corporate Ideology in *World of Warcraft*. In *Digital Culture, Play, and Identity: A World of Warcraft Reader*, ed. H. Corneliussen and J. Rettberg, 19–37. Cambridge: MIT Press.

Rheingold, H. 1993. *The Virtual Community: Homesteading on the Electronic Frontier*. New York: HarperPerennial Paperback.

Rickadams.org. n.d. http://www.rickadams.org/adventure/a_history.html. Last accessed August 2008.

Ryan, P. 2008. Building Social Communities for Your Game: A Primer. *Gamasutra*, October 22. http://www.gamasutra.com/view/feature/3828/building_social_com munities_for_.php.

Salen, K., and E. Zimmerman. 2005. *The Game Design Reader*. Cambridge: MIT Press.

Scacchi, W. 2004. Free/Open Source Software Development Practices in the Computer Game Community. *IEEE Software* 21:59–67.

Schechner, R. 1977. *Performance Theory*. London: Routledge.

Schoolcraft, H. 1990. *The Hiawatha Legends*. AuTrain, MI: Avery Color Studios. First published 1856.

Schramm, Mike. 2007. Breakfast Topic: WoW in the World. http://www.wowinsider. com/2007/06/14/breakfast-topic-wow-in-the-world/. Last accessed August 2008.

Seay, F., and R. Kraut. 2007. Project Massive: Self-regulation and Problematic Use of Online Gaming. In *Proceedings ACM Conference on Human Factors in Computing Systems*, 829–38. New York: ACM Press.

Second Life. n.d. http://forums.worldofwarcraft.com/thread.html;jsessionid=C715AA 292A37AD9A1EE1CE436A654B1B.app11_06?topicId=2765961752&sid=1&p ageNo=7. Last accessed August 2008.

Seed, P. 2007. Looking Back: A Decade of Using Games to Teach History, 1996–2006. In *Proceedings of the First International Humanities, Arts, Science, and Technology Advanced Collaboratory Conference*, 193–200.

Sharritt, M. 2009. Evaluating Video Game Design and Interactivity. In *Interdisciplinary Models and Tools for Serious Games: Emerging Concepts and Future Directions*, ed. R. Van Eck, 19–39. Hershey, PA: IGI Global.

Sicart, M. 2008. Defining Game Mechanics. *Game Studies* 8. http://gamestudies. org/0802/articles/sicart. Last accessed February 2009.

Spinuzzi, C. 2008. *Network*. Cambridge: Cambridge University Press.

Squire, K. 2005. Changing the Game: What Happens when Video Games Enter the Classroom? *Innovate: Journal of Online Education* 1:25–49.

Steinkuehler, C. 2006. The Mangle of Play. *Games and Culture* 1:199–213.

Steinkuehler, C., and M. Chmeil. 2006. Fostering Scientific Habits of Mind in the Context of Online Play. In *Proceedings of the International Conference of the Learning Sciences*, 723–29. Mahwah, NJ: Erlbaum.

Steinkuehler, C., and S. Duncan. 2008. Scientific Habits of Mind in Virtual Worlds. *Journal of Science Education and Technology* 17:530–43.

Steinkuehler, C., and D. Williams. 2006. Where Everybody Knows Your (Screen) Name: Online Games as "Third Places." *Journal of Computer-Mediated Communication* 11.

Stevens, P. 1978. Play and Work: A False Dichotomy. In *Proceedings Further Studies of Work and Play,* ed. H. Schwartzman. West Point, NY: Leisure Press.

Stewart, K., and H. Choi. 2003. PC-bang (Room) Culture: A Study of Korean College Students' Private and Public Use of Computers and the Internet. *Trends in Communication* 11:61–77.

Strathern, M. 2004. *Commons and Borderlands.* Wantage: Sean Kingston Publishing.

Sutton-Smith, B. 1975. Play as Adaptive Potentiation, *Sportswissenschaft* 5:103–18.

Takhteyev, Y. 2009. Coding Places: Uneven Globalization of Software Work in Rio de Janeiro, Brazil. Ph.D. diss., University of California, Berkeley.

Tang, J., N. Yankelovich, B. Begole, Van M. Kleek, F. Li, and J. Bhalodia. 2001. CoNexus to Awarenex. In *Proceedings Conference on Computer–Human Interaction,* 221–28. New York: ACM Press.

Taylor, T. L. 2003a. Multiple Pleasures: Women and Online Gaming. *Convergence* 9:21–48.

Taylor, T. L. 2003b. Power Gamers Just Want to Have Fun? Instrumental Play in an MMOG. In *Proceedings Digra Conference,* 300–311.

Taylor, T. L. 2006a. *Play between Worlds: Exploring Online Game Culture.* Cambridge: MIT Press.

Taylor, T. L. 2006b. Beyond Management: Considering Participatory Design and Governance in Player Culture. *First Monday,* September.

Taylor, T. L. 2008. Does *World of Warcraft* Change Everything? In *Digital Culture, Play, and Identity: A World of Warcraft Reader,* ed. H. Corneliussen and J. Rettberg, 187–201. Cambridge: MIT Press.

Thelwall, M. 2008. Fk Yea I Swear: Cursing and Gender in a Corpus of MySpace Pages. *Corpora* 3:83–107.

Thomas, S., and T. Lang. 2007. From Field to Office: The Politics of Corporate Ethnography. *Procedings Ethnographic Praxis in Industry Conference,* 78–90. Portland, OR.

Thott. n.d. Afterlife Dragon Lotto Rules. DKP explanation. http://www.afterlifeguild.org/dkp-explanation. Last accessed August 2008.

Toma, C., J. Hancock, and N. Ellison. 2008. Separating Fact from Fiction: An Examination of Deceptive Self-Presentation in Online Dating Profiles. *Society for Personality and Social Psychology* 4:1023–36.

Tschang, F. 2007. Balancing the Tensions between Rationalization and Creativity in the Video Games Industry. *Organization Science* 18:989–1005.

Turkle, S. 1995. *Life on the Screen: Identity in the Age of the Internet.* New York: Simon & Schuster.

Turkle, S. 1998. At Heart of a Cyberstudy, the Human Essence. Interview by Katie

Hafner. http://web.mit.edu/sturkle/www/nytimes.html. Last accessed January 2009.

Turner, V. 1982. *From Ritual to Theatre: The Human Seriousness of Play.* New York: PAJ Publications.

Vandenberg, B. 1998. Real and Not Real: A Vital Developmental Dichotomy. In *Multiple Perspectives on Play in Early Childhood Education,* ed. O. Saracho and B. Spoedek, 226–50. Albany: SUNY Press.

von Bertalanffy, L. 1968. *General System Theory: Foundations, Development, Applications.* New York: George Braziller.

Vygotsky, L. 1986. *Thought and Language.* Cambridge: MIT Press.

Wakeford, N. 2003. The Embedding of Local Culture in Global Communication: Independent Internet Cafes in London. *New Media and Society* 5:379–99.

Whitehead J., B. McLemore, and M. Orlando. 2008. *World of Warcraft Programming.* New York: Wiley.

Williams, D. 2006. Why Game Studies Now? Gamers Don't Bowl Alone. *Games and Culture* 1:13–16.

Williams, D., N. Ducheneaut, L. Xiong, Y. Zhang, N. Yee, and E. Nickell. 2006. From Tree House to Barracks: The Social Life of Guilds in World of Warcraft. *Games and Culture* 1:338–61.

Williams, M. 2007. Avatar Watching: Participant-Observation in Graphical Online Environments. *Qualitative Research* 1:5–24.

Willis, P. 1978. *Profane Culture.* London: Routledge.

Wilson, S., and L. Peterson. 2002. The Anthropology of Online Communities. *Annual Review of Anthropology* 31:449–67.

Wine, C. 2008. How Big Is Your Epeen? A Study of Hegemonic Masculinity in Communication on the World of Warcraft Forums. Women's Studies honors thesis, University of Massachusetts.

Winner, L. 1977. *Autonomous Technology: Technics-out-of-Control as a Theme in Political Thought.* Cambridge: MIT Press.

World of Warcraft.com. 2007a. Nihilium Recruiting: Females Need Not Apply. http://www.wowinsider.com/2007/03/20/nihilum-recruiting-females-need-not-apply/. Last accessed July 2008.

World of Warcraft.com. 2007b. Nihilium response. http://forums.worldofwarcraft.com/thread.html;jsessionid=0C50640F6A9B1D710B5F66235ACACA56?topicId=2720292344&sid=1&pageNo=9. Last accessed January 2009.

Wright, T., E. Boria, and P. Breidenbach. 2002. Creative Player Actions in FPS Online Video Games: Playing Counter-Strike. *Game Studies* 2. http://www.gamestudies.org/0202/wright/.

Wynn, E., and R. McGeer. 2006. Collaboration Environments for Large Engineering Projects: 3d Open Source Options. IT Innovation Collaboratory, Intel Corporation.

Yee, N. 2005. *WoW* Gender–Bending. http://www.nickyee.com/daedalus/archives/001369.php. Last accessed April 2008.

Yee, N. 2006. The Labor of Fun: How Video Games Blur the Boundaries of Work and Play. *Games and Culture* 1:68–71.

Yee, N., J. Ellis, and N. Ducheneaut. 2009. The Tyranny of Embodiment. *Artifact* 2.

Index

Page numbers in italics refer to illustrations.

Aarseth, E., 89
active aesthetic experience, 85, 198
activity, hybrid physical-digital spaces of visual-performative, 181–82, 194, 196, 201
activity, participatory design, 70–72, 79–83, 199. *See also* modding and mods; theory-craft
activity theory, 30, 41–42, *42,* 56–57, 62, 65, 85, 102
addiction to video games: described, 128; heterogenous mix of resources and, 135; intermittent reinforcement of unpredictable rewards and, 39–40; negative connotation of, 126–27; positive connotation of, 125–26, 133–34; psychological problems as trigger for, 127–28; school and, 124, 125, 127–28, 132; self-regulation and, 125, 129–33; summary, 123, 135–36; video games as cause of, 124–25
aesthetic experience: encoded rules and, 45, 54; game play as, 104; mods as, 151; phases and, 45–46, *46;* play and, 6–7, 41, 48; work versus, 44, 49, 94–95, 198; *WoW* and, 45–46, 54
aesthetic experience theory: activity and, 41, 151; balance and proportion qualities and, 123; flow and, 47, 85; human activities and, 43; means-ends relations and, 44–45; mods and, 151; participatory aesthetic experience and, 41, 48, 68, 70, 79–80,
82–85, 92–93, 194, 197; passion and, 123–24; play and, 101, 151; on relations sustained by an activity, 128; relations sustained by an activity and, 128; remaking of material of experience and, 47–48, 79, 139, 204; sociality and, 47–48, 50–51; subjective disposition toward activity and, 43, 46; summary, 41, 48–51. *See also* aesthetic experience
aggro: RL, 109, 116–17, 161, 162; in *WoW,* 109, 147, 206n1
alchemy profession, 9, 12, 112, 209n7
Alliance races, 16, 60. *See also specific races*
American Medical Association (AMA), 125
Ang, C. S., 5
Apadwe.com, 127
arena play, 55, 206nn2–3
Art as Experience (Dewey), 41
artistry in visual design: awards for, 12; described, 54, 168; of druids, 52, *53,* 86, 87, 89, 169; encoded rules and, 74, 76; of gear, 87, 89, 169, *170,* 208n20; gear and, 87, 208n20; medium as artistic production and, 80, 198; nostalgia runs due to, 83–84, 208n18; participatory design activity versus, 79–80, 83; resource role of rules and, 83–84, 208nn17–18
Ashby, R., 71
Auctioneer (mod), 147–48
autonomy, and performance, 7, 101, 205–6n1

bag slots, *10*, 75, 146
Bainbridge, W., 8, 21, 134, 186, 196, 200, 208n16
Bakhtin, M., 161
Bandura, A., 121
Barab, S., 5
Bardzell, J., 43, 56–57, 165
Bardzell, S., 43, 56–57, 165, 209n1
Baudrillard, J., 92, 93
Beavis, C. H., 179
Begole, B., 148
Bell, M., 22
Blizzard Entertainment: on Chinese *WoW* culture, 176; community, and role of, 83, 149–50, 210n6; design changes by, 62, 80, 206n5, 206–7n6; encoded rules in digital entities, and preoccupation of, 35, 199; ethnographic research, and culture of, 35; feedback and, 62, 80, 206n5, 206–7n6; masculinist video games by, 211n13; mods and, 149–50, 210n4, 210n6; TBC, and software design alterations by, 62–68, 83–84, 208nn17–18; time-consuming activities to slow down game and, 112
BlizzCon, 6, 18, 21, 35, 80, 117, 150
Blomberg, J., 83
Blood Elves, 16, 159, 169, *170, 208n22
Boellstorff, T., 28, 35, 77, 102
Bohannon, J., 200
boredom and monotony: game play, and respite from RL, 12–13, 48, 115–16; in RL, 97, 104–5, *104–6*, 113, 120, 200
boyd, d., 165
Brown, B., 22
buffs and debuffs, 5, 9–11, 115, 149, 210
Burning Crusade, The (TBC), 62–68, 83–84, 208nn17–18
business practices, and applications for video games, 5–6, 109–10, 200
Butler, J., 54

Cacioppo, A., 39
Callois, R., 95, 103, 200
Callon, M., 62
Cassell, J., 166, 174
Castronova, E., 108
Cefkin, M., S., 5
CGAlliance, 26
character leveling, 12, 15, 39–40, 45–46, 55, 184, 205n1, 206–7n6

cheating, 182–83, 184
Chee, F., 124, 127, 179
Chen, M., 203
Cherny, L., 93
Chinese *WoW* culture: cross-cultural encounters in, 202–3; demographic data on players of, 190; fraud in, 182–83, 184; gender-bending and, 189–90, 196; gendered practice in, 187–92; gold farming and, 106–7, 176; gold raiding and, 176–77, 183; guilds, and sociality in, 194; heterosexual flirtation and, 190; hybrid physical-digital spaces and, 181–82, 194, 201; Internet cafes and, 7, 26, 177–82, *178*, 211n1; ladyboy characters, and male players playing female characters in, 187–89; men, and gendered interactions in, 187–90, 191–92; mods and, 179, *179;* participatory aesthetic experience in, 194–96, *195;* PK in, 191–92, 211n2; players' introduction into, 192; point cards in, 183–85; political realities and, 185–86; PvE play in, 190–91, 192; PvP play in, 190–91; raiding as social experience in, 193–94; real money/game transactions in, 106; real money transactions and, 184–85; small living spaces and, 180, *180;* sociality and, 21, 179, 180, 193–94, 212n3; summary, 196; TBC release and, 62; women's introduction into, 192; women's mastery of performance in, 190–92; work-like activities in game play and, 99
Chmeil, M., 141–42
Choi, H., 179
Choontanom, T., 30, 57, 110
classes: players' social, 19, 24–25; in *WoW,* 15, 210n5. *See also* healing class
CNNIC, 179
Cohen, S., 124
collaboration, and sociality, 5, 21, 55, 193, 212n3
collective order. *See* encoded rules in digital entities; resource role of rules
combat log, 57–58, 206n3
community, in context of encoded rules, 83, 149–50, 210n6. *See also* sociality
Consalvo, M., 61, 69, 166, 207n11
contingency element, in games and game play, 103, 104, 142, 155
Corneliussen, H., 156, 159, 166, 168, 171, 172, 199, 212n1

corpse camping, 17
Counter-Strike (video game), 143, 210n1
Crabtree, A., 181
critical thinking skills, and theorycraft, 139–42
cross-cultural encounters, 194–96, *195,* 202–3
Csikszentmihalyi, M., 47
cultural logics of *WoW. See* addiction; Chinese *WoW* culture; gendered practice; modding and mods; theorycraft

damage meters, 58, *59,* 207n15
Damer, B., 93, 205n2
Deadly Boss Mods (DBM), 81–82
debuffs and buffs, 5, 9–11, 115, 149, 210n5
decursing, 149, 210n5
Decursive (mod), 149
Delwiche, A., 6
De Meyer, G., 93
Derelict (pseud.) guild, 31, 67, 109
design. *See* encoded rules in digital entities; resource role of rules
Dewey, J., 41, 44. *See also* aesthetic experience theory
Dibbell, J., 106–7
Dicki, M., 185
DiGiuseppe, N., 21, 29, 158
DKP (Dragon Kill Points), 177, 207n10
Draenei, 16, 209n5
druids: artistry in visual design of, 52, *53,* 86, 87, 89, 169; critical thinking skills, and customizing, 141–42; cross-cultural encounters and, 202–3; described, 15, 52, *53*
Ducheneaut, N., 14–15, 16, 21, 39, 166, 208n19, 209n8
Duncan, S., 142
dungeons: described, 15–16; instances and, 119; nostalgia runs and, 208n18; raiding, 58–60, 209n10; TBC and, 62–67, 83–84. *See also specific dungeons*
Dutton, W., 109
dwarfpriest.com, 139–41
Dwarfs, 16, 139–41, 159, 203

Ellis, J., 70
Ellison, N., 165, 182
Ellul, J., 62
empowerment, 57, 148

encoded rules in digital entities: activity theory and, 62; aesthetic experience and, 45, 54; artistry in visual design and, 74, 76; community in context of, 83, 149–50, 210n6; constitution of technology and, 72–73; corporate preoccupations reflected in, 35, 199; feedback, and discourse about, 62, 80, 206n5, 206–7n6; game play and, 117–18, 137, 210n1; gear and, 75, 209n5; hackers and, 69–70, 73, 198; human activities in video games, and impact on, 7, 18, 46–47, 61; life online shaped by, 61; magic circle and, 118; mangle notion and, 70–73, 207n8; mods and, 70–72, 80–83, 149, 210n6; participatory aesthetic experience and, 198; *Second Life* and, 77–79, 207n13; TBC, and changes to, 62–68, 83–84, 208nn17–18; video games and, 61–62, 206n5, 206–7n6; in *WoW,* 61, 62–68, 80–82, 83–84, 208nn17–18. *See also* resource role of rules
Engeström, Y., 65
enterprise resource planning systems, 68–69, 72, 207n7
ethnographic research, 4–7, 27–35, 56, 177; activity theory and, 30; author's introduction to *WoW* and, 4–5; Blizzard culture and, 35; dates for, 6; described, 27–29; invitations to guilds and, 32–33; mastery of performance and, 34, 56; methodology in, 28, 29–30, 34, 177; participant-engagement in, 35; participant-observation in, 28, 30–31, 34–35; participant researchers' identification and, 35; perturbance in, 32; sites for, 7, 29–30; sources for information and, 33–34
European *WoW* culture: Corneliussen and, 156, 159, 166, 168, 171, 172, 199, 212n1; gold farming and, 176; guilds and, 59, 99–100, 163–64; hybrid physical-digital spaces and, 182, 201; TBC release and, 62, 66
Everquest (video game), 4, 13–14, 57, 166, 171

family: guilds and, 25, 26, 31, 154; masculine rhetoric and, 155; self-regulation and, 100, 101, 107, 109, 124, 125, 135; video games, and play with, 21, 26, 179, 182, 192
Farmer, R., 70, 93

farming: as capitalist labor, 112–13; defined, 59, 110; gold, 106–7, 176; RL, and links with, 110–16, *114,* 209nn4–7; as time-consuming activity to slow down game, 112; worklike activities in game play and, 98–99, 102

Fawcett, B., 12

feedback on changes in design, 62, 80, 206n5, 206–7n6, 209n5

Fields, D., 5

Final Fantasy (video game), 4, 187

Flanagan, M., 174

flow, 27, 44–45, 47, 85–86

fraud, 182–83, 184

Freire, P., 156

Fron, J., 61, 73, 159, 166, 173, 207n9

Fujimoto, T., 88

Fullerton, T., 19, 166, 167–68, 172, 173, 174, 211n12

game geography coordinates, 146

game mechanics, and encoded rules, 137, 210n1

game play: as aesthetic experience, 104; apart together feelings in, 116; boredom and monotony, and respite in world of, 12–13, 48, 115–16; business practices and, 6, 109–10, 200; contingency element in, 103, 104, 142, 155; encoded rules in digital entities and, 117–18, 137, 210n1; in Korea, 8, 19, 107–8, 176, 179, 203; mastery of performance valued in, 55, 57; not-play and, 108–16, 120; professional gaming and, 106–8; RL, and links with, 108–16, 120; Skinnerian dynamics and, 55, 133; subjective dispositions toward activity and, 104, 199; summary, 94, 103, 120, 199–200; violence and, 14, 205nn3–4; worklike activities in, 95, 98–99, 98–100, 102, 106–8, 110, 111, 200. *See also* activity theory; magic circle; mastery of performance; play

games, 4, 7, 73, 94, 103–4, 142, 199, 207n9. *See also* game play; play

Games, I., 5

ganking, 17, 71, 119

Garvey, C., 98, 103, 118

Gatherer (mod), 147, 148

gear: arena play and, 206n2; artistry in visual design of, 87, 89, 169, *170,* 208n20; encoded rules and, 75, 209n5; feedback on changes in design of, 209n5; fraud and, 184; metrics and, 61; mods for organization of, 146; performance, and impact of, 58, 65–66, 113–14, 177; raiding and, 63–66; sociality and, 65–66, 74; TBC and, 83–84; theorycraft, and analysis of, 139–41; worklike activities, and materials for, 100, 110, 200

Gee, J., 5

Geertz, C., 199

gendered practice: Chinese, 187–92; cross-gendered activities and, 169, 171–72; dampened heterosexual interactive and, 160–61; demographic data on players and, 19–20; dominant plane of gendered interaction, 158–61, 166, 173, 211nn9–10; emotes and, 9, 160, 164–65; female character design and, 159, 166–75, *170;* female players playing male characters and, 172–73; female-unfriendly practices and, 163–64; feminine design of and, 167–69, 211n12; gender-bending and, 160, 189–90, 196; gender dynamics and, 161, 172; gendered language, 20, 153–56; heterosexual flirtation and, 158, 162, 164–66, 190, 211n8, 211n11; homophobic language, 20, 153, 154, 156, 157; ladyboy characters and, 187–89; magic circle and, 157, 173; male character design and, 168, 169, *170,* 171, 211n14; masculine adjectives for vernacular names, 15; mastery of performance and, 57, 190–92; NPCs and, 168–69; secondary plane of gendered interaction, 158, 162–66, 164–66, 211n8, 211n11; sexual fun in chat and, 190; summary, 152, 173–75, 199; unaccountablity for rhetoric and, 155. *See also* men players; women players

gendered sensibilities, and design of video games, 167–68, 172, 174

Gnomes, 16, 67, 203

gold, game, 46, 106–7, 176–77, 183. *See also* money transactions, real

Golub, A.: citations, 28, 56, 59, 124, 185; on homophobic language, 156; on men's rhetoric, 157; on mods, 81–82; on perfor-mative demands of raiding, 56; on sexual-

ized language, 153–54, 156; on worklike activities, 209n5
Graner Ray, S., 166, 173
Greenberg, S., 148
grinding, 99, 110. *See also* farming
Grohol, J. M., 125
Groleau, C., 65
group play, 74–75, 207n10
guilds: Chinese, 194; described, 9, 14–15; family and, 25, 26, 31, 154; hierarchy, 202; Hoodoos, 31, *32;* invitations to, 32–33; shared characteristics of players in, 25–26; sociality and, 25–26, 194; TBC, and software change effects on, 63–66; Terror Nova, 31, 163; website postings for, 33–34. *See also* Scarlet Raven (pseud.) guild; *specific guilds*
Gutwin, C., 148

hackers, and encoded rules, 69–70, 73, 198
Hansen, S., 77
Harris, J., 21, 22, 29
HAWT descriptor, 87, 208n20
Hayes, E., 103, 159, 161, 166, 173, 174
healing class: alchemy profession and, 9, 12, 112, 209n7; decursing and, 149, 210n5; described, 15; metrics, 58, 81, 206n3, 207n15
Heath, C., 148
hierarchy, 41–42, *42,* 85, 102, 202
Hoodoos guild, 31, *32*
Hook, S., 43
Horde races, 16
Huhtamo, E., 93
Huisman, J.-W., 84–85
Huizinga, J.: on apart together feelings, 116; on game play, 103; on moral principles, 101; on play, 95, 97, 102, 116, 118, 200, 208–9n2
human activities: aesthetic experience theory and, 43; and impact in video games, 7, 18, 61; in video games, and impact on encoded rules in digital entities, 7, 18, 61; in visual-performative media, 7, 8
Humans, 16, 159
humor, 60–61, 67, 130
Hunter, D., 13–14, 76, 93
hybrid physical-digital spaces, 181–82, 194, 196, 201

Innikka (pseud.): emotes used by, 160, 165; game play and, 9–12; gendered practice and, 154–55; gold raiding by, 177; as healer, 81, 207nn14–15; mastery of performance by, 34, 56; mods and, 82, 207n14; Night Elf race and, 5, 16, 159; participant-observation ethnographic research, 30; participant-observation in ethnographic research and, 28, 30–31, 34–35; screenshot of, *13*
instances (instanced play): magic circle and, 118–20
Internet cafes *(wang ba):* access to digital technologies and, 179, 211n1; Chinese *WoW* culture and, 7, 26, 177–82, *178,* 211n1; as hybrid physical-digital spaces, 181; sociality and, 180, 181, 193
Isenberg, Karl, 143–44
Ito, M., 28, 137, 150

Jackson, P., 43
Jenkins, H., 92, 137, 166, 174
Jerz, D., 88, 92, 143
Jha, P., 19
Jordan, W., 69, 73, 207n9
Juul, J., 88, 94, 102, 103, 110, 118

Kafai, Y., 5, 142, 166
Kallinikos, J., 61, 62, 68–70, 72–73, 207n7
Kaptelinin, V., 40–41, 43, 62
Karazhan (Kara) dungeon, 63, 67, 68, 71, 76, 90, 168
Kavetsky, J., 17, 154, 173
Kelty, C., 145
Kendall, L., 137
Kennedy, H., 57, 103, 166, 172, 192
Kensing, F., 83
Klastrup, L., 17, 166
Korea, game play in, 8, 19, 107–8, 176, 179, 203
Kow, Y. M., 30, 146, 150, 183, 210n2
Kraut, R., 123, 125, 128, 129, 130
Kucklich, J., 137, 143
Kuutti, K., 85

LambdaMoo (video game), 76, 93
Lampe, C., 182
LandoverBaptist.org, 26
Lang, T., 181, 193

Lastowka, F., 13–14, 76, 93
Latour, B., 62
Leontiev, A., 6, 18, 40–41
leveling, 12, 15, 39–40, 45–46, 55, 184, 205n1, 206–7n6
Li, Z., 6
Lin, H., 45
Linden Lab, 35, 77–79. See also *Second Life*
Lindtner, S., 21, 29, 179, 181
Lineage (video game), 71–75, 120, 211n12
Lingley, K., 124, 185
Liuning, Z., 180
lonely player stereotype, 20–21, 29, 127
Lowood, H., 137
Luff, P., 148
Ly, S., 202
Lyotard, J.-F., 73

magic circle: encoded rules and, 118; gendered practice and, 157, 173; instances and, 118–20, 209nn9–11; not-play and, 116; play and, 102, 108, 116, 117; RL and, 108; summary, 123; *WoW* and, 118–20, 157, 173, 209nn9–11
Magtheridon's Lair, 56
Malaby, T., 28, 35, 77, 78–79, 102–3, 108, 199
Malliet, S., 93
Malone, K.-L., 33
mangle notion, 70–73, 207n8
Mankekar, P., 92
Marckmann, H., 84–85
mastery of performance: described, 59; flow and, 85–86; game play, and valued quality of, 55, 57; metrics of, 57–58; performative challenges and, 52, 55; play, and valued quality of, 14, 40; valued quality of, 14, 40, 55, 57–58; in video games, 52, 55; women and, 57, 190–92; in *WoW,* 15, 34, 55–56
medium, visual-performative media. *See* visual-performative media
men players: about, 187–92; female characters played by, 158–61, 173, 187–89, 211nn9–10; female-unfriendly practices by, 163–64; gender-bending and, 160, 189–90, 196; gender dynamics and, 161, 172; gendered rhetoric and, 20, 153–56, 210nn1–4; heterosexual flirtation and, 158, 162, 164–66, 190, 211n8, 211n11; homophobic rhetoric by, 20, 153, 154, 156,

157; ladyboy characters and, 187–89; men's disputes with, 162–63; rhetorical practices of, 20, 153, 156–57, 210nn1–2, 210n4, 210–11n7. *See also* players
metrics: combat log and, 57–58, 206n3; damage meters mods for, 58, *59,* 207n15; gear and, 61; healing class and, 58, 81, 206n3, 207n15
Miller, D., 28
Miller, S., 101, 103, 115, 116
MMORPG, 17–18, 202
Mnookin, J., 93
mobs (monster/mobile), 10, 56, 80, 82, 84, 90, 110, 153
modding and mods: as aesthetic experience, 151; Blizzard and, 149–50, 210n4, 210n6; Chinese, 179, *179;* community, and role of, 149–50, 210n6; creation of, 70–72, 80–83, 143–47, 199; damage meters and, 58, *59,* 207n15; data on, 143, 210n2; distribution of, 58, 143; empowerment and, 148; encodes rules and, 70–72, 80–83, 149, 210n6; fame and, 145; function of, 146–48; game geography coordinates, 146; gear organization and, 146; history of, 143; participatory design activity and, 70–72, 80–83, 199; resource role of rules, and effects of, 81–82, 207n14; sociality and, 148, 150–51; updates, and care for, 143, 145, 146
money transactions, real, 106, 184–85. *See also* gold, game
monster/mobile (mobs), 10, 56, 80, 82, 84, 90, 110, 153
Moore, R., 21
moral principles, 101, 124, 129–30, 186–87
Morningstar, C., 70, 93
Mortensen, T., 166
Mulvey, L., 159
Mumford, L., 62
Murray, J., 88

Nakamura, L., 176
Nardi, B.: on business applications for video games, 6; citations, 40–41, 43; on fraud, 183; on male players playing female characters, 158; on mods, 146, 148, 150, 210n2; on power of technology, 62; productive play seminar and, 70; on sociality, 21, 22

Night Elves, 5, 16, 159
Nihilum (pseud.) guild, 59, 99–100, 163–64
Nissenbaum, H., 174
Noël, S., 16
nonplayer characters (NPCs), 17, 90, 116, 143, 159, 168
nostalgia runs, 83–84, 208nn17–18
not-play, 95–98, 97, 104–5, 104–6, 108–16, 120
NPCs (nonplayer characters), 17, 90, 116, 143, 159, 168

Odom, W., 209n1
Orcs, 16, 119, 159
Orlikowski, W., 69

participant-engagement, 35
participant-observation, 28, 30–31, 34–35
participant researchers, identification of, 35
participatory aesthetic experience: aesthetic experience theory and, 41, 48, 68, 70, 79–80, 82–85, 92–93, 197; in Chinese WoW culture, 194–96, 195; common core of, 194, 195; encoded rules and, 198; performance and, 57, 84–86, 93; resource role of rules, and nurtured, 76, 198; in WoW, 85, 92, 137, 194
participatory design activity, 70–72, 79–83, 199. See also modding and mods; theorycraft
Pearce, C., 28, 35, 70, 95, 137, 156, 210n6
performance: arena play and, 55, 206nn2–3; autonomy and, 7, 101, 205–6n1; described, 54; gear, and impact on, 58, 65–66, 113–14, 177; humor, and salience of, 60–61, 67; metrics of, 57–58, 206n3; participatory aesthetic experience and, 57, 84–86, 93; progression and, 58–60, 66, 72, 74, 86; raiding and, 55–56; sociality, and effects on, 64–65; subjectivity and, 56–57; video games and, 55–61. See also raiding
Perkins, C., 39
Peterson, H., 21, 182
Peterson, L., 28
phases, 45–46, 46
Pickering, A., 70–71
pickup groups (pugs), 18, 46, 74–75, 160, 184, 211n10
PK (player kill), 191–92, 211n2
play: as aesthetic experience, 6–7, 41, 48;
aesthetic experience theory and, 151; arena, 55, 206nn2–3; autonomy and, 101; characteristics of, 14, 102–3; group, 74–75, 207n10; heterosexual flirtation and, 162, 190; hierarchy of activities and, 102; instanced, 118–20, 209nn9–11; magic circle and, 102, 108, 116, 117; meaningfulness of, 116; professional gaming and, 106–7; progress as motivation in, 39, 40; rewards as motivation in, 39–40; RL, and links with, 108, 113, 120; Skinnerian dynamics and, 39, 40; summary, 94, 120; value of, 95, 97, 200, 208–9n2; of video games with family, 21, 26, 179, 182, 192; in visual-performative media, 203–4; voluntariness of, 97–98, 101, 106, 208–9n2; work, and subjective separation from, 95, 97–98, 100, 102, 209n3; worklike elements in, 102. See also activity theory; aesthetic experience theory
player kill (PK), 191–92, 211n2
players: "alone together" feelings of, 209n8; demographic data on, 18–19, 19–20, 26, 83, 190, 208n16; diversity of, 20–21; introduction into WoW and, 4–5, 152–53, 192; shared characteristics of, 25–26; social classes of, 19, 24–25. See also men players; women players
point cards, 183–85
Polin, L., 5
political realities and WoW, 185–86
Poole, S., 95, 111, 112, 209
Postigo, H., 137, 143, 150
Powell, A., 179
power leveling services, 46, 184
priest forums, 57, 82, 207n15
problematic use of video games. See addiction to video games
professional gaming, 106–8
progression, 58–60, 66, 72, 74, 86
pugs (pickup groups), 18, 46, 74–75, 160, 184, 211n10
pwning opponents, 16, 71, 171, 173

Qiu, J., 180
Quake (video game), 57, 172

races, 16, 203. See also specific races
Raessens, J., 84, 85, 86
raiding and raiding guilds: about, 9, 31;

raiding and raiding guilds (*continued*)
  causal, 11; damage meters and, 58, *59,*
  207n15; gear and, 63–66; gendered rhetoric, 154; gold, 176–77, 183; mastery of
  performance and, 34, 55–56; performance
  and, 55–56; performative demands of, 56;
  pickup groups and, 18, 46, 74–75, 160,
  184, 211n10; raiding described, 9, 15; sociality, 65, 193–94; worklike activities and,
  100. *See also* Scarlet Raven (pseud.) guild
Rea, S., 107, 179, 203
real life (RL): aggro and, 109, 116–17, 161,
  162; farming, and links with, 110–16,
  114, 209nn4–7; game play, and links with,
  108–16, 120; hybrid physical-digital spaces
  and, 181–82, 194, 196, 201; magic circle
  and, 108; play, and links with, 113, 120;
  power leveling services and, 46, 184; self-
  regulation and, 130–33; third space and,
  120, 127, 209n11; *WoW,* and links with,
  108–16, 120
Recount (mod), 58, *59,* 81, 207n15
Reeves, B., 6
remaking of material of experience, 47–48,
  79, 139, 151, 204
resource role of rules: artistry in visual design
  of and, 83–84, 208nn17–18; group play
  and, 74–75, 207n10; loot distribution as
  example of, 75–76, 207nn11–12; mods,
  and effects on, 81–82, 207n14; participatory aesthetic experience of being nurtured
  and, 76, 198
Rettberg, S., 95, 111, 113, 124, 209n6
Rheingold, H., 93
rhetoric: gendered, 20, 153–54, 210nn1–4;
  HAWT descriptor and, 87, 208n20;
  homophobic, 20, 153, 154, 156, 157,
  210n1; negotiated, 20, 26; school, and
  gendered, 155–56, 157; sexualized, 20,
  153–54, 156, 157; unaccountablity for,
  155; unequal position of women, and
  men's, 154–55, 210n5; video games, and
  gendered, 20, 153, 210n1; video games,
  and role in travel of, 203; women players and, 153, 156, 157, 210n2, 210–11n7;
  work, and gendered, 155–56, 157
Rickadams.org, 92
Rodden, T., 181
rules. *See* encoded rules in digital entities;
  resource role of rules

Ryan, P., 69

Salen, K., 117
Scacchi, W., 145
Scarlet Raven (pseud.) guild: damage meters
  and, 58; demographic data, 31, 33;
  described, 11; dissolution of, 67; ethos, 33;
  as family, 25; fraud in, 184; gender data,
  31; members described, 30–31; participant-observation ethnographic research,
  30; TBC, and software change effects on,
  63–65
Schechner, R., 118
school: boredom, and monotony at, 97,
  104–5, 113, 120, 200; gendered rhetoric
  and, 155–56, 157; as not-play, 97, 104–5;
  rhetorical practice to deploy unequal
  position of women in, 155; self-regulation
  and, 129–30, 133; vacancy in student's life
  and, 133; video games, and applications
  in, 141–42; *WoW* addiction and, 124, 125,
  127–28, 132
Schoolcraft, H., 27
Schramm, M., 110
Seay, F., 123, 125, 128, 129, 130
Second Life: adult-themed activity reputation
  of, 134, 209n1; citation, 134; described, 6,
  17, 77, 78–79; design, and impact on, 79;
  encoded rules in, 77–79, 207n13; gamelike environments for business and, 6, 200;
  Linden Lab and, 35, 77–79; participant
  researchers in, 35; as virtual world, 17–18
Seed, P., 142
self-regulation: addiction to video games,
  125, 129–33; family and, 100, 101, 107,
  124, 125, 135; moral principles and,
  129–30; work and, 100, 101
Serpentshrine Cavern (SSC), 9–12, 58, 99,
  119
servers, 16–17, 190–93
Sharritt, M., 5
Sicart, M., 210n1
Skinnerian dynamics, 55, 133
Slater, D., 28
Smith, R., 124
sociality: "alone together" feelings and, 209n8;
  boys' tree house metaphor for, 153, 210n3;
  in Chinese culture, 21, 179, 180, 193–94,
  212n3; collaboration and, 5, 21, 55, 193,
  212n3; diversity of players and, 20–21;

gear and, 65–66, 74; guilds and, 25–26, 194; performance, and effects of, 64–65; problematic use and, 129–30; raiding, and contradiction to, 65; self-regulation and, 129–30; sociable chats, 3–4, 15, 22–23; social classes of players of, 19, 24–25

software modifications: participatory design activity and, 70–72, 79–83, 199; TBC and, 62–68, 83–84, 208nn17–18. *See also* modding and mods; theorycraft

spectacle of images in visual design, 86–92, *91*, 198, 208nn19–22

Spinuzzi, C., 43

Squire, K., 5

SSC (Serpentshrine Cavern), 9–12, 58, 99, 119

Starcraft (video game), 211n13

Steinkuehler, C., 200; citations, 5, 21, 48, 106, 127; on interactive stabilization, 70–71, 72; on pedagogical value of video game activities, 141–42; on *WoW* as third space, 120

stereotypic lonely player, 20–21, 29, 127

Stevens, P., 47, 95, 208–9n2

Stewart, K., 179

Strathern, M., 28

subjective separation from: work, 95, 97–98, 100, 102, 209n3

subjectivity: activity theory and, 56–57; dispositions toward activity and, 43, 46, 104, 199; performance and, 56–57; work and play separation and, 95, 97–98, 100, 102, 209n3

Sudden Attack (video game), 203

Sun, C., 45

Sutton-Smith, B., 109, 113, 147

Takhteyev, Y., 210n4

Tang, J., 148

Taylor, T. L.: citations, 15, 21, 33, 73, 81, 103, 159, 174; on design of female characters, 166, 171; on encoded rules in digital entities shaping online life, 61; on *EverQuest,* 14, 57; on females playing male characters, 173; on females' sense of safety, 211n11; on instancing, 120; on metrics of mastery of performance, 57–58; on mods, 82; on participatory design activity, 79–80, 82; on violence in video games, 14

TBC (The Burning Crusade), 62–68, 83–84, 208nn17–18

television, 92, 134, 136, 197, 202–3, 208n23

text-based role-playing games, 88–89, 92–93

Thelwall, M., 156, 210n7

theorycraft, 137–42, 151

third space, 120, 209n11

Thomas, S., 181, 193

Thottbot.com, 60–62, 137, 177, 205–6n1, 206–7n6

Toma, C., 165

Tschang, F., 12

Turkle, S., 57, 92, 135, 159

Turner, V., 14, 95, 110, 113, 120, 209n3

Ultima Online (video game), 14

Undead, 16, 185–86

Upper Black Rock Spire (UBRS) dungeon, 66, 67

Vandenberg, B., 101, 155, 156, 162

Victorian memes, 13–14

video games: critical thinking skills and, 141–42; culture, and applications for, 5–6, 109–10, 141–42, 200; described, 197; encoded rules and, 61–62, 206n5, 206–7n6; gendered rhetoric in, 20, 153, 210n1; gendered sensibilities, and design of, 167–68, 172, 174; impact of human activities in, 7, 18, 61; language travel, and role of, 203; masculinist, 167, 168, 172, 211n13; mastery of performance in, 52, 55; performance contours in, 55–61; play in, 7; vacancy in student's life and, 133. *See also* addiction to video games; visual-performative media; *specific video games*

violence, and game play, 14, 205nn3–4

virtual world/experience, 8, 13–14, 17–18

visual design, and spectacle of images in, 86–92, *91*, 198, 208nn19–22

visual-performative activity, 85, 181–82, 194, 196, 198, 201

visual-performative media: accessibility of, 54; autonomy and, 7; complexity in, 7, 9, 54; described, 7, 8; design of female characters off-putting to women and, 166; educators on, 5; engagement in RL activities and, 197–98; as global artifact alternative to traditional media, 196, 202–3; human activity in stimulating visual environment and, 7, 8; hybrid physical-digital spaces and, 182, 196, 201; interactive stabiliza-

visual-performative media (*continued*)
tion in, 70–72; MMORPG and, 17–18,
202; moral principles and, 124, 129–30,
186–87; performative described, 52, 54;
play in, 14, 40, 203–4; real world visual-
performative activities and, 54; rewards
and, 7, 39–40, 55, 72, 113, 116, 197; as
spectacle of images, 86–92, *91,* 208nn19–
22; texts and narrative in, 88–89; third
space in, 120, 127, 209n11
voluntariness of play, 97–98, 101, 106,
208–9n2
von Bertalanffy, L., 71
Vu, T., 29
Vygotsky, L., 18, 68

Wakeford, N., 179
wang ba (Internet cafes). *See* Internet cafes
(*wang ba)*
whispers, 9–10
Whitehead J., 143
Williams, D., 21, 48, 120, 127, 210n3
Williams, M., 28
Willis, P., 143
Wilson, S., 28
Wine, C., 57, 82, 199, 207n15, 210n4
Winner, L., 62, 190
wipe, 11, 55–56, 208n17
women players: acceptance into for, 153, 173–
75; heterosexual flirtation and, 158, 162,
164–66, 190, 211n8, 211n11; introduction
into for, 152–53, 192; male characters
played by, 172–73; mastery of performance and, 57, 190–92; men's rhetorical
practice to deploy unequal position of,
154–55, 210n5; place in dominant plane of
gendered interaction for, 160–61; rhetorical practices of, 153, 156, 157, 210n2,
210–11n7. *See also* players
work: aesthetic experience versus, 44, 49,
94–95, 198; boredom, and monotony

at, 97, 104–6, 113, 120, 200; gamelike
environments for work and, 5–6, 147,
200; gendered rhetoric and, 155–56, 157;
hierarchy of activities and, 102; moral
principles and, 101; as play, 85; play versus,
95, 97, 106–8, 200, 208–9n2; professional
gaming and, 106–8; RL, and links with,
110–16, *114,* 209nn4–7; self-regulation
and, 130–31; subjective separation from,
95, 97–98, 100, 102, 209n3; unequal
position of women, and rhetoric at, 155;
visual-performative media, and role in
global, 202
worklike activities: Chinese *WoW* culture, 99;
complaints about, 209n5; farming and,
98–99, 102; feedback about, 209n5; in
game play, 95, 98–99, 98–100, 102, 106–8,
110, 111, 200; gear materials and, 100,
110, 200; as not-play, 95–98, 104–6; in
play, 102; raiding and, 100
World of Warcraft (WoW): accessibility and
appeal of, 8, 54; active aesthetic experience and, 85, 198; activities pursued while
playing, 134–35; as aesthetic experience,
54; demographic data on players of, 18–19,
26, 83, 190, 208n16; described, 12, 16,
197, 205n1, 206n4; multiple characters in,
14, 146; players' introduction into, 4–5,
152–53, 192; servers in, 16–17, 192, 193;
texts and narrative in, 88, 89
worldofwarcraft.com, 163, 210n6, 222
WoW Web Stats (WWS), 58, 81
Wright, T., 210n1

Yee, N.: citations, 6, 95, 137; on demographic
data on players, 19–20; on farming, 209n6;
on game play, 99, 111, 112; on gendered
practice, 160

Zaphiris, P., 5
Zimmerman, E., 117